LOYALISTS

OTHER TV BOOKS BY PETER TAYLOR

Behind the Mask: The IRA and Sinn Fein

LOYALISTS

War and Peace in Northern Ireland

PETER TAYLOR

New York

Publisher's Cataloging-in-Publication Data
Taylor, Peter, 1942–
    Loyalists : war and peace in Northern Ireland / Peter Taylor.
      p. cm.
    Includes bibliographical references and index.
    ISBN: 1-57500-047-4
    1. Unionism (Irish politics) 2. Northern Ireland—Politics and government—20th century. 3. Ulster Volunteer Force. 4. Terrorism—Northern Ireland—History. I. Title.
    DA990.U46T39 1999   941.6
                         QBI99-416

PICTURE SOURCES
David Barker: pages 1 *bottom*, 11 *bottom*, 14 *top*
Courtesy of the Giles Family: page 1 *top*
Courtesy of James Murdock: pages 4 *bottom, 5 top*
PA News: pages 6, 12, 16 *bottom*
Pacemaker: pages 7 *top right* and *bottom*, 8, 13, 14 *bottom*, 15, 16 *top*
Public Records Office of Northern Ireland: page 3 *bottom*
Courtesy of the PUP: page 9
Courtesy of Gusty Spence: pages 10, 11
Courtesy of the UDA: page 7 *top left*
The Ulster Museum: pages 2 *bottom*, 3 *top*

First published in Great Britain by Bloomsbury Publishing Plc.

TV Books, L.L.C.
Publishers serving the television industry.
1619 Broadway, Ninth Floor
New York, NY 10019
www.tvbooks.com

Manufactured in the United States.

To *the people of Northern Ireland*

Acknowledgements

I had always intended to follow *Behind the Mask* with *Loyalists*, conscious that *Behind the Mask* only told the recent history of the conflict through one set of eyes. Those same events, when seen from a loyalist perspective, invariably present a totally different picture, which is familiar to their own community but far less so to most people outside it. My purpose in making the *Loyalists* BBC television series and in writing this book was to provide an insight into what made the loyalist paramilitaries, their community and politicians act in the way they did. Thus people might gain a greater and more balanced understanding of recent history, which has tended to be told more from a nationalist and republican point of view. My hope is that *Loyalists* will add a new dimension to the account of the violent forces that have made the past three decades so bloody, in a conflict that now may finally be coming to an end.

I could not have made the television series or written the book without the help, trust and support of many people, primiarily the loyalists themselves. The paramilitary organisations, the UDA, UVF and others, gave me remarkable access to many of the men who had fought their 'war'. They spoke with astonishing and often chilling candour about what they did, and why, as I attempted to chronicle their remarkable journey from 'war' to peace. The same goes for the loyalist and unionist politicians who spoke with unaccustomed frankness about contentious attitudes and events. I am grateful both to them and to the many members of the Protestant community for all their kindness and confidence in what I was trying to do, especially to John Beresford Ash for his family history, and to the Giles family in Belfast who helped me write 'Billy' at a time of great grief. I am also grateful to those in the RUC, Northern Ireland office and elsewhere who so generously gave their help.

As ever, I am indebted to my BBC colleagues in London and Belfast, and in particular the *Loyalists* production team who gave me the space and support without which I never could have written the book. Above all my thanks are due to my producer, Sam Collyns, who generously gave me the time to write at no small cost to himself and whose patience, good humour and perseverance with E-Mail, kept me and the television series on course; to Andy Kemp, our video-tape editor who, with Sam, produced miracles from the mountain of material; to Julia Hannis who performed astonishing feats of research in addition to keeping us all organised; to Stuart Robertson for his mastery of archive film; to Mary Moss for her stunning titles and graphics; to Yolanda Ayres, Maria Ellis and their colleagues on the *Panorama* desk for their back-up; to our executive producer, Peter Horrocks, for his support of the project (and the book) and fine editorial judgement; to Mark Damazer, who first encouraged me to undertake *Loyalists* and to Helen Boaden who carried his enthusiasm on; to BBC Northern Ireland's Chief Security Correspondent, Brian Rowan, who shared his vast experience with me and made critical initial introductions to individuals on the Shankill Road; to the Controller BBC Northern Ireland, Pat Loughrey, and Keith Baker, Andrew Colman and their colleagues in the newsroom and elsewhere for their guidance, wisdom and advice; and to June Gamble and Danny Cooper in BBC Belfast News and Information for diligently searching out mountains of cuttings; and to Mark Thompson, Controller BBC2, for commissioning the series.

No writer could have asked for a more supportive, enthusiastic and professional publisher than Bloomsbury. Thanks to Alan Wherry who, after *Behind the Mask*, first encouraged me to write a book about the loyalist paramilitaries: to David Reynolds who confidently commissioned it knowing how tight the deadline was; to Helena Drakakis who so coolly and professionally co-ordinated the operation in a nail-bitingly tight schedule; to production manager Polly Napper who helped her do it; to editor Bela Cunha who turned my manuscript round in record time and improved it in the process; to Shane Weller who so expertly read the proofs; to Ben Murphy who compiled the index with lightning speed; and to my agent, John Willcocks, who sorted out the contractual details with his customary efficiency.

Finally, greatest thanks of all to my wife and family—Sue, Ben and Sam, not forgetting 'Josh' who barked to take me for walks to breathe the fresh air and think. Without them I would never have survived. Ben and Sam were as supportive and encouraging as any sons could be whilst Sue always urged me on with the warning not to look at the summit whilst climbing the mountain, and assured me that I would get there in the end. I am relieved to say that I finally did.

Contents

Introduction

Billy

Billy's story is typical of that of hundreds of young loyalists who lived through the thirty years of slaughter euphemistically known as the 'Troubles'. Typical, that is, except in one respect.

William Alexander Ellis Giles – 'Billy' – was born into a working-class Protestant family in Island Street in the loyalist heartland of East Belfast. It was 1957 and the IRA's border campaign was already one year old, not that it would have affected anyone in the back-to-back terrace houses where the Giles family lived in the shadow of the shipyard. But it would have registered. To Protestants living in a state that had been born out of conflict, the IRA remained an ever present threat however distant the reality may have been. Billy was the eldest of a close-knit family of six, with three brothers – Sam, Thomas and Jim – and two sisters – Sylvia and Margaret. He described his mother, Lily, as 'a housewife' and there was no shame in that in a world refreshingly untouched by political correctness. His father, Sam, was a plater in the Harland and Wolff shipyard which had provided the menfolk of East Belfast with employment since before the yard launched the *Titanic* in 1912. The number of Catholics who worked there could almost be counted on the fingers on one hand. There were jobs for the boys under the giant gantries that dominated the Belfast skyline – but only if they were Protestants. In those days the word 'discrimination' had hardly entered the political vocabulary. 'We were a hard-working, ordinary family,' Billy told me. 'Hard-working and quiet.' Loyalism – loyalty to the Protestant faith, Queen and country and the constitutional link with Britain – ran through the family, as it does through the veins of just about every Protestant in Northern Ireland. Sam was a member of the Orange Order, the Royal Black Preceptory and the Apprentice Boys of Derry, the masonic-like 'loyal orders' whose secret rituals have bound together Protestant males down the centuries. He was also a former British soldier and still proudly wears his Royal Electrical and Mechanical Engineers tie today. Service life ran in the family and all of Billy's brothers joined the British army. Photographs of the boys in their army uniforms proudly adorn the living-room walls.

Church lay at the heart of family life, and for Billy and his brothers and sisters, Sunday school was obligatory on the Sabbath. 'When you went on holiday, you went with the church,' Billy remembers. 'You visited some seaside in the rain. It was a day away and the only holiday you had.' Although the family did not attend the Reverend Ian Paisley's Free Presbyterian church, the 'Big Man' had a profound effect on the young Billy. 'He was the man,' he said. 'I thought that whatever Paisley said was true. Being affected by Paisley is part of being a Protestant. We went to his rallies. Tens of thousands followed him, just to hear what he had to say. He was preaching about the situation as if it was the gospel or a biblical text and, because of our upbringing, we were a ready audience. When you're young and caught up in that kind of atmosphere, you can't distinguish one thing from another. On reflection now, I realize he was full of hate.'

The Giles family was not political beyond the politics that all Protestant working-class families embraced. They accepted the *status quo* because they were part of it. When I asked Billy if he thought he was better off than his Catholic neighbours, he said there was no difference since they all lived in the same conditions. The family was brought up in a two-bedroom house with a toilet in the yard until it was condemned as unfit to live in. When they moved to a council house in 1972, it was the first time they had had hot water or a bathroom. It was only when Billy saw the private housing estate next door that he realized there were differences, not between Protestants and Catholics but between the working and middle classes.

Although the family now lived in the relative security of a staunch loyalist estate, Billy's father, Sam, joined the Ulster Defence Association, the umbrella body of the vigilante groups which had sprung up in loyalist areas across the city as defence against the anticipated IRA attack. It was the normal thing for Protestant fathers and sons to do in the early days of the Troubles. 'At that time, almost everyone would have been involved in some sort of organization,' Billy said. 'It was part of growing up in Belfast.' But as the conflict became increasingly bloody, he found himself attending more and more funerals of friends he had lost and people he had known. Day after day, he witnessed the horrors of the IRA's campaign. He saw a policeman 'shovelling bits of body into a bag' on 'Bloody Friday' when the IRA blitzed Belfast in July 1972 with twenty-six bombs that slaughtered eleven people. 'I saw a lot of things, just like everyone else.'

By 1975, Billy felt he could no longer stand on the sidelines and watch the security forces fail to come to grips with the IRA. He too enlisted, but not in the army his brothers had joined. Two days after his eighteenth birthday, just after his holiday in Blackpool, he joined the illegal Ulster Volunteer Force (UVF) – by invitation. He felt the UDA was too large – by this time tens of thousands had enlisted – and he had always had a romantic admiration for the original UVF which was founded by the loyalist hero, Sir Edward Carson, in 1913 to resist the British Government's decision to give Ireland Home Rule. 'They were soldiers. A private army,' he said. 'They were people I could identify with in terms of my history.' Billy never told his parents what he had done and did everything he could to keep his paramilitary involvement from them. He knew they would have been horrified had they known, and his mother, Lily, would have been heartbroken. 'I was living a lie,' he told me. 'After I'd been on the phone, they'd say "Who's that?" and I'd say "Nobody". When I was going out, they'd ask "Where are you going?" and I'd say "Nowhere". When they later found out, they just cracked up. I didn't really appreciate what I was doing to them at the time.'

Billy spent his first two years as a UVF Volunteer being trained by former British soldiers, some of them veterans of Aden and Borneo. Many had escaped the poverty of Northern Ireland in the sixties to see the world and make a better life elsewhere but had returned to the province once violence had erupted, to offer their military expertise to their fellow Ulstermen in their hour of need. Billy was trained in how to use weapons and explosives. At the time he joined the UVF, there were genuine fears that a 'doomsday' situation was fast approaching when there would be civil war. The British Government was already conducting a clandestine face-to-face dialogue with the IRA via the Secret Intelligence Service, MI6,[1] and there was growing concern among Protestants that they were about to be sold out to Dublin. Loyalists felt they had to be armed and ready to resist the anticipated IRA onslaught.

By the early 1980s loyalist fears had intensified following the 1981 IRA hunger strike in which ten republican prisoners demanding to be treated as political prisoners not criminals starved themselves to death. The Prime Minister, Margaret Thatcher, was unbending and refused to give way. The result was cataclysmic and produced undreamed-of political and propaganda dividends for the Republican Movement – the IRA and Sinn Fein. By the time of the hunger strike, Billy had drifted away from the UVF but the ancient fears reawakened by the deaths of the ten republican prisoners brought him back again into its ranks. 'Protestants were fearful of what was going to happen,' Billy said. 'They feared there was going to be an uprising and they were all going to be slaughtered. They would have appreciated the Provos [the Provisional IRA] actually coming to war with them but they never did so. They never actually went to war in the "war" sense.' Sharing the forebodings of his community, Billy became active again. 'Many of us who had left, came back. My whole mentality at that time would have been to prepare for war. We were expecting to fight along the border and we went off to train in fields.' But one attack made Billy go further.

On 25 September 1982, a twenty-year-old Protestant woman, Karen McKeown, was fatally wounded by a gunman from the republican splinter group, the Irish National Liberation Army (INLA). Karen was a Sunday-school teacher and was outside a church hall in East Belfast when a gunman came up and shot her in the back of the head. She died in hospital three weeks later. Billy did not know the young woman but was profoundly affected by the callousness of the killing that had taken place in his own area. 'She was getting into a car and a guy stuck a gun in the back of her head and said, "You're dead",' at least that's how Billy remembers what happened. 'The story goes that she thought it was one of her friends playing. And the guy shot her. I don't know why it happened. I didn't think. It was probably her innocence and she was coming out of church. It changed me dramatically.' Neither Billy nor his family was every sectarian. Sam remembers Billy often bringing home a young Roman Catholic called Michael Fay, with whom he worked, for a cup of tea and a video. Billy admits that he became indifferent to the sectarian killing of Catholics by the loyalist paramilitaries, as by this time were many other members of his community. 'When they heard reports of a Catholic shot here or a Catholic shot there, they would have thought, "So what?" I don't believe I was ever like that until that particular shooting. Now I wanted to see people killed over it. I wanted the IRA stopped, and I thought that was the only way. You can talk to republicans until you're blue in the face but they still go on killing innocent people.' Up to that point, Billy expected others to pull the trigger as he felt that close-up killing was not the role he was cut out for. He had been training for 'doomsday' when he was prepared to defend his community and his country in the conventional military sense. 'I had a soldier's mentality. I had to be prepared to fight over a ditch or in a road or in a street, but I'd be fighting as part of an army with a reason behind it. The enemy would have been there and I would have fought and that would have been all right. I was prepared for shooting with a rifle or preparing bombs but I was never into actually assassinating someone.' But after Karen McKeown's death, all that was to change despite the fact that her parents had asked for no retaliation. The grieving family's plea was lost on Billy. 'Now I wanted to kill the other side,' he told me. 'The only way to stop them was to terrorize them. It was them and us.'

Shortly after the killing, Billy ran into another UVF colleague whom he had not seen for a long time. The man said how terrible it was about the 'wee girl' and thought they should be doing something about it. Billy got a gun and a target was selected. It was to be his friend and workmate, Michael Fay.

He was a guy the same age as myself. It didn't matter who it was to me, like. It wouldn't have mattered who he was.

He was your workmate.

He was someone I knew, yes.

You lured him into a trap.

That's right. It's not something I'm proud of.

He was a Catholic.

That was enough. It didn't matter because at the end of the day I was thinking that if they could shoot us, we could shoot them.

Them being?

Catholics, nationalists, republicans. Put whatever slant you want upon it. They were all the same.

But they weren't all the same. They were different.

They were all the same in my thinking then.

But you're supposed to be non-sectarian.

I know. But everything went out of the window. That's just the way it affected me. What would have been classed before as a decent young man, suddenly changed.

The plan was carefully laid, and the unsuspecting victim was to be lured into a trap at the end of November 1982, the month after Karen McKeown had died from her injuries. But on 16 November, Lenny Murphy, a senior UVF figure and leader of the notorious 'Shankill Butchers',[2] who had been released from prison only four months earlier, was shot dead, presumably by the IRA, outside his girlfriend's home. The UVF decided that retaliation had to be swift, and the plan to kidnap Michael Fay was suddenly brought forward by a week. The Protestant Action Force – a pseudonym for the UVF – issued a statement saying that three Catholics would die 'to avenge Murphy'.[3] On 19 November 1982, the day of Lenny Murphy's funeral, Billy put the plan into operation, driving off with Michael Fay in Fay's blue Ford Escort. Michael's wife, Mary, thought her husband had gone to the hospital to visit their fourteen-month-old daughter, Jennifer, who was sick.[4] When the car stopped, Billy pulled out a gun and shot Fay through the back of the head. 'It was quick and it was dirty and a guy lost his life.' His body was then bundled into the boot, Billy knew he was capable of killing and now he had done it – without hesitation. He told me how he thought this killing would be the last and that once it was done, the 'war' would be over. The effect was traumatic. He described the impact with a pain that had not diminished with the years. His face and eyes told it all.

The split second it happened, I lost part of myself that I'll never get back. You hear the bang and it's too late. Standing over the body, it hits you. I felt that somebody had reached down inside me and ripped my insides out. You've found somewhere you've never been before and it's not a very nice place. You can't stop it. It's too late.

Did you ever come back from that place?

No. I never felt a whole person again. I lost something that day that I never got back. How do you put that back? You can't. You'll never get that back no matter what people say to you or what you say or think. I've done something and been involved in something that I can't ever change and I have to live with it. What would have been classed before as a decent young man, suddenly turned into a killer. That's Northern Ireland.

But it wasn't the environment that turned you into a killer. You were responsible for it.

All responsibility went out of the window. If I'd have been born in England, I wouldn't have killed somebody because of their politics or their religion or anything else. Up until that time, it wasn't part of me. But now it is.

Michael Fay's widow, Mary, was devastated. 'Please, God, let there be no more killings,' she pleaded. 'If only the killers could see the grief and heartbreak they cause. I feel sorry for the people who did this.' Billy's parents were horrified at the killing of Billy's friend and workmate but had no idea that their son was responsible.

Billy was later arrested and taken to the RUC interrogation centre at Castlereagh where he made a full confession after 'just a wee bit of pressure'. It was a relief to unburden himself of his guilt. 'My whole upbringing was to respect the police. They were somebody to look up to. When they told me that what I had done was wrong, they were telling me what I already knew. There was no problem. I went to trial and pleaded guilty.' Billy's parents were shattered. They could not believe that their son had become a killer. 'My mother blamed herself. She felt guilty for what I was. I know I was to blame and not her, but she didn't see it like that.' Billy was remanded for two years and seven months before finally being sentenced to life imprisonment for murder, conspiracy to murder, possession of firearms and membership of an illegal organization. Eight other men were tried with him, charged with a catalogue of over eighty terrorist crimes, including five sectarian murders. Five of them received life sentences along with Billy Giles.[5] Before his son went off to serve his sentence in the Maze prison, Sam Giles was allowed to see him. 'He touched my hand across the table and just broke down,' Billy remembers.

At first prison was a relief, as he no longer had to live a life of deceit. 'I got that off my shoulders. I didn't have to tell lies any more. People knew what I was involved in and what I was doing.' The people with whom he lived on the wings of the 'H-Blocks' – the cell units so called because of their shape – were Billy's own, the loyalist paramilitaries of the UVF and

UDA, who ran their own lives in the gaol and, like the republican prisoners, organized their wings along military lines. The command structures of the organizations outside were replicated inside. Billy made good use of his time. Education had never been his strong point: he had left school without any qualifications and without 'hardly lifting a pen'. In the Maze, all that changed. With hours, days, months and years stretching before him, Billy decided to make up for the opportunities he had never had or taken advantage of. Encouraged by a number of skilful and caring tutors, he took several GCSEs, getting an A in English, and then went on to do an Open University degree in Social Sciences. 'Billy was remarkable,' one of his tutors told me. 'He very much struggled against the tide and was often the only person on his wing studying at that level. He just kept at it, flowering in a relationship with his tutors that he'd never experienced before. It wasn't a pupil–teacher relationship at all. It was very much an interaction between equals. Billy really pioneered education on the loyalist wings.' After taking his degree, he did a course in creative writing and wrote a play about his childhood called *Boy Girl*, which was later produced in Belfast with only a handful of the audience aware of the fact that it was the work of a UVF prisoner. Sam and Lily, Billy's proud parents, were in the audience.

It was seven years before Billy finally became adjusted to life in the Maze, and it was then that I first met him. It was the summer of 1990 and the conflict showed no signs of abating, with the loyalist paramilitaries intensifying their retaliatory killings as the IRA entered the third decade of its campaign. I was making a documentary for the BBC inside the Maze prison and remarkably had been given unrestricted access to prisoners in both the republican and loyalist wings of the 'H-Blocks'. We spent several weeks that summer virtually living in the prison, leaving only at 'lock up' in the evening and returning for breakfast the following morning. Our Northern Ireland Office 'minder' never came on to the wings with us and left us alone to talk to the prisoners without someone in authority looking over our shoulders. The arrangement suited both parties. I remember first meeting Billy in his cell. We sat and talked, with me on the metal chair by his desk and Billy propped up by a pillow at the head of his bed. Whereas most prisoners, clad in their blue Glasgow Rangers football shirts, looked pictures of fitness and health, thanks to regular use of the modern multi-gym at the end of the wing, Billy was pale and drawn as if he had never seen the sun. He was quiet and softly spoken and at times it was difficult to make out what he said. His eyes were never still as they darted from me to the ceiling to the window of the cell – anywhere and everywhere, as if permanently searching for something. It may have been nerves or just his manner conditioned by the years inside. He had just served around half his sentence and the other half seemed interminable. Gradually, Billy told me his story, reliving in graphic and painful detail what he had done and why. Billy, I thought, was a tortured soul and perhaps this was a form of catharsis.

I visited his parents, Sam and Lily, and found them simple and dignified people, still trying to come to terms with what Billy had done and still uncomprehending as to how and why their son could have become a killer. I knew that hundreds of parents from both communities felt the same as they saw their sons arrested, tried and sentenced to long years inside the Maze prison. I believed that in most cases it was not the parents but history and the conflict itself that made the sons what they were.

I interviewed Billy for the documentary and he was pleased with the result. He said it was good for people outside, in particular throughout the rest of the United Kingdom, to see men as they were, without masks, and realize how ordinary they were underneath. I recall once asking a young IRA prisoner from Derry, serving life on the republican wings for murder, what an IRA man was doing reading Tolstoy and Hardy, whose works I had noticed lining the shelf of his cell. He looked me straight in the eye and said, 'Because an IRA man's normal just like everybody else.' When I pointed out that 'normal' people did not go around killing other people, he said 'normal' people elsewhere did not live in Northern Ireland. The same applied to loyalist prisoners – although their reading matter was not always the same.

Most years, Billy sent me a Christmas card with a few words about himself and how he was getting on, always asking too how my family was. From time to time I thought his sentence must be nearing its end and wondered what he would do when he got out after spending fourteen years in gaol. Billy was finally released on 4 July 1997 and immediately threw himself into the real world as part of the UVF's political wing, the Progressive Unionist Party (PUP). In particular, he focused his energies on the enormous problems of trying to rehabilitate loyalist prisoners after many years in gaol. Billy was perfectly placed to do so. Although I was outside government buildings at Stormont in the long, cold hours that led up to the signing of the Good Friday Agreement on 10 April 1998, I was not aware that Billy was in the warmth inside as part of the PUP's negotiating team. He had gone there on the Monday and left on the Friday just before the Agreement was signed. 'The job had been done,' he later told me. 'It felt good that it was over and here was a document that we all could live with.' Billy said he now saw a future for the 'kids coming up'.

I met Billy again in the early summer of 1998 when my producer, Sam Collyns, and I were carrying out the initial research for the BBC-TV *Loyalists* series. I did a double-take when Billy walked into the hotel lobby where we had arranged to meet him. I had told Sam all about Billy and he too was astonished at what he saw. Billy was utterly transformed. In place of the gaunt, haunted figure I had met in prison eight years earlier was a smart, middle-aged man in a dark, neatly pressed suit with white shirt and tie, carrying a black executive briefcase. Billy, like most prisoners following their release, had put on a few pounds but not as many as some. He talked about his work for EPIC (Ex-Prisoners Interpretative Centre) – the organization that helps loyalist prisoners to resettle in the community – and of how the workload was increasing with the numbers of men soon to be released under the Good Friday Agreement. But he did so with confidence not anxiety. We talked once again about his life and how he felt now. The remorse and the pain were still there. 'Getting out of the prison gates didn't stop me thinking about what I did. For me personally, it's never going to go away.' The soul, I felt, was still tortured. I recalled again the phrase that the veteran former UVF leader and life-sentence prisoner Gusty Spence had used when he announced the loyalist ceasefire in October 1994 – 'abject and true remorse'. I felt that if ever it applied to anyone, it applied to Billy Giles. Whether Michael Fay's family would have accepted it is another question. Billy seemed to have paid the price over the years with intense emotional suffering. I asked him if he had ever said anything to Michael Fay's family. He told me he had not because he felt he could never say enough. It would have been easy to take the remark as a cop-out but I believed Billy meant it. At the end of our conversation, I asked Billy what he planned to do next. 'Be happy!' he said with a smile as he got up and left.

On the evening of Thursday 24 September 1998, Billy got ready to go to Scotland the following day for a stag night organized for his future brother-in-law, Steve. Steve was to come round and collect him early the next morning from the house Billy shared with his partner, Cathy. Cathy had taken her children by a previous marriage and gone off to spend the night with her mother. At 9.10 that evening, with the house now empty, Billy lifted the telephone and ordered a Chinese take-away. Five minutes later, he took out some lined paper and a pen and began to write. The first words he wrote were 'I'm sorry'. They were double underlined. 'Cathy and the children are at her mum's so I'm alone,' he continued. 'I wanted it that way because I've been working out what I've being going to do for a long time now.' He then wrote a four-page letter.

As everyone knows, my life is an open book. I was involved in something that is often described as 'the troubles' and I took Michael Fay's life. I wanted to do it. I was so sick of hearing about the big, bad Protestants and living every day with what the other side were doing that I grew to hate with a passion. My mind became diseased. The moment the gun went off that day of 18 November '82, it was too late.

The take-away arrived but Billy was no longer hungry. He sat down to record what had happened in gaol and following his release.

When I went to gaol, I was glad. I tried to make amends by not causing anyone any harm. I was co-operative, educated myself and although I wouldn't have shamed the Lord by declaring myself to be a Christian, I tried to live as such. I saved 'screws" [prison officers] lives on two occasions, once when another inmate and me stopped another prisoner from cutting an officer's throat and the second time – during the March '95 riot – when I stopped the wrecking and quietened the bloodlust amongst my more militant and embittered colleagues and convinced them to allow free passage to the Block staff – they surely would have died a death that morning. Not a word was ever said about it.

Billy then went on to describe how he was 'assaulted and battered' by prison staff later that day and 'treated like an animal' for days on end after that. He described his anger and frustration and the compensation for his injuries that was finally offered in August 1998. 'I couldn't win,' he wrote. 'That was the final straw.' He told of how he had put his time in prison to good use and the expectations he had on release of a 'good job with a good salary' that would enable him to buy things and give his family and himself the chance to 'live a comfortable life'. 'I'd served my time,' he wrote, 'and all I wanted was a chance.' Billy never got it. 'A life sentence means life.' He described how 'wrecked' he felt when his expectations were dashed, and he could not get a job despite his degree and his newly acquired skills. He did, however, find government-assisted employment at the Somme Heritage Centre but the wage amounted to little more than income support. After a prison sentence of fifteen years, Billy found himself living without 'a thing in the world'. He gambled to try and make some extra money, all the while hating himself more and those who would not let him 'have the chance to prove that I was able and capable of better things'.

After about ten o'clock, Billy stopped writing and went to see his mother. Gripping the arms of the chair, he bent over and kissed her and told her how much he loved her. She smiled and said she knew. 'No, I mean I really, really love you,' he insisted. He then said goodbye. Sam and Lily thought he seemed his normal self and was going home to bed, presumably because of the early start for Scotland the following morning.

Billy returned home just after eleven o'clock and sat down again to continue his letter. By this time he had prepared a noose. 'I'm just back from visiting my mother. God love her,' he wrote. 'Tried on the noose for size. Cried some.' He took a second drink of alcohol. 'I hurt,' he continued. 'I've been hurting for years and soon the hurting and the pain and suffering will be over. Everyone is going to say, "fool". To me, it's the easy way out. I'm sick of suffering, soon I'll be free of it all – that's the driving force – freedom from having to live with my conscience and the recognition that I was a victim *before* my imprisonment, *during* my imprisonment and *after* my imprisonment. I was a victim too . . . now hopefully I'll be the last. No more. Please don't let any kid suffer the history I have. I didn't deserve it and they certainly don't. Please let our next generation live normal lives. Tell them of our mistakes and admit to them our regrets. Steer them towards a life that is "troubles" free. I've decided to bring this to an end now. I'm tired.' He offered his 'sincerest apologies' to all those whom he knew he was going to hurt. 'I'm going to pray to God before I die,' he wrote. 'He's the one that will set me free. I feel sure that when I die, I'll go to heaven. I'll watch over you's.' He then started to pray. He took his shoes off, had a few drinks, and fell asleep. He woke up at four o'clock, quite sober, and an hour later wrote his final words: 'Have just made myself a cup of tea, set things up, will pray and go back to sleep again.' He signed the letter, Billy Giles.

When Steve came to collect his future brother-in-law at 6 a.m., he found Billy. I was shattered when I heard the news. Billy had seemed so confident, happy and in control of his life when I had seen him only a few months earlier. I even thought the demons might have gone.

On the eve of the funeral, Sam Collyns and I went to see Mr and Mrs Giles and the family. Billy was lying in the sitting room in an open coffin, dressed in his best suit, with his white shirt and tie. A small bronze UVF badge inscribed with the words 'For God and Ulster' was pinned to his lapel. He was just as I remembered him from our last meeting but now the spirit had gone. Lily sat at the head of the coffin with her hand resting gently on her son's brow. Her eyes were tired and red from crying as she had kept vigil all night, refusing to leave his side. His father's eyes were red too. We sat and talked of the Billy whom they and I had known. I looked at Billy's face from which the colour had gone and thought that at last he had found peace. His eight-year-old niece, Ysabell, also came to say goodbye to her uncle whom she adored. As she sat by the coffin, she wrote the following verse:

Look out the window,
Look out it now.
If you don't look out the window
I think you'll cry.
So, come on, and look out the window,
Uncle Billy,
Look out it now.

Although his death would never be recorded as such, Billy was, as he had written, a victim of the Troubles. I recalled the words in his last testament, that future generations would be spared the agony that Northern Ireland had gone through, and hoped that his final wish would come true.

Chapter One

Under Siege

John Beresford Ash's family is one of the four oldest Protestant families in Northern Ireland. The ancestral home is Ashbrook, a graceful house of grey stone nestling in rhododendron-covered grounds between the River Faughan and the foothills of the western Sperrin mountains just outside Londonderry. John was educated at Eton from 1951–6, as were his father, grandfather, great-grandfather and great-great-grandfather, and does not look or sound like most people's idea of a Northern Ireland Protestant. The family has lived at Ashbrook for over 400 years and has played a historic role down those turbulent centuries. For the past three decades, violence has been on John's doorstep since he lives only a few miles outside the city of Londonderry, or Derry as nationalists call it, where the Troubles began in 1968 when the civil rights movement first erupted into violence. In that time, John has watched the number of his fellow Protestants in the city decline as they fled what they saw as the tide of Irish nationalism sweeping Catholic families into traditionally Protestant areas. Loyalists have seen the pattern repeated all over the province in what they regard as a nationalist take-over of Ulster. The notion of siege is burned deep in the Protestant psyche.

John and his family have not been immune from the Troubles, which is not surprising given who they are and where they live. John himself has faced death at least twice. The first occasion was in the early years of the Troubles, when the violence in Derry was at its height and the IRA had set up the 'no-go' area of what it called 'Free Derry' in the nationalist Bogside and Creggan estates. These areas which had also sprung up in Belfast were so called because they had become IRA strongholds and were 'no-go' to the police and army. In Derry, the area was sealed off by barricades and patrolled by masked IRA men with guns, many of them under the direction of the young Martin McGuinness, who was then commander of the Provisional IRA's Derry Brigade.

Late one December night in 1972, John found himself in 'Free Derry'. His unscheduled visit was prompted not by curiosity but necessity. 'I'd just listened to the ten o'clock news and I looked at my packet of cigarettes and saw to my horror that it was empty,' he told me. 'I was a fifty-a-day man in those days and I thought, "Help! What am I going to do?" All the cigarette machines were being blown up or robbed, the pubs used to close at ten and there were no hotels or cafés. I was simply dying for a "gasper" so I had to go out and search for any place that was open.'

Without realizing what he was doing or thinking of the danger involved, John wandered into the Bogside in his desperate quest and suddenly found himself confronted in the pitch dark by a barricade and masked men. Faced with John Ash's military bearing and Eton accent, the IRA not unreasonably thought they had captured a British army spy. He was taken out of the car and escorted through the narrow streets to a house in the Creggan estate which stands above the Bogside. There he says he was confronted by the Brigade Staff of the Provisional IRA. 'It was classic. A bare room with one armchair and the inevitable naked light bulb. I was made to sit in it with two men on either side holding submachine-guns to my head. Then the Brigade Staff trooped in, all masked bar one. It was all rather unnerving. They started the interrogation by asking my name, rank and number but as I didn't have one I couldn't tell them anything. It was an extraordinary situation. Here was I, a citizen of the United Kingdom, being held illegally in part of the United Kingdom that wasn't under the control of the UK armed forces. It was totally unreal.' John told his interrogators who he was and what he was doing, that he was searching for cigarettes and not intelligence on the IRA. They probably thought it an unlikely story, but established it was true once they checked with the local Catholic population. They said his family had always been 'decent with their people'. 'I wouldn't say I was treated with kindness but there was a certain amount of courtesy and there was certainly no physical violence at all.' The IRA admitted they had made a mistake and told him he could go. John returned to Ashbrook a relieved man – but without his cigarettes.

As the IRA had been told, their captive was well regarded by his Catholic neighbours, some of whom he employed on his modest estate. Down the centuries, the family had never been absentee landlords who had left it to others to exploit their land and the people who worked it, and as a result they had remained largely untouched since Ashbrook first became the family home at the end of the sixteenth century.

Ashbrook was originally a gift from Queen Elizabeth I to John Beresford Ash's ancestor, General Thomas Ash, in grateful recognition of the services he had rendered to the Crown in helping put down rebellion in Ireland. When the General first came to Derry in the late 1590s, he was a stranger in the hostile land then known as Ulster, the most northern of the four ancient provinces of Ireland – Leinster, Munster, Connaught and Ulster.

The precise year he arrived is unknown as John's family records were destroyed in 1922 when the Four Courts in Dublin, which housed the Public Record Office, were burned during the civil war that followed partition. General Ash had soldiered in Ireland in the wars at the end of the sixteenth century when Queen Elizabeth was confronted by a rebellion led by the O'Neills and the O'Donnells, the powerful Gaelic chieftains who wished to maintain their independence and resisted the Crown's attempt to bring them and their tribes under central Tudor control. Her Majesty gave the warlords the choice: surrender peacefully to the new order in which their lands would be confiscated and then regranted, or fight. The earls chose the latter course and war ensued, in which the rebels were seen as sixteenth-century 'terrorists'. But Elizabeth's war with the Irish rebels had a wider European dimension – as had most of Ireland's wars – because Protestant England's Catholic enemy, Spain, still smarting from the loss of her great Armada, was the insurgents' ally. England's abiding fear, which persisted down the centuries and through the First and Second World Wars, was that Ireland would be used as a base for a back-door attack by England's European enemies, be they Spanish, French or German. That is why the cardinal principle of British Government policy was to keep Ireland loyal and secure.

General Thomas Ash served with honour in the war and Ashbrook was his reward. The rebel leaders admitted defeat and fled to the Continent, leaving behind their lands that became the Crown's spoils of victory. The ground was now laid for what became known as the 'plantation' of Ulster under Elizabeth's successor, James I, at the beginning of the seventeenth century, in which thousands of English and Scottish Protestants, many of them Presbyterians from the Scottish lowlands, flocked across the Irish Sea to make new lives for themselves in a new, albeit inhospitable, land. Most of the Protestants of Northern Ireland today trace their ancestry back to that original plantation and others that followed in the decades to come. From the beginning, the settlers felt under siege from the dispossessed native Catholic population whose lands they now occupied. Ashbrook was not just a gift to the General but a defence for the new settlers. 'The General was a professional soldier,' John told me. 'He'd been sent over to pacify and colonize this part of Northern Ireland. I imagine the local population resented these intruders coming from a foreign country and the settlers needed a certain amount of protection. Thomas Ash was the fellow who provided it. It was essential from England's point of view to virtually own the place.' The ruins of the old 'bawn', the fortified enclosure that all landowners were legally obliged to construct, are still visible today in the kitchen and deep cellars at Ashbrook.

The area around Derry, the city's original name taken from the Gaelic

word 'Doire' meaning 'place of the oaks', was especially rich and potentially profitable with fertile soil, rivers teeming with fish and forests thick
with the oak trees that were in great demand for building ships. General
Ash, an entrepreneur as well as a soldier, cut down thousands – and
unpatriotically sold them to the Spanish. Derry became a natural magnet
not only for the settlers but for the merchant companies of the City of
London who saw its mouthwatering commercial opportunities. 'The
plantation was a successful effort by the British to exploit the natural
resources of this part of Ireland and a natural opportunity to make money,'
say John. 'It was started by the "Young Turks" – the merchant adventurers.
I suppose one would have said, as with the Wild West, "Go West, young
man!" There were fortunes to be made and that's how Northern Ireland
was colonized. The settlers had this thing called the Protestant work ethic
and they made the thing a great success.' Soon, three-quarters of the
inhabitants of the newly settled parts of Ulster were Protestants with no
previous ties, interest or connection with the original inhabitants of the
land they now worked.

Another ancestor, Sir Tristram Beresford, from whom John takes the
Beresford part of the family name, became the first land agent for the
London merchant companies, looking after administration as their interests
as well as providing protection for the new settlers. In 1613, when the
Royal Charter was granted enabling the merchant adventurers to colonize
Ulster, the name of the city was changed to Londonderry. John thought it
was to make the settlers feel at home. 'I think it was to give some
encouragement to the people working here because rather naturally they
found it rather unpleasant. They were constantly being attacked and never
being paid. It was a sort of bribe to make them think that they were doing
something for their own home town.' A contemporary account of the
plantation records that revolt was inevitable as the dispossessed Catholics
withdrew to the woods from where they became the scourge of the settlers
'upon whom they descended when the occasion offered to plunder and
assault'.[1] In 1641, the 22,000 Protestants of the now well-established
colony saw their enduring nightmare come true as embittered Catholics
attacked the settlers. The rising was part of a wider rebellion by Catholics
throughout the country who had seen the new Puritan parliament in
England pass a decree suppressing the Catholic religion in Ireland. The
Great Rebellion, as it became known, marked the beginning of the English
civil war, which claimed the lives of about one-third of the native Irish
Catholic population during the eleven years in which it raged on both sides
of the Irish Sea.[2] What began as a political uprising by Irish and English
Catholics throughout Ireland – the English had settled in the other three
ancient provinces long before the plantation – descended into an orgy of

sectarian killing in Ulster where 4,000 settlers were murdered in Porta-down. Catholics were massacred by Protestants in reprisal. The events of 1641 reinforced the idea in the mind of every settler and his family that they were defenders of their faith in an alien country besieged by hostile natives who would shrink from no atrocity to retrieve their lands. Fifty years later, in Derry, the siege became real.

To defend the Londonderry plantation and their commercial interests, the merchant companies had fortified the city with huge walls designed to keep even the most determined enemy at bay. In 1689 they served their purpose dramatically during an epic siege of the city by the army of the Catholic King James II during the war for the English throne. Ireland was caught up in the wider European power struggle in which Catholic France and Protestant Holland were the superpowers and deadly rivals of the time. Fearing that England was becoming a Catholic satellite of King Louis XIV of France, the Dutch Prince William of Orange invaded England, chased King James from the throne, became King William III and proclaimed the 'Glorious Revolution' of 1688 in which the Protestant faith and succession were assured. In panic, James fled to France and then with his French allies came to Ireland to attack England from the rear – which is how his Jacobite army (the word for the supporters of King James's Stuart dynasty) came to be laying siege to Derry.

The city which had a peacetime population of around 2,000 was swollen to an estimated 30,000 as families from the surrounding countryside sought refuge within its walls from the advancing army of King James. 'My family was living at Ashbrook,' John recalls, 'and there was obviously no security at all in a private house. You had to have a full-scale castle to survive those sort of troubles. So they did what everybody else did, they went inside the walled city and rode out the siege as best they could.' The siege began on 7 December 1688, when thirteen young Protestant Apprentice Boys closed the gates in the face of the enemy after the Governor of Derry, Colonel Robert Lundy, decided that resistance was futile and proposed to negotiate terms of surrender. Lundy was deposed and smuggled out of the city as cries of 'No Surrender' echoed from the walls. As a result, the word 'Lundy' entered the loyalist vocabulary as a term of abuse for anyone prepared to betray Ulster. Conditions during the siege were horrendous, as another of John's ancestors, Captain Thomas Ash, recorded in a famous contemporary diary. On 26 July, almost eight months into the siege, he wrote the following entry:

> God knows, we never stood in such need of supply; for now there is not one week's provisions in the garrison. Of necessity we must surrender the city, and make the best terms we can for ourselves. Next

Wednesday is our last, if relief does not arrive before it. This day the cows and horses, sixteen of the first, and twelve of the last, were slaughtered; the blood of the cows was sold at four pence per quart, and that of the horses at two pence . . . There is not a dog to be seen, they are all killed and eaten.[3]

Other contemporary accounts describe unburied corpses being devoured by rats and the rats then being devoured by desperate humans. Everything had its price: a dog's head was two shillings and sixpence; a cat was four shillings and sixpence; a rat was a shilling; and a mouse, sixpence.[4] Fifteen thousand men, women and children are estimated to have died through starvation, malnutrition and disease. The day after Captain Ash wrote that entry, two ships loaded with supplies – the Protestant fifth cavalry – broke the 'boom' that the besiegers had placed across the neck of Loch Foyle to prevent re-supply of the besieged city. The captain of the flagship of the squadron, the *Mountjoy*, was Michael Browning, who was also coming to the aid of his wife, Elizabeth Ash, who had taken shelter with her mother inside the walls after Ashbrook had been overrun by the advancing Jacobite army. But Captain Browning never saw his wife or mother-in-law. 'It was rather sad really,' explained John, 'because almost within sight of the walls of Derry, he stopped a bullet and so never had this joyful reunion.' Captain Thomas Ash recorded the scene in his diary:

Captain Browning stood upon the deck with his sword drawn, encouraging his men with great cheerfulness; but a fatal bullet from the enemy struck him in the head, and he died on the spot. King William did his widow the honour of tying a diamond chain round her neck, and settled on her a pension.[5]

A copy of a famous painting, *The Relief of Derry*, now hangs in Ashbrook showing Governor Walker (who replaced the disgraced Colonel Lundy) surrounded by joyful citizens, pointing to the *Mountjoy* as the ship broke the 'boom'. Elizabeth Ash is depicted in the foreground tending the sick and the dying alongside her mother and son, the diarist Captain Thomas Ash. Elizabeth is unaware of the fate of her husband, Captain Browning.

The siege of Derry became one of the most powerful symbols in Protestant history. 'They were hard men in those days and even harder women and they stuck it out and became national heroes,' said John. 'The notion of Derry, the "Maiden City" – because her walls were never breached – has been built up and built up to commemorate what would have been a catastrophic defeat.' The Apprentice Boys became the symbol of Protestant defiance, the name 'Lundy' synonymous with treachery and

'No Surrender!' the battle cry of loyalists down the centuries. The siege remains living history today, as every year the Apprentice Boys of Derry, the Brotherhood founded at the start of the nineteenth century to cherish their memory, commemorate the siege by burning a sixteen-foot-high effigy of Lundy to mark its start in December and march round the walls to mark its relief the following August. It was the Apprentice Boys' parade on 12 August 1969 to celebrate the 300th anniversary of the lifting of the siege that provoked the rioting that led to the deployment of British troops and the effective beginning of the current conflict.

The Protestants' victory was sealed a year later on 11 July 1690 when their champion, King William III of Orange, defeated King James II's army at the Battle of the Boyne. The Protestant succession to the English throne was now secure and 'Remember 1690' entered the handbook of Protestant slogans alongside 'No Surrender!' The Orange Order was founded over a century later in 1795, following a skirmish with Catholics near the village of Loughgall in County Armagh, to sustain 'the glorious and immortal memory' of King William and the Boyne.[6] The huge parades throughout areas of Northern Ireland on 12 July every year celebrate 'King Billy's' famous victory, traditionally seen by many working-class loyalists as a victory of the 'Prods' over the 'Taigs' (a traditional term of abuse for Catholics), which is why marching is such a politically sensitive issue today.

With the siege of Derry over and King William III now firmly established on the throne of England, John's family returned to Ashbrook and rebuilt the house that the Jacobite troops had burned. More than a century later, another of his ancestors, John Beresford, who was a minister in the Irish parliament in Dublin that ran Ireland on behalf of the Crown, achieved lasting fame by writing the Act of Union of 1800 that created the United Kingdom of Great Britain and Ireland. After another rebellion in 1798 had underlined not only Ireland's instability but its vulnerability to foreign invasion, once again at the hands of the French, William Pitt, the English Prime Minister of the day, decided that Ireland should be brought under direct control. The Irish parliament in Dublin was to be abolished and Irish members were to be elected to the House of Commons at Westminster. 'John Beresford was Commissioner of the Revenue in Dublin, a Privy Councillor and the power behind the throne,' John explains. 'In fact he was known as the "uncrowned king of Ireland". He was a member of the Irish parliament and had a finger in almost every pie there was. He was also an extremely forceful character. There was tremendous opposition to the change among the British aristocracy over here and the Anglo-Irish gentry because they rather naturally thought they could run the country to their own advantage far better without inter-ference from London. But he finally managed to cajole the landowners

into voting for the Act of Union, the principle being that the island of
Ireland would be far better governed by a parliament in London than a
parliament in Dublin. My ancestor, John Beresford, actually wrote the
small print of the Act of Union. The significance of the Act was vast. It was
of tremendous strategic importance to have Ireland under British control.
We now had garrisons here and troops to defend the place.'

But despite – or perhaps because of – the Act of Union, Ireland was
never at peace. The nineteenth century was marked by constant political
agitation as social, economic and constitutional grievances forced their
unwelcome attention on successive British governments faced with the
growing emergence of Irish nationalism and widespread violence and civil
unrest. The greater the nationalist menace, the more determined Protestants became to resist, fearing for all they held dear should the constitutional position of Ireland be changed and they become thrall to the Roman
Catholic Church. Sectarian riots in Belfast and Derry broke out in decade
after decade in the second half of the century, often fuelled by the
inflammatory speeches of the Reverend 'Roaring' Hugh Hanna, a nine-
teenth-century fundamentalist preacher who was one of the Reverend Ian
Paisley's predecessors. By the end of the century, the Irish Question
continued to dominate British domestic politics with parties at Westminster taking sides on the issue. The British Prime Minister, William Ewart
Gladstone, who recognized that Ireland had a separate national identity,
twice endeavoured to solve the Question by introducing bills in 1886 and
1893 to grant Home Rule, a form of semi-independence, to Ireland, but
both bills were defeated – the first in the House of Commons and the
second in the House of Lords. Gladstone finally resigned, defeated by
Ireland as most of his successors also proved to be. In the process he had
split his own Liberal Party and forged the alliance between the Conservative Party and the Ulster Unionists from which the Conservative and
Unionist Party finally emerged. The Conservative champion of the
unionist cause at Westminster was Lord Randolph Churchill who be-
queathed to loyalists yet another historic slogan, 'Ulster will fight and
Ulster will be right'.

But the cause of Home Rule did not die with Gladstone. His Liberal
successor as Prime Minister, Herbert Henry Asquith, who was John's aunt's
grandfather, also took up the Irish challenge and in 1912 attempted to push
a third Home Rule bill through parliament, this time with every chance of
success as veto by the House of Lords had been removed by the Parliament
Act of the previous year, under which their lordships could only veto
legislation from the House of Commons three times. Now it was no longer
a question of if Home Rule would be introduced but when. With that
realization came the critical question for Asquith's Government: would

Ulster Protestants resist and if so, how? The question was soon to be answered.

In 1912, a new champion emerged for Ulster loyalists, beleaguered yet again, in the form of Sir Edward Carson, a Protestant barrister from Dublin who was also a unionist MP for Trinity College Dublin in the Westminster parliament. Even before Home Rule became an issue once again, Carson had acquired a high public profile by his acclaimed defence of the Marquis of Queensbury in the 1895 trial of Oscar Wilde. In 1910 he became leader of the Irish Unionist Parliamentary Party and spoke eloquently against the third Home Rule bill, but he came into his own two years later when he led over half a million Ulster and Irish Protestants in signing the Solemn League and Covenant against Home Rule. It was the climax of eleven rallies held over ten days in September 1912 in what became known as the 'Covenant Campaign' (imitated by Ian Paisley in his 'Carson Trail' of 1981), in which Carson addressed cheering crowds all over the North, having warned Asquith's Government, 'It is you who are prepared to break the law and it is I who am prepared to resist you when you break it.'[7] On 28 September 1912, Carson marched through tens of thousands of cheering loyalists thronging Belfast's Royal Avenue and Donegal Square and into the foyer of the magnificent City Hall, to sign the Covenant with a special silver pen. To Protestants, the Covenant was the equivalent of England's Magna Carta or America's Declaration of Independence. It set out Ulster's position in one extremely long sentence.

> Being convinced in our consciences that Home Rule would be disastrous to the material well-being of Ulster as well as the whole of Ireland, subversive of our civil and religious freedom, destructive of our citizenship, and perilous to the unity of the empire, we, whose names are underwritten, men of Ulster, loyal subjects of his gracious Majesty King George V, humbly relying on the God whom our fathers in days of stress and trial confidently trusted, do hereby pledge ourselves in solemn covenant throughout this our time of threatened calamity to stand by one another in defending for ourselves and our children our cherished position within the United Kingdom, and in *using all means that may be found necessary* [author's emphasis] to defeat the present conspiracy to set up a Home Rule parliament in Ireland.[8]

John's grandfather and grandmother both signed Carson's Covenant. All those who did so also pledged to refuse to recognize the authority of any Home Rule parliament that was set up. But it was the scarcely veiled threat in the phrase 'all means that may be found necessary' that caused greatest concern to Asquith and his Government. Effectively Ulster Protestants were threatening rebellion against the wishes of the sovereign parliament of the United Kingdom. The sentiment was to be often repeated at various stages in the present conflict by Ian Paisley and other loyalist leaders, who believed the British Government was bent on selling them out to a united Ireland.

Carson was Paisley's hero. 'He was the man that taught the people of Northern Ireland the traditional unionism that I have espoused and fought for all my political life,' he told me. 'He's the founding father of our state.' The paradox of loyalism iş that although many who would describe themselves as loyalists have always professed loyalty to the United Kingdom and Crown, their first loyalty has been to the preservation of their own position within it. That is why the British Government and loyalist politicians frequently clashed. Carson's speeches put into words what the Covenant did not. The word was force. 'We have one object in view and that is the object of victory, and we are going to win,' he told his audience. 'As you [the Government] have treated us with fraud, if necessary we will treat you with force.'[9] By 1913 Carson had raised a private army of around 100,000 men between the ages of seventeen and sixty-five, drawn exclusively from those who had signed the Covenant – proof positive that 'all means that may be found necessary' meant military resistance. It was known as the Ulster Volunteer Force (UVF) and given the blessing of the Ulster Unionist Council, which was – and still is – the governing body of the Ulster Unionist Party. Finance was never a problem since it was underwritten to the sum of over a million pounds by the Ulster business community.[10] Regiments were raised all over Ulster, some trained by former British soldiers in Orange Halls and fields across the province. In the words of one partisan historian, class distinctions were set aside.

> Such was the measure of their commitment that after a hard day's toil in the fields or the factories, men walked for miles to attend parades and drills. Social distinctions were forgotten. Gentry cheerfully obeyed orders from their tenants and company directors from their employees.[11]

The UVF itself was commanded by an illustrious senior officer of the day, Lieutenant-General Sir George Richardson.[12] Carson raised the temperature and the anxiety in Downing Street still further when he announced that he had 'pledges and promises from some of the greatest generals in the army, who have given their word that, when the time comes, if it is necessary, they will come over and help us keep the old flag flying'.[13] He criss-crossed Ulster inspecting Volunteers drilling with wooden rifles, telling them they were 'a great army' and asking for their trust with the assurance that 'we will select the most opportune methods, or if necessary take over ourselves the whole government of this community in which we live'.[14]

It was seditious talk, but nothing was done to stop it. There were even plans for the Ulster Unionist Council to become a Provisional Government with Carson at its head. Moreover, at the beginning of 1914, there was a further development that gladdened the hearts of Ulster loyalists. In March, sixty British cavalry officers based at the Curragh camp near Kildare resigned their commissions rather than face the prospect of being used to coerce Ulster unionists and take on the UVF. The War Office refused to accept their resignations and declared that it did not intend to undertake any military operations against recalcitrant Ulster unionists, but the assurance was given without the authority of the Cabinet and the Secretary of War and the Chief of the Imperial General Staff. Both were forced to resign.[15] Nevertheless, the message was clear: there was no guarantee that British soldiers would obey orders should they be called upon to put down a loyalist rebellion in Ulster.

Initially the English press made a mockery of Ulstermen drilling in fields with dummy rifles, but soon began to take them more seriously once the wooden guns became real. In a daring plot approved by Carson, 35,000 rifles and 3 million rounds of ammunition were secretly smuggled into the port of Larne from Germany on board a freighter called the *Clyde Valley*. The consignment was landed during the night of 24/25 April 1914 and its contents distributed to the UVF throughout Ulster, much of them being stowed away in the roofs of Orange Halls. The chief gun-runner was one of Carson's lieutenants, Major Frederick Crawford, who had signed the Covenant in his own blood. But battle was never joined as, just over three months later, on 4 August 1914, Britain was at war with Germany. The showdown was postponed.

The Ulster Volunteer Force did go to war but not against the enemy it had expected. Three days after the opening of hostilities, the newly appointed War Minister, Lord Kitchener, said, 'I want the Ulster Volunteers.' He finally got them and 10,000 new uniforms were ordered from Moss Bros. in London.[16] The Volunteers went into battle not as the UVF but as the 36th Ulster Division, but as long as the word 'Ulster' was in their title, few of them complained. Thousands of Ulstermen enlisted to fight for King and Country, answering Lord Kitchener's famous poster call 'Your Country Needs You!' Many never returned. John Beresford Ash's family paid a heavy price. Seventeen of them were either killed, gassed or wounded during the course of the war. On 1 July 1916 – the original calendar anniversary of the Battle of the Boyne – the 36th Ulster Division was thrown at the German lines in the Battle of the Somme. Some are recorded to have rushed from the trenches with cries of 'No Surrender' and 'Remember 1690' into a barrage of enemy shells and deadly machine-gun fire. Many wore Orange ribbons and one sergeant wore an Orange sash. The loss of life was awesome. Two thousand Ulster Volunteers were killed and over 3,000 wounded. The West Belfast battalion of the UVF, known as 'the Shankill Boys', was 700 strong when it left the trenches. When the slaughter was over, only seventy were left.[17] John Beresford Ash's father was a professional soldier and fought at the Somme as a junior captain in the Royal Fusiliers, not as an officer in the UVF which was made up entirely of volunteers.

I asked John why the Somme had such an emotional place in loyalist history. 'Don't forget, they were volunteers,' he said. 'They were not regular soldiers. They had joined out of love of their country and they really believed they had a higher duty to perform. They were fighting against the evil of Kaiserism. In all, nearly 100,000 men from all regiments were lost that first day. I think 20,000 were lost in the first hour. They always say that patriotism died on the Somme. People just did not believe that such carnage could take place.'

The memory of the Somme remains still fresh in the minds of loyalists today, especially those who became members of the reincarnated but illegal Ulster Volunteer Force in the present conflict, whom successive British and Irish governments branded 'terrorists'. Augustus 'Gusty' Spence became the legendary leader of the modern UVF and served a life sentence for murder.[18] His father was a member of the original UVF and he says he took in the history of loyalism 'with his mother's milk'. Today the study in his small bungalow off the Shankill Road stands as a shrine to the Somme and his fellow Ulstermen who made the ultimate sacrifice. 'There was something like 5,200 casualties,' he told me. 'Now one can imagine in a place like Belfast – or as small as Northern Ireland – that the telegrams and lists of the dead and wounded, the killed and the missing, had a profound impact. The whole province was plunged into mourning. We were born and reared with the sacrifice of the Somme.'

Nineteen sixteen was the great watershed year in both loyalist and republican history, marked by two dramatic events that were to condition the paths the two traditions were to take for the remainder of the century. The Somme was one. The Easter Rising was the other. On Easter Monday 1916, republicans who were the forerunners of the Irish Republican Army (IRA) seized the Post Office in Dublin and proclaimed the Irish Republic.[19] With the country at war, the rebellion was seen as a stab in the back and Britain executed the leaders of the Rising for treason, thus creating martyrs and the notion of 'blood sacrifice'. Just over two months later, loyalists made their own blood sacrifice at the Somme.

When the Great War was over and the Ulstermen who survived returned home, they discovered that the issue of Home Rule, which they had initially volunteered to fight, had not gone away. They now saw the old enemy, Irish republicanism, with a new name, the Irish Republican Army, fighting a savage guerrilla campaign to force Britain to leave the whole of Ireland. To Irish nationalists it became known as the War of Independence. The British would have regarded it as a war against 'terrorism', although the British auxiliary forces known as the 'Black and Tans' indulged in savagery every bit as vicious – if not more so – than that of their enemy. After two years of bloody fighting, a compromise was reached and a Treaty signed on 6 December 1921 that recognized the partition of Ireland under which Britain was to withdraw from twenty-six of Ireland's thirty-two counties. The Treaty did not give Ireland her independence but what the IRA's leader, Michael Collins, called 'the freedom to achieve freedom' in the form of the semi-independent 'Eire' or Irish Free State. Eire had its own parliament in Dublin known as Dail Eireann and no longer sent MPs to Westminster. Even today the term 'Free State' is still used disparagingly by many loyalists despite the fact that 'Free State' became the Irish Republic in 1937.

The partition of Ireland that had been ratified by the Government of Ireland Act before the signing of the Treaty, divided the country and created for unionists the state of Northern Ireland that was to remain an integral part of the United Kingdom. Partition was brought about because of the continuing threat of a loyalist rebellion that had not been diminished by the intervention of the Great War. But from the outset, the division was artificial. Only six of the nine counties of the ancient province of Ulster were excluded to guarantee Protestants an overriding two-thirds majority within the new state. Northern Ireland's new parliament at Stormont was regarded, with good reason, as a 'Protestant parliament for a Protestant people'.

From its birth, Northern Ireland was a state under siege born amidst widespread sectarian violence, in particular in Belfast and Derry. In the first two years of its existence, 557 people were killed in inter-communal rioting – 303 Catholics, 172 Protestants and 82 members of the police and British army. Belfast witnessed the most vicious sectarian rioting of all that led to mass expulsions of Catholic workers from the Protestant-dominated shipyards and engineering works. It is estimated that around 10,000 Catholic workers were put out of their jobs and 23,000 Catholics were driven out of their homes.[20] The IRA was active too, trying to destabilize the state from the very beginning and complete the business that partition had left unfinished. To most loyalists, the minority nationalist population was seen as the IRA's sleeping partner as it shared the same aim of achieving a united Ireland. Nationalists were regarded as the enemy within, a Trojan horse for the IRA and the Dublin Government that loyalists were convinced was plotting with its allies to bring about the downfall of their state. Partition and the violence that came with it only reinforced Protestants' siege mentality. The civil war that followed partition between the pro- and anti-treaty forces tore the new Irish Free State apart between 1922 and 1923. The bitter fighting, in which family was set against family and Irishman against Irishman, left almost a thousand people dead and confirmed Northern Protestants in their conviction that they wanted to have nothing to do with the South.

The defensive 'wall' of the new state was a formidable security apparatus that consisted of an armed police force and draconian laws against subversion. The new police force, the Royal Ulster Constabulary (RUC), reflected in its name the allegiance of the majority population and was aided by an armed force of special constables known as the Ulster Special Constabulary (USC). The largest and most effective arm of the USC was the 'B' Specials, a unit of 16,000 men who volunteered their services one night a week, on the understanding that they were only to be used in an emergency. Many of them were former members of the original Ulster Volunteer Force. They were unpaid, armed by the state and exclusively Protestant. The 'B' Specials, whose job was to keep an eye on potential subversives in their areas, were hated by nationalists, who saw them as a nakedly sectarian force, and revered by loyalists, who saw them as the defenders of their community and their state. Today loyalists and their politicians still speak warmly of the 'B Men' whom they fondly remember as their bulwark in a golden age when the their state was secure and the IRA kept firmly in its place. They also lament the ending of the Special Powers Act, the statute that gave the Northern Ireland Minister for Home Affairs sweeping powers to fight subversion without any undue concern for civil liberties. It was introduced in 1922 to combat the violence and was intended to last for only a year but finally became permanent until its abolition in 1972. It gave the Minister unprecedented powers to ban organizations, impose curfews, make arrests without warrant and intern suspects without trial.[21]

This was the state in which the young John Beresford Ash grew up. When he returned to Northern Ireland and the family home at Ashbrook in 1959 after Eton and a brief spell in the army in accordance with the family tradition, he was not happy at what he found, in particular in his home town of Derry where, although nationalists were in a majority, the electoral boundaries had been so gerrymandered that unionists ran the city. 'It was an extraordinary situation,' he said. 'There was blatant discrimination against the Roman Catholic population. They were kept in certain wards so that regardless of their numbers, they could never have proper representation at local government level.' John also saw that however hard they tried, many Catholics found it difficult to escape the poverty to which they had long been consigned because of the discriminatory nature of employment. Although in Derry itself there was work for Catholic women in the shirt factories along the banks of the River Foyle, there was little work for their menfolk, and what jobs there were were largely taken by Protestants. 'I was the only Protestant person who employed Catholics here and so they were kept as a financial underclass. Consequently they never had any money and they couldn't buy a house. The only housing they could get was public housing and that was all concentrated in one ward of the city. So they had a genuine grievance.'

John saw trouble coming a decade before it erupted and, on his return to Northern Ireland, warned the Young Unionist Council of which he was a member that 'if the Protestant people didn't make some normal, reasonable concessions to normal, reasonable requests from the Catholic population, there was going to be big trouble ahead and they were riding for a fall'. To most unionists in those days, such thoughts bordered on treachery. John was told he was a 'blow in', did not know what he was talking about and should keep his mouth shut. Disgusted by the response and the clear indication that neither attitudes nor the situation were going to change, he gave up politics altogether. He did not even bother to resign but simply stopped going to meetings, as he watched violence flare in 1968 and Northern Ireland slip ever closer to the abyss. His prophecy came true and, almost thirty years later, John Beresford Ash narrowly escaped death for the second time.

In the small hours of 15 August 1997 John and his French wife, Agnès, were asleep in bed when they were awakened by the tinkling of breaking glass. As they were having repairs done to the outside at the time, John thought that one of the chandeliers in the hall had fallen down. He remembers the tinkling going on for about five seconds before he heard 'a tremendous bang' as a concrete block was thrown through one of the windows in the hall, followed by a petrol bomb. 'Suddenly our bedroom was bathed in brilliant white light. We rushed down the main staircase and found five fires in the hall which we managed to put out before they really got hold.'

Six months later to the day, on 15 February 1998, there was more blinding white light as the fire-bombers struck again, once more in the middle of the night. This time it was a more calculated attack. A window in the dining room was smashed and a petrol can dumped on the window seat which was then ignited with paraffin and more petrol. Fortunately for the family, the petrol can had leaked so the 'bomb' never properly went off. Had it done so the Beresford Ash family and Ashbrook would probably have been finished. As John fought the flames, coughing and choking in the dense billowing smoke, he could see around him the portraits of his ancestors looking down from the walls. 'I thought to myself, "Don't worry, chaps. I'm here. I'll put this bloody fire out." I felt really quite emotional. I also felt that if I died, there was no better place to go.'

But that was not the end. Four months later, on 12 June 1998, the fire-bombers struck for a third time, but now in a more sinister way. Again, John and his wife were asleep in bed when they heard a crash, but it was not followed by the sound of breaking glass. 'We followed our by now set routine. As I came down the main staircase, I could see there was a tremendous glow of fire but this time it was outside the house not in. I flung open the door and to my absolute amazement saw five little fires in a semicircle about ten yards from end to end. I immediately realized what it was. We'd recently had a family photograph taken outside our front door for my sixtieth birthday that had been in the local papers. There were five of us there, my three daughters and my wife and myself. I assumed this was meant to represent the five of us being burned.' I suggested that most people who had been fire-bombed three times in ten months would want to move; was not he minded to do so now? 'Good Lord, no!' he said, looking horrified at the thought. 'We're devoted to our house. This is our family home. I shall never leave.' I asked him if the bombers had ever been caught. 'No,' he said, 'and they never will be.' Today, John Beresford Ash and most of the Protestants of Northern Ireland still feel themselves a community under siege.

Chapter Two

Gathering Storm

If there is one dominant loyalist figure who runs through the entire history of the current conflict, he is the Reverend Ian Kyle Paisley. To his tens of thousands of supporters – and he never tires of reminding his opponents that he has repeatedly topped the poll in the elections to the European Parliament – he is Ulster's true defender and guardian of the Protestant faith. To his equally numerous critics, he is the sectarian bigot who has fanned the flames of the Troubles from the very beginning with a vocabulary of one word – No. Whatever the reality, and it is far more complex than any black and white judgement, there is no doubt that Ian Paisley has had a profound influence on the course of events. He has been written off more times than many care to remember by those ever eager to write his obituary, but all predictions of his demise have proved premature. Paisley exists only because Protestant Ulster exists, and he is the rock on which it stands.

For almost half a century – for his influence goes as far back as 1951 when he founded his own Free Presbyterian church – he has instilled a messianic devotion in his followers, who see 'the Big Man' as the true prophet of his time, the heir of Carson, the sworn enemy of Rome, the opponent of ecumenism, the scourge of the IRA, the denouncer of 'Lundys' and the thorn in the side of countless British governments whom he is convinced are determined to sell out Ulster and hand it over to Dublin. The key to understanding Paisley, whatever view may be held of him, is to recognize that as with Islamic fundamentalists, the politics flow from the deep religious conviction. Paisley preaches 'Christ Crucified', believing that every word in the Bible is true. The questions may be difficult but the answers are simple and they are all there in the Good Book. For the loyalist community that for thirty years, if not four centuries, has felt itself permanently under threat from what it sees as the Roman Catholic enemy, the religious and political certainties of Paisley's message have always had an instant and powerful appeal. When I interviewed him for *Loyalists*, he brushed aside the charges of his enemies. 'I live my life before God and my country and to tell you the truth I couldn't care less what people say about me – either when I'm living or dead. It's something that will be repeated as long as the world exists that Paisley is a "bad boy". They said the same about Carson. All I can say is that I'll not be changing. I will go to the grave with the convictions I have.'

Noel Docherty was a disciple who fell under Paisley's spell as long ago as the 1950s. Docherty was a printer by trade and in the mid-sixties set up the Puritan Printing Press that published Paisley's newspaper, the *Protestant Telegraph*, whose pages were full of anti-Catholic diatribes with lurid stories such as 'The Love Affairs and the Vatican' and the 'Harlot of Rome'.[1] Docherty played a highly controversial role in one of Paisley's early political organizations, the Ulster Protestant Volunteers, and went to gaol as a result. On his release he disappeared without trace. There were rumours that he had gone to Rhodesia to fight the 'terrorists' and then to South Africa, where he was reported to have set up another printing business. Over the years, journalists had tried to track him down as the guardian of Paisley's secrets, but without success. Noel Docherty appeared to have gone for ever and taken his past with him. But as the result of an astonishing piece of detective work, Julia Hannis, one of our *Loyalists* team, finally found him in England. He agreed to a meeting and gave us directions for a rendezvous at a Pizza Hut in a Northern town. We were several minutes late after a long drive from London and literally bumped into him as he was coming out of the door. Perhaps he was using our lateness as an excuse to change his mind. He was bearded and wore a battered trilby hat which I initially suspected might be a disguise, but it was not. He was clearly nervous and suspicious at first, fascinated to know how we had found him and curious to hear what we were doing. For two hours, he sat drinking coffee and eating garlic bread. He was not a pizza lover. Gradually he began to tell his remarkable story.

Docherty had first been drawn to Paisley in the mid-fifties when he was a young pupil at high school and involved in intense debates on the true meaning of the Bible. There were fierce arguments over whether what it said could be taken literally.

As a young man I was religious and I was having trouble with my class-mates about the Creation story and the Virgin Birth. Paisley explained them in his sermons and did so with conviction. His fundamentalism greatly appealed to me. He was forthright and he wasn't afraid. I saw him as a true disciple of Christ. He thundered the message forth in a way that brought joy to my heart and I was spellbound by his oratory. I felt he was going places and I wanted to go with him.

Why did you feel he was going places?

The ecumenical movement [the *rapprochement* between the Protestant and Catholic churches] was a big thing in Belfast at the time and Paisley was the only person I had seen who was preaching against it. I felt ecumenism had to be destroyed and Paisley was the man to do it.

Why did you want to go with him?

One likes to be led. There was power with Paisley – power in his mannerisms and power in his preaching. He was like a breath of fresh air. His sermons brought the Bible alive. I felt this is a man that's doing the Lord's work and if he's going to do the Lord's work, then I'm going to do it with him. I saw him as a great Ulsterman and a second Carson.

In the fifties, when the young Docherty was spellbound by Paisley, politics were not an issue. 'There was really no threat to Ulster from any quarter that I could see. Unionists were running everything and the police force was in control.' As soon as he was old enough, Docherty joined the 'B' Specials simply because he saw them as an arm of the Protestant religion. 'It was an exclusively Protestant organization,' he said. 'When I joined, I didn't care what its role was. It was just a back-up for the RUC – guarding things like Carson's monument and power stations if needed. When you joined they just used to say, "Can you fire a .45?" Answer: "Yes." "Can you hit that aperture?" Answer: "Bang! Yes!" and then they'd say, "Next!" But then I came to realize that its role was to protect Ulster people against the IRA. We knew who the enemy were. The IRA never went away.'

Although politics were not an issue when the young Docherty first joined the 'B' Specials and Paisley's Free Presbyterian church – he saw both as serving the same purpose – all that was to change in the sixties. By 1963, Northern Ireland had a new Prime Minister, Captain Terence O'Neill, who displayed all the liberal and ecumenical tendencies that Paisley and his growing band of followers felt threatened the stability of Protestant Ulster and the primacy of the Protestant faith. In Paisley's eyes, the process that he was convinced would eventually lead to a united Ireland had to be confronted and stopped at every opportunity, regardless of how trivial the issue may have seemed at the time. Barely two months after Captain O'Neill became Prime Minister on 25 March 1963, Pope John XXIII died. He had done much to open up the Roman Catholic Church and embrace the growing spirit of ecumenism, and his attempt to break down denominational barriers had struck a chord in the Protestant and Catholic congregations of Northern Ireland. As a mark of respect, O'Neill sent an unprecedented letter of condolence to Cardinal Conway, the head of the

Roman Catholic Church in Ireland, and approved the lowering of the
Union Jack on Belfast City Hall as a mark of respect. Swiftly Paisley made
the maximum capital out of what he saw as an act of treachery and
summoned his supporters to the Ulster Hall, which was to become his
favourite theatre and stage in the years ahead. He lambasted O'Neill and
the Protestant churchmen who had also sent condolences as the 'Iscariots of
Ulster', and assured his followers that 'this Romish man of sin is now in
hell' to cries of 'Hallelujah!' and 'Amen!' He then led a march to the City
Hall to protest against the lowering of the flag.[2] It was the tactic that was to
become a familiar sight in Northern Ireland, as Paisley would call a rally,
fire up his supporters and then lead a march to protest.

A year later, another flag became the focus of Paisley's wrath. A general
election had been called in Britain for the autumn of 1964, and in the West
Belfast constituency Sinn Fein was running a candidate called Liam
McMillen, who had been interned during the IRA campaign of 1956–
64 that had just ended. McMillen subsequently went on to become the
commander of the IRA's Belfast Brigade before the organization split in
1969. An Irish Tricolour was displayed in the window of the Sinn Fein
election office located at the bottom of Divis Street that runs from the
nationalist Falls Road into the city centre. Under the Flags and Emblems
Act, such displays were illegal only if the police deemed they were likely to
cause a breach of the peace, and generally a blind eye was turned since
taking action would be likely to cause more trouble than leaving it alone.
But Paisley's eye was not blind nor were those of his supporters once their
attention had been drawn to the display of the offending flag. Now
Docherty was incensed. 'We called it the "murderers' flag",' he recalls. 'It
was like flying the swastika in London during the Second World War. It
represented something that was anathema to every Ulsterman. We had to
get that flag down and maybe burn the place where it was flown. That was
the idea. Nothing was going to stop me. Come hell or high water, that flag
was going to burn!' Paisley was determined to force a showdown and have
the flag removed. The now familiar pattern emerged. A summons went
out in the form of an 'SOS to Ulster Protestants!', a rally was convened in
the Ulster Hall, and Paisley laid into republicans who dared to fly their flag
and the pusillanimous authorities who declined to take it down. 'If that flag
is not removed tomorrow,' he boomed, 'I will organize a march and
remove it myself.'[3]

Faced with the threat of a Paisley march into republican West Belfast
with the attendant risk of serious public disturbance, the police moved in
and removed the offending flag. Fighting erupted between Sinn Fein
supporters and the police. Three days later, the Tricolour was back in the
window following more clashes with the police. The RUC moved in once

more, smashed the window with pick axes and removed the flag again. This time fierce rioting broke out. Petrol bombs were thrown and the IRA even brought out a few guns. The RUC responded with water cannon to try to disperse the protesters. They were the worst disturbances Belfast had seen since the riots of the 1930s, and police reinforcements were called in, wearing military helmets and backed by armoured cars. Fifty civilians were taken to hospital.[4] One observer of the riot was a young republican called Gerry Adams. Paisley claimed a great victory and established himself in the eyes of loyalists as the man prepared to stand up to republicanism, warning a victory rally in the Ulster Hall that those who had kicked policemen in Divis Street would be kicking Protestants tomorrow.[5]

Today, Paisley has no regrets about his actions or the violent emotions he stirred up. I pointed out that the flag was only in the window and not flying on a pole outside the Sinn Fein election office. 'It doesn't matter where the Tricolour was,' he told me. 'It was an act of defiance and the IRA made it clear they were defying the law and thumbing their nose at the authorities.' But were not his actions provocative and simply asking for trouble? 'It was the only way you could move the jellyfish who were in government. It wasn't as if I was a lone voice crying in the wilderness. I was voicing the strong resentment of the Ulster people at the time.'

The following year, Paisley was presented with another ready target to swell his band of supporters and confirm his reputation as the scourge of 'Lundys' within the governing Unionist Party. In 1965, Prime Minister O'Neill broke with tradition and, as part of his growing *rapprochement* with the Irish Republic, invited its Prime Minister, Sean Lemass, to Belfast. Since Articles Two and Three of the Irish constitution of 1937 claimed territorial jurisdiction over Northern Ireland, it had been unionist policy since partition to have no dealings with the Dublin Government until it recognized Northern Ireland's right to exist. Despite the fact that no such recognition had been given or even considered by Dublin, O'Neill went ahead and, without the prior knowledge of his Cabinet colleagues, hosted the Lemass visit. Inevitably, Paisley paraded his supporters outside the Stormont parliament with placards declaring 'No Mass! No Lemass!', 'Down with the Lundys!' and 'IRA Murderer Welcomed at Stormont!'[6]

But in the increasingly tense atmosphere – and unknown to all but a few – other developments of a far more sinister nature were under way, involving loyalists who were prepared to carry guns not placards to counter what they perceived to be the growing republican threat. The fact that the IRA had put its arms away the previous year, although not decommissioned them, after the failure of its 1956–64 campaign cut no ice with the loyalist hard men who believed their enemy was merely preparing for its next campaign. They came together to form an armed group that they called the Ulster Volunteer Force, after Carson's UVF that had fought at the Somme, no doubt believing that the adoption of that title would give them standing and respectability within the loyalist community. They adopted the same motto, 'For God and Ulster'. And so, in the loyalist stronghold of Belfast's Shankill Road, the 'new' UVF was born. One of its earliest recruits was Gusty Spence, who had taken in loyalist history 'with his mother's milk'. He still has a vivid recollection of being sworn in in a barn near Pomeroy in County Tyrone. No doubt the secret ceremony took place so far from Belfast to avoid prying eyes. The UVF became the most secretive of all the loyalist paramilitary organizations that were to emerge over the coming years. Spence told me he was approached by two unionist politicians, whom he refused to name, who invited him to join the UVF. 'I willingly agreed,' he said.

> There were four of us and we were transported to a place outside Pomeroy. It was like a big barn with hurricane lamps. I guess there might have been about forty people there. We all raised our right hands and took the oath. I was later told that the man who swore us in was an ex-colonel in the British army. I was tickled pink to join and proud that someone would have chosen me to become a member of the Ulster Volunteer Force. There was still a sense, like with the old Ulster Volunteers, that you were for the cause. You would fight and die for it – yes, fight and die for the cause.
> **Who was your enemy when you joined the UVF?**
> Oh, the IRA.
> **But in 1965 the IRA barely existed.**
> Well, that may be the case. It's all right in hindsight looking back on all these things but if the people are telling you that the IRA is a threat, we had no reason to disbelieve them. Irish history has been permeated by republican activity. It may seem foolish now, even silly, but that's how it was at the time.

The killing did not start until 1966, the fiftieth anniversary of the Easter Rising and the Somme and the year that effectively marks the beginning of the current conflict. As Easter approached, there were intelligence reports that the IRA was preparing to launch a new campaign to coincide with the anniversary of the seizure of the GPO in Dublin in 1916. According to the secret Cabinet papers of the day, British Intelligence had warned Harold Wilson's new Labour Government that thirty-four IRA training camps had been identified where there were 'lectures on the use of explosives, live firing practice and advice on the mounting of attacks on government buildings'. The intelligence briefings went on to indicate, perhaps somewhat over-optimistically, that the IRA had '3,000 trained members or supporters' who were 'adequately supplied' with guns and ammunition.[7] The fact that republicans had blown up Nelson's statue in Dublin the month before the Easter Commemoration seemed to indicate to the authorities that the intelligence reports were not a work of fiction. Ian Paisley had no doubt about the threat nor had his lieutenant, Noel Docherty, who was one of the 'B' Specials ordered to guard Carson's statue outside the Stormont parliament building. 'I think every Special was alerted at that time,' he told me. 'I think I was on duty twice a week. We were expecting attacks on power stations, post offices and police stations. There was a lot of tension and a lot of nervousness. I remember standing at Carson's monument the whole night with the RUC on either side of me with their hot tea flasks, their Bren guns and their blankets. I stayed there all night drinking coffee in a greatcoat.'

As the Easter Commemoration approached and loyalists expected the IRA to take to the streets any moment, Paisley and Docherty wanted to be ready with an organization that could be mobilized both to meet the IRA threat and to challenge O'Neill. At the beginning of 1966, they set up an organization known as the Ulster Constitution Defence Committee (UCDC) with Paisley as chairman and Docherty as secretary. Docherty cannot remember whether it was he or 'the Bishop' (the word he constantly used when referring to Paisley) who had the original idea. The Committee was an umbrella group of a dozen 'Protestant patriots' – who came to be referred to as Paisley's 'Twelve Apostles' – who under the UCDC constitution 'pledged by all lawful methods to uphold and maintain the Constitution of Northern Ireland as an integral part of the United Kingdom as long as the United Kingdom maintains a Protestant Monarchy and the terms of the Revolution Settlement [of 1688]'.[8] Not surprisingly, the organization's constitution stipulated that 'no one who has ever been a Roman Catholic is eligible for membership' – not that any Roman Catholic would have rushed to join. The UCDC constitution also made it clear that it would expel anyone connected with 'subversive or lawless activities' but, like Carson's Covenant that reserved the right to use 'all means that may be found necessary to defeat the present conspiracy', the Committee also stated it would 'take whatever steps it thinks fit' to maintain Northern Ireland's constitutional position within the United Kingdom.

But the Committee itself was little more than an umbrella for the organization that Docherty helped set up beneath it called the Ulster Protestant Volunteers (UPV), whose numbers ran into many thousands, with a membership fee of ten shillings a head. It adopted the same motto as the reincarnated UVF, 'For God and Ulster', thus adding a degree of confusion to the loyalist paramilitary picture that was now beginning to emerge. Docherty's role was to set up branches or 'divisions' of the UPV across Ulster. Paisley insists that the word 'divisions' referred to parliamentary boundaries and had no military connotations. Docherty, whose brainchild the UPV was, saw it differently. When we spoke, he never once mentioned the word 'divisions' but repeatedly referred to 'cells'. 'The idea was to have cells all over Ulster – in every hamlet, every town, and every major city. Anybody could have been a member of the UPV. It wasn't a secret and there were no oaths. If we needed a demonstration, the support was already organized and sitting there. We could do it at the toss of a coin. The "Bishop" liked the idea.' But Docherty also had other plans and set about organizing 'a secret cell structure' within the existing UPV cells, which he then proposed to arm. 'We already had government-issued .45 Webleys and government-issued Sten guns [as "B" Specials], so we thought, "Why not have our own – under the floorboards", and that's what we started to do. My idea was to have the [secret] cells made up mainly of "Specials" so that at the snap of a finger or a secret code word we could have had a private army just like Carson did with the signing of the Covenant. So Paisley would have had his own private army and he'd have been a second Lord Carson. That was my idea.' Docherty says that he never told Paisley what he was up to as Paisley had to be protected. 'The "Bishop" couldn't be caught,' he said, 'because he was more important than any member of any cell. It wasn't in our interests and it wasn't in his interests to discuss details. He knew I was forming cells but he didn't know about the arms. I trusted him with the future of Ulster but he had to be protected. He would have liked the idea of an armed militia with him the leader. He would have loved that idea but that was in his head. There was no action on his part.' Only a handful of Paisley's supporters were privy to what Docherty was up to. One of those whom Docherty took into his confidence was a Sunday-school teacher called Billy Mitchell who, like Docherty, idolized Paisley and had joined his church in the mid-sixties. 'You felt you were part of the cause,' Mitchell told me. 'You were part of the organized band of people – the chosen few – who would defend Ulster.' Mitchell subsequently joined the UVF, became one of its senior commanders and was later convicted of a double murder carried out as the result of a loyalist paramilitary feud.

Despite all the dire forebodings, the republicans' Easter Commemoration passed off without serious incident. The IRA had not come down from the hills to slaughter its enemies. Not that loyalists thought for one moment that the threat had gone away. According to Docherty, it was around this time that Paisley told him he had been informed by his supporters in the Portadown area that there was a group of Protestants in the nearby village of Loughgall who were interested in joining the Ulster

Protestant Volunteers. Paisley suggested that Docherty should get in touch with them. Docherty spoke to Mitchell, whom he now regarded as a 'trustworthy, tough young man'. They decided to go down together, and the meeting was set up for the evening of 21 April 1966 at the house of a local farmer called James Murdock, another Free Presbyterian and fanatical supporter of Paisley. 'Paisley was our leader,' Docherty told me. 'He was our saviour, our Moses, our champion prepared to resist to the death to oppose the Roman Catholic Church and ecumenism. O'Neill spelled the end of the Ulster we all knew. In a "doomsday" situation, we felt that in some mystical way, the UPV was going to save Ulster.' As Paisley had a speaking engagement in Armagh the same evening, which was only a few miles from Loughgall, he agreed to give Docherty and Mitchell a lift. After he dropped them off, introduced them to Murdock and the others at the meeting – all of whom were 'B' Specials – and had a cup of coffee, Paisley went on to his engagement in Armagh. During the course of the evening, the group discussed the supposed IRA threat and what they would do if the 'B' Specials were disbanded and the army was not around to protect them. James Murdock told me had no recollection of the conversation. They then discussed arming themselves. 'There was general talk about arms,' Docherty recalls. 'We needed shotguns, Sten guns, revolvers and explosives – the paraphernalia of weaponry.' Docherty remembers one of the new recruits, a quarryman, saying that he had, or could get, gelignite. Docherty says he stored the offer away in his head. 'There were a couple of monuments in Ulster I would have been quite happy to get rid of,' he said. 'Not me personally because I wasn't a gelignite ace, but I would have been quite happy to supply someone else that wanted to.' Paisley returned around midnight, picked up Docherty and Mitchell and set off for Belfast. On the journey, Paisley apparently asked Docherty how things had gone. 'Paisley would have said to me, as he would have said on a number of occasions, "How did it go? Have they got many members?" He would have been more interested in the volume. He would want a hundred where I was looking for five good guys. So I'd say, "Yeah, we're going to have a big group down here."'

Did you say to Dr Paisley, 'Oh, by the way, we can get hold of gelignite and guns'?
Never. Never, never, never. I would never trust him.
It just seems very strange that here is the man that you all idolize. You're setting up what is effectively a private army for him, an armed private army, and yet the subject of the arms is never raised with Dr Paisley. He never asks about it. You never tell him about it. Do you expect us to believe that?

Maybe it sounds a little bit like that movie *Mash*, where the
Colonel doesn't know what his doctors are doing. Let's put it that
way. Paisley was the Colonel. He was OK as a figurehead whilst we
would do the job underneath him. He didn't know. He may have
had an inkling. He may have, but certainly we never told him.
   **Did he ever say to you, 'Look, Noel, I don't want you
messing around with guns'or any of that sort of stuff'?**
   No.

Billy Mitchell gives the same account of the trip home. As neither man
today has any love for Paisley, and neither knew I was interviewing the
other, there is no reason to believe they are being economical with the
truth. I also questioned Dr Paisley about that return journey from
Loughgall.

   **Did you ask them what they had been talking about, what they
   had been up to?**
   No. If it was a UPV meeting, I would ask them how it went, but
they never told me that they were discussing any such matters, and
certainly I was not in any way aware of it, nor was I associated in any
way, and I'd be very surprised at this long juncture now that I was in
on such a thing.
   **Did you have any suspicions about what Noel Docherty was
   up to?**
   Yes, I had suspicions about a lot of people in those days and what
they were up to, and I was trying to direct them along the political
path. There were a lot of people who were so angry about what
would happen that they were prepared to take the law into their own
hands.

The meeting at Loughgall proved Noel Docherty's undoing. Through
Billy Mitchell, he subsequently helped the Shankill Road UVF acquire the
gelignite that had been mentioned at the meeting. He took three of their
members to the Portadown area, blindfolded them and took them to
Loughgall where they were shown the gelignite. 'Whether they took it
that night, I don't know. I was probably having tea with the farmer.' The
connection came to light when James Murdock's business card was found
in the possession of one of the members of the UVF, who had taken it from
the farmer's home. 'It was that business card that connected me and the
UPV – which was Paisley – to the UVF on the Shankill Road,' Docherty
remembers ruefully.
   On 18 October 1966, Docherty was sentenced to two years' imprison-

ment for explosives offences. The farmer, James Murdock, was acquitted and the quarryman was fined £200. Paisley was greatly embarrassed when the local press began to run stories that a senior member of his organization was involved in terrorism. At Docherty's trial, the activities of the secretary of the UCDC, the organizer of the Ulster Protestant Volunteers and member of Paisley's church came to light. Paisley expelled Docherty from the organizations he had helped found and told journalists outside Crumlin Road gaol where Docherty was incarcerated that his disciple had been disowned. Docherty remembers the moment with some bitterness.

It would have been nice if Paisley had taken me aside and said, 'Look, you've been up to no good and you know the price. You have to go. You're caught now. Disappear. Bye-bye. But he didn't do that. He just ignored me and changed the lock on the printing house doors. Close friends of mine became strangers. I was just ostracized. And when I eventually did go into gaol, the first night he had a meeting outside the prison and said, 'I knew nothing of what this man has done. I wash my hands of him.' That was worse than the two-year gaol sentence.

Were you using Dr Paisley or was he using you?
I think it's six of one and half a dozen of the other. It's swings and merry-go-rounds. Yes, I was trying to use Paisley and he certainly was using me.

Despite Paisley's denial of knowledge of the clandestine activities in which Noel Docherty and Billy Mitchell were involved, what happened at Loughgall and the subsequent prosecution of members of the UPV and UVF clearly illustrate just how close to the wind Paisley was sailing, even in those early days, in associating with men who were prepared to use violence. It was to happen again on more than one occasion in the future.

At the conclusion of the interview, I asked Noel Docherty if he had started the Troubles, as his was one of the very first convictions. 'I may have,' he said. 'I hope I didn't. I hope I didn't start pulling the first trigger. If I can be held responsible for what happened, then I'm just as guilty as the rest.' He put on his hat, said good-bye and disappeared into the anonymity he had enjoyed for the past thirty years. Part of loyalist history had gone.

Chapter Three

Murder

In the aftermath of the Easter Commemoration in 1966, the Shankill Road UVF, with whom Noel Docherty and Billy Mitchell had begun to associate, started its campaign of sectarian intimidation under the guise of attacking the IRA. One of their targets was thought to have been an off-licence off the Shankill Road that was owned by a Roman Catholic. In those days, the Shankill was not as exclusively Protestant as it became later when Belfast divided into clearly defined Catholic and Protestant areas as the violence intensified and each community sought safety in the company of its own. The house next door to the off-licence, like the vast majority in the Shankill, was rented by Protestants, a seventy-seven-year-old widow called Mrs Matilda Gould and her son, Samuel. The walls of their home had already been daubed with the familiar sectarian slogans, 'Remember 1690', 'Pope-head' and 'This house is owned by a Taig', presumably by bigots who thought that Mrs Gould's house was part of the Catholic-run off-licence. At 10.40 on the evening of 7 May 1966, a petrol bomb was thrown through Mrs Gould's window while she was asleep in bed. The house went up in flames and Mrs Gould died in hospital from her injuries seven weeks later.

At the inquest, the RUC officer who investigated the attack, Detective James McComb, said, 'I think the act was part and parcel of the activities of an organization known as the Ulster Volunteer Force.' Samuel Gould was awarded £336 compensation for the loss of his mother's care and assistance. Making the award, Mr Justice Gibson, who was later assassinated by the IRA on 25 April 1987, said the attack had been carried out by 'a seditious combination or unlawful organization whose activities were directed to asserting and maintaining Protestant ascendancy in areas of the city where there was a predominantly Protestant majority of the population, by overt acts of terror.'[1] Historically, Mrs Gould was the first victim of the current Troubles. A fortnight later, the UVF issued a chilling statement to the Belfast newspapers from 'Captain William Johnson, Chief of Staff of the UVF'. The name, as with all such statements from the paramilitaries on both sides, was fictitious.

From this day, we declare war against the IRA and its splinter groups. Known IRA men will be executed mercilessly and without hesitation. Less extreme measures will be taken against anyone sheltering or helping them, but if they persist in giving them aid, then more extreme methods will be adopted . . . we solemnly warn the authorities to make no more speeches of appeasement. We are heavily armed Protestants dedicated to this cause.[2]

Although Gusty Spence was a member of the UVF when the statement was issued, he insists he was only 'a reasonably small cog in a big piece of machinery', but nevertheless does not distance himself from it.

That statement would be made in your name because you were a member of the organization.
Oh, yes, yes, yes.
And did you agree with that statement?
Well, at that time, yes. Oh, absolutely, yes.
'Executed mercilessly and without hesitation'?
Yes.

The Shankill UVF met in a back room of the Standard Bar, where it appears a decision was made to kill a republican called Leo Martin, who was believed to be a leading member of the Belfast IRA. Four men were ordered to carry out the operation and trawled the Clonard area off the Catholic Falls Road where Martin was thought to live. They failed to find him. Presumably not wishing to return to the Standard Bar with mission unaccomplished, they shot a Catholic called John Patrick Scullion, whom they had encountered in the area drunk and allegedly singing republican songs. Like the victims of the hundreds of loyalist murders that were to follow, John Scullion was an innocent Catholic who happened to be in the wrong place at the wrong time when loyalist paramilitaries were looking for a victim. Astonishingly, when his body was discovered, it was assumed that he had fallen over in a drunken stupor, injured himself and subsequently died. Three weeks later, 'Captain William Johnson' phoned the Belfast press again and, claiming that he was 'Adjutant of the First Battalion of the Ulster Volunteer Force', said that Scullion was their victim.[3] What appeared to have been a case of death by misadventure suddenly became a murder hunt. Scullion's body was exhumed and the belated discovery was made that the abdominal wound was the result of a gunshot.

In June 1966, the loyalist marching season began and the tensions, as always, started to rise, but now perhaps more so than usual given the events of the first six months of the year. On the evening of Saturday 25 June, after a parade down the Shankill, Gusty Spence went to the Standard Bar where he met other members of the UVF. It appears that it was decided that a second attempt should be made to hit Leo Martin, who was named as 'the target for the night'.[4] Two UVF men were ordered to go to Martin's house to kill him. But Martin was not at home. For the second time, the UVF had failed to find and shoot him. The two men returned to the Standard Bar and later in the evening, with Spence and the others, moved on to the Malvern Arms, a pub well known for its after-hours drinking.

That night, three young Catholic barmen – Peter Ward, Richard Leppington and Liam Doyle – had been working late in the International Hotel in Belfast city centre, a mile or so away. As it was Saturday night and it had been a long and busy evening, their manager, Andrew Kelly, also a Catholic, suggested they go off for a drink. The only pub that he knew was open, albeit unofficially, at that time of night was the Malvern Arms off the Shankill Road. In those days, Catholics had no problem going up the Shankill or Protestants up the Falls. 'I'd been there before without any problems,' Andrew Kelly told me. 'I knocked on the door – the door in those days was kept closed at night – and the publican, who knew me, took us in. It was around midnight. There was no problem at all. We had a drink and stayed in our own company. The bar was quite busy that particular night.' I asked him how the regulars would have known that they were Roman Catholics. 'I understood that some of them had been talking to Peter Ward. I don't know what the conversation was and he may have told them that he came from the Falls Road.' One of the UVF men who had gone to the Malvern Arms with Gusty Spence was Hugh McClean who subsequently made a statement to the police about what happened that night.

> The conversation came up about the religion of these fellows. Spence asked the company if they would be Catholics . . . Spence then went up to the bar beside the four lads to buy a drink. When he returned to our table, he said, 'I've been listening to their conversation and they are four IRA men.' We had some more drinks . . . Spence said, 'These are IRA men, they will have to go.'[5]

The four young Catholics left the Malvern Arms about 1.45 a.m. by the side door, with Peter Ward leading the way and Andrew Kelly behind him. Kelly remembers suddenly seeing flashes and hearing the sound of gunfire. 'Somebody gave a signal to start shooting. Peter Ward was hit first. Apparently the bullet went in through the fifth rib and came out through the ninth. He was dead when he hit the ground. I was shot too and dropped down but they kept on shooting at me. There were four gunmen.

They didn't say anything. All I remember are the flashes and the shooting.' Andrew Leppington and Liam Doyle, who were following Peter Ward and Andrew Kelly out of the bar, were also shot and seriously wounded. Doyle survived because he rolled up into a ball when he hit the ground and made himself a more difficult target. Miraculously, Andrew Kelly also survived. 'I don't know why they did it. We were ordinary working people with no IRA connections. We were shot just because we were Catholics.'

Peter Ward's mother, Mary, was sitting at home looking out of her bedroom window, waiting for her son to come in. Although she knew there were often late-night functions at the International Hotel on a Saturday evening, she had started to worry because it was getting so late. Then a priest knocked at the door and said he had 'bad news' about Peter and gradually explained that he had been shot. Mary was devastated and remains so to this day. 'They shot at Peter and Peter fell. It was the UVF shot him and he was shot for nothing, just because he was a Roman Catholic. My Peter had nothing against any religion. He worked with everybody, Catholics and Protestants. Everybody was Peter's friend. He never had no enemies.' I asked Mary Ward what the past thirty years had been like. 'It has been a heartbreak,' she said. 'I never go anywhere or never look to go anywhere because Peter's always there.'

Gusty Spence, Hugh McClean and Robert Williamson, another UVF man were arrested after the biggest murder hunt in the province's history. In the course of the interview during which he made his confession, McClean was asked how he had come to join the UVF. According to the police, he replied, 'I was asked did I agree with Paisley and was I prepared to follow him. I said that I was.' After being charged, he is alleged to have said, 'I am terribly sorry I ever heard of that man Paisley or decided to follow him.'

Paisley immediately repudiated the murder of Peter Ward and told the Protestant daily paper, the *Belfast Newsletter*, 'Like everyone else, I deplore and condemn this killing, as all right-thinking people must.' His own paper, the *Protestant Telegraph*, made clear its leader's position: 'Mr Paisley has never advocated violence, has never been associated with the UVF and has always opposed the hell-soaked liquor traffic which constituted the background to this murder.'[6]

Gusty Spence was charged with the murders of Peter Ward and John Scullion, the UVF's inebriated victim of earlier that summer. After complex legal wranglings, the charge of murdering Scullion was dropped, and Spence and two of his colleagues, Hugh McClean, a former naval seaman, and Robert Williamson, a former British soldier, stood trial for the murder of Peter Ward. The Crown's star witness was a man called

Desmond Reid, who had been at the initial meeting with Spence and others at the Standard Bar on the night of the murder. Reid had come to the attention of the police in the round-up that followed the murder, when gelignite had been found at his home, gelignite which Reid had collected from the quarryman who had been at the Loughgall meeting earlier that year to which Paisley had driven Noel Docherty and Billy Mitchell. Reid struck a deal with the police whereby he agreed to give evidence against Spence in return for the police dropping the explosives charge. In his statement Reid said that he had been sent out to collect some of the gelignite and then returned to Spence's sister's house later that evening. After 1.30 a.m. Spence, Williamson and McClean had come in and gone into the scullery where Reid overheard one of them say, 'That was not a bad job.'[7]

On 14 October 1966, Spence, McClean and Williamson were found guilty after a week's trial and given a minimum recommended sentence of twenty years by Lord Chief Justice McDermott. Four days later, after a much longer trial, Noel Docherty was sentenced to two years for possession of explosives. The two trials indirectly tied in the UVF and the UVP. To this day, Gusty Spence maintains his innocence of the killing of Peter Ward, which may be significant given that, with barely an exception, all the other former UVF members I interviewed for *Loyalists* freely admitted that they were guilty of the offences for which they had been sentenced – and many of them were for murder. Spence admitted to me that he had been 'carrying a gun all that day' and had been 'carrying a gun for weeks', but insists he was not there when Peter Ward was shot. He lodged an appeal and the UCDC petitioned for his release or retrial. Both were turned down.

Spence was released from the Maze prison in 1985, having served eighteen years of his sentence, and went on to play a prominent role in the UVF's political wing, the Progressive Unionist Party (PUP). It was Spence who was chosen to deliver the ceasefire statement of the combined loyalist paramilitaries on 13 October 1994 in which he expressed 'abject and true' remorse for the victims of loyalist violence. I asked him if that included Mrs Mary Ward. 'The most important thing to do was to apologize to Peter Ward's mother,' he said, 'and to apologize to all the mothers'. Mary Ward told me that Spence had telephoned her. 'He said he wanted me to forgive him. I said, "Yes, I'll forgive you on one condition, that you bring peace to this country, because I don't want any other mother to go through what I have gone through." My Peter is in my mind every day and every night. I said, "I know it's not going to bring Peter back, but please try and bring peace here." ' I asked Mary if she now forgave Gusty Spence. She said she did.

The murder of Peter Ward shocked both communities, not least the law-abiding loyalists of the Shankill Road and elsewhere. Many of the young men who later became involved at various levels with the loyalist paramilitaries were barely teenagers at the time and had been brought up by their parents to be courteous to their elders, respectful of the police and regular attenders at Sunday school. To Protestants, the thought of a sectarian murder committed by members of their own community on their own doorstep was deeply shocking. Such things were unthinkable in the mid-sixties when crime of any kind was virtually non-existent in Northern Ireland. Even those who rose to the highest ranks within the loyalist paramilitaries, like Andy Tyrie, who later became the supreme commander of the Ulster Defence Association (UDA), had an upbringing that bore little relation to what they were to become. Tyrie remembers his childhood and what his parents taught him with affection.

My mother and father were very hard-working people. They provided for all the family and looked after them very well. We had a very good childhood. My parents always said you had to do as you're told. We were taught manners and how to behave yourself when you went visiting anybody else's home. We were taught to respect other communities. My mother used to do a lot of handicrafts – quilt-making and embroidery and stuff like that. She shared her skills with the Catholic community who lived around the corner in the Falls Road, so there were no sectarian attitudes from our family. People in the Shankill Road and the Falls Road had to work to survive. It was almost like a market economy at the bottom end of the Shankill and the Falls. They exchanged things and helped each other out as much as they possibly could.

On occasions like the 12th of July or republican commemorations, we could actually look down the street and see each other. But I don't remember any real bitterness. If there was, it didn't last. It was almost seasonal and then everybody went back to their normal ways of doing things and normal ways of living.

William 'Plum' Smith was also born and reared on the Shankill and remembers an upbringing that was just as typically strict. Because there was said to be some native American blood in his family, he was known from an early age as 'Plum', after a character in the *Beano* comic known at 'Little Plum – Your Redskin Chum'. The name stuck. 'Plum' went on to join the Red Hand Commando, a paramilitary organization associated with the UVF, and was later sentenced to ten years for attempted murder. 'The concern for my mother was getting her dinner ready that night. The concern for my father was trying to get the money to pay for that dinner. So politics weren't really talked about as such in my house. All the Protestant kids were taught to be very law-abiding types. I went to Sunday school and I went to church like many of the kids from round about the area. If you were playing football in the street and the policeman came along, everybody would run. You wouldn't really do anything outside the law. Everybody was brought up in that strict way.' Billy Mitchell, who came from an earlier generation, had an even tougher upbringing but one that still inculcated in him all the traditional Protestant values. His father died when he was two years old and his mother brought up Billy and his brother single-handed, relying on the few shillings she earned from her work as a stitcher and the ten shillings a week she received from National Assistance. Billy came from 'a good Christian home' with a mother who was a Baptist Sunday-school teacher. He was a regular churchgoer. Some time in the late sixties, Billy Mitchell joined the UVF, and he was later sentenced to life imprisonment for the murder of two members of the rival UDA. How was it then that people like Billy Mitchell, 'Plum' Smith and Andy Tyrie, and literally hundreds of other young loyalists from similar law-abiding and God-fearing Protestant families, came to fill Northern Ireland's prisons as the years went by? Billy Mitchell gave an explanation, no doubt speaking for the vast majority of his contemporaries:

> Someone didn't fly over Northern Ireland and drop some sort of 'loony gas' and suddenly people woke up one morning as killers. We didn't go to bed one night as ordinary family men and wake up the next morning as killers. Conditions were created in this country whereby people did things they shouldn't have done. While I'll accept responsibility for what I have personally done, I won't accept responsibility for creating the conditions that allowed me to do it and that allowed other people to do it.

Although history had already made it inevitable that periodically down the centuries Ireland would erupt into violence, the particular conditions that sparked the current conflict were already well established by the time Peter Ward was murdered by the UVF. The events that were to follow in the years ahead only accelerated the process as more and more 'ordinary family men', on both sides, became killers.

Chapter Four

Insurrection

On 29 January 1967, three months after Gusty Spence was sentenced for the murder of Peter Ward, a meeting took place in Belfast that would have far-reaching consequences. A decision was made that day to set up a broad-based civil rights movement to demand fair treatment for Northern Ireland's Roman Catholic minority and an end to the discrimination nationalists felt they suffered at the hands of the unionist state and its local authorities. The group that was formed at that meeting became known as the Northern Ireland Civil Rights Association (NICRA), and its activities over the following three years would have a profound effect on the growing instability in the province.

The notion of agitating for civil rights was not new, but had hitherto been confined to a predominantly middle-class pressure group, known as the Campaign for Social Justice, run by Dr Conn McCluskey and his wife, Patricia, from their home in Dungannon, County Tyrone. They endeavoured to draw the attention of a wider audience, in particular British public opinion, to the way politics worked in their own town where, although there was a narrow Catholic majority (53 per cent), the electoral system was rigged in such a way that the local council consisted of fourteen Protestants and only seven Catholics. The system whereby electoral boundaries were rigged to produce a result that defied the composition of the community was known as 'gerrymandering'. Historically, the state of Northern Ireland itself was a gerrymander since its border had been drawn deliberately to guarantee a Protestant majority. The most blatant gerrymander of all was in Derry where 14,000 Catholic voters elected eight councillors, while 9,000 Protestant voters elected twelve. As a result, Londonderry City Council was controlled by unionists although there was an overwhelming nationalist majority in the city. The anomaly was achieved because most of the Catholics were concentrated in one of the three electoral wards of the city known as the Bogside. As the other two wards had Protestant majorities, a Protestant council was elected.[1] Nationalists also complained that the voting system was rigged against them as only householders or lease owners had the vote and therefore, as the Catholic community was the more impoverished, Protestants had more votes.

There was also widespread discrimination in housing and jobs. Because local authorities allocated council housing, Protestant councils tended to provide houses for Protestants – although in areas like Newry, where there was a nationalist council, the majority of houses went to Catholics. Although in some cases discrimination worked both ways, in jobs it did not. Because most of the businesses in Northern Ireland were Protestant-owned, most of the jobs went to Protestants. Often giving your address on a job application or at an interview was enough to guarantee acceptance or rejection. The most notorious example of job discrimination lay with the largest employer in the province, the Belfast shipbuilders Harland and Wolff, whose workforce consisted of 10,000 workers only 400 of whom were Catholics. The shipyard lay at the heart of Protestant East Belfast and that is where most of its workers came from.[2]

The McCluskeys tried to make Harold Wilson's Labour Government at Westminster sit up and take notice of the injustices that were endemic in part of the United Kingdom, but Westminster declined to do so. The Labour Government, which coincidentally had been elected in the year that the Campaign for Social Justice had been formed, 1964, and raised great expectations of reform, also turned a deaf ear to warnings of the trouble in store. Paul Rose, one of the Labour MPs who had taken up the McCluskeys' cause, was parliamentary private secretary to the Labour Cabinet Minister Barbara Castle, and was told to put his energies elsewhere when he raised the subject with her.

> I remember her patting me on the head and saying, 'Why is a young man like you concerned about Northern Ireland? What about Vietnam? What about Rhodesia?' I just looked at her with incomprehension and said, 'You'll see when they start shooting one another.' She was totally oblivious to this. I think their priorities were focused on other things to the extent that they were totally blinded as to what was going on in their own backyard.[3]

But most Protestants did not see the issue of civil rights in the same way as most Catholics and bitterly resented the suggestion that because Catholics claimed they were second-class citizens, Protestants, by definition, must have been first-class. Nothing, they insist, could have been further from the truth. Certainly the fact that most of the Protestant working class was equally impoverished in terms of social conditions tended to be conveniently ignored by many of those who agitated for change. The issue remains a sore point with loyalists today. Billy Mitchell was brought up outside Belfast 'in a wooden hut'; he was not prepared to grace his dwelling with the term 'wooden bungalow'.

> I remember in the kitchen one time the cooker fell through the floor because the floorboards were rotten. It was infested with woodworm. We had an outside dry toilet. You went to the toilet in a bucket and emptied the crap in your pit. It was hard going. The fresh water was about two miles away. It had to be carried in buckets and mother had to go to the well to draw the water. And there was no hot water. Your bath was one of those big galvanized things that was filled with boiling kettles. That was the way we were brought up.

Conditions for Protestants in Belfast were materially little better. Bobby Norris was brought up in the Lower Ormeau Road, which, in the sixties, was a mixed area where Catholics and Protestants worked, played and drank together. Today, the Lower Ormeau is entirely Catholic and one of the sectarian flashpoints since all Protestants have long fled.

> Our housing was the same as our Catholic next-door neighbour – two-up and two-down with an outside toilet. It irks me when I hear about the disadvantages that the Catholics had and the agenda for equality that they go on about now. I just wish that we had some of that equality as well because it certainly affected myself and my family just as much as it affected the Catholics who lived next door to me.
> **But as a Protestant, weren't you a first-class citizen?**
> Absolutely not. There was no difference. The guys that I ran about with had the same conditions as I did. So please don't call me advantaged.
> **Bath night?**
> Tin bath and a rub down like the people next door. There was discrimination but not just against Catholics. The ordinary working class were discriminated against just as much as any Catholic.
> **But you were supposed to feel superior, weren't you, because you were Protestants, that's what the politicians were telling you.**
> Yes, those they called 'politicians'. We were election fodder. They'd come down every four or five years with their 'kick the Pope' bands and we were happy enough to cheer them on. They'd wave their Union Jacks and flags at us and wind up my parents and people like that. At the end of the night, we went back to our ghettos and they went back to their big houses. Then we didn't see them for

another four or five years. We didn't realize it at the time. It's taken
years for us to evolve this sort of thinking.

In Derry, too, where Protestants controlled the council, living conditions
were little better. Gregory Campbell, who was to become one of Ian
Paisley's most articulate political spokesmen, still resents the way his
community was portrayed as the civil rights movement gained strength.

> I was from very much a working-class background. We had two small
> rooms downstairs, two bedrooms upstairs, no hot running water and
> the old outside toilet. We lived in small, steep streets with terraced
> houses. You almost felt that if you took the bottom one away, all the
> rest would collapse like a deck of cards. Not only was I *not* a first-class
> citizen, I remember the absolute sense of indignation and outrage
> whenever I was accused of being one. There was this explicit
> inference to Catholics being second-class citizens and therefore this
> inference that I was in some way depriving them of their rights. I can
> distinctly recall, even as a sixteen-year-old, looking round my humble
> surroundings at home and saying, 'Well, if this is second-class citizen-
> ship, I really wouldn't want to meet the third-class citizens.'

But Protestants resented the civil rights movement not just because they
thought it misrepresented their social conditions – a misrepresentation they
felt the media willingly swallowed – but because they saw it as representing
a challenge to their state. The Cameron Commission, the Government's
official inquiry into the violence that was to follow, understood how the
majority community felt.

> It was in the circumstances inevitable that the civil rights movement
> should be mainly (though not exclusively) supported by Catholics and
> also attract support from many who had been prominent in Nation-
> alist and Republican politics. Officially, the Association [NICRA]
> campaigned only on civil rights issues, but in practice its activities
> tended to polarize the Northern Ireland community in traditional
> directions. It was bound to attract opposition from many Protestant
> Unionists who saw or professed to see its success as a threat to their
> supremacy, indeed to their survival as a community.[4]

From the beginning, unionist politicians saw the civil rights campaign, and
in particular its umbrella body, the Northern Ireland Civil Rights Association, as an IRA front, whose purpose was to destabilize Northern Ireland
and achieve by political agitation on the streets what it had failed to achieve

by force of arms. Barely five years earlier, the IRA had called off the campaign it had waged along the border between 1956 and 1962, recognizing that it had been a failure. It had never managed to ignite partition as an issue and, unlike the IRA in its current campaign, had failed to mobilize any significant support. Its leadership had then decided that the way to further its goal of uniting Ireland was to mobilize the Catholic and Protestant working classes so that unionism, stripped of its grass-roots electoral support, would simply fall apart. However attractive the analysis in theory, it bore little practical relevance to the increasingly sectarian politics of Northern Ireland, so that far from uniting the working classes, civil rights only drove them further apart.

There is no doubt that the IRA was involved in the civil rights campaign from the outset, although never to the extent that loyalists believed. It was not an IRA conspiracy, and there were genuine grievances to be addressed. Certainly, the IRA was prominently represented at NICRA's first Annual General Meeting in February 1968 when, according to RUC Special Branch reports, nearly half of those who attended – thirty out of seventy – were 'known republicans or IRA' and six of the fourteen members of NICRA's subsequent national executive – again nearly half – were 'members of the Republican Movement'.[5] The fact that other organizations represented on the executive, such as trade unions and the Campaign for Social Justice, had nothing to do with republicans is evidence of how broadly based the movement was. That is not to say that the IRA was not determined to use and exploit the civil rights issue in every way it could. That was an integral part of its strategy. Nevertheless, the composition of NICRA's executive, and the role played by IRA members in stewarding its marches, was more than enough to confirm loyalists' conviction that the IRA was masterminding the civil rights campaign to further its own ends. This was certainly the view of the Stormont Government of the day. John Taylor, who today is Deputy Leader of the Ulster Unionist Party (UUP), still holds the same view of civil rights as he held almost thirty years ago when he became Minister of State in the Department of Home Affairs. 'It was seen by myself and fellow Unionists as a new means of overthrowing Northern Ireland and forcing Northern Ireland into a united Ireland,' he told me. 'It was seen as a nationalist plot to overthrow the state.'

William Craig was the Stormont Minister for Home Affairs at this critical period in Northern Ireland's history and went on to become one of its most controversial political figures. Craig was not known as a 'unionist hardliner' for nothing. He effectively retired from political life in the late seventies and, exhausted and ill, became a recluse, tending his roses and walking his dog in the peace and solitude of County Down. In 1998, when I first approached him, there were many who thought that William Craig was no longer alive, but a name and memory from a turbulent past. But he was, although now a frail man. I had met him in the early seventies when he was strong and fit, but I barely recognized the person who came to the door. I had forgotten how tall he was, but his face was now drawn and his voice was faint. Standing on the doorstep, I explained what I was doing and asked if he would talk to me about that period in Northern Ireland's history in which he had played such a leading role. He said he had never talked about it before and had no wish to talk about it now: it was all in the past and, anyway, he was not feeling well. I apologized for the intrusion and asked if I could come back again when he might be feeling better. He nodded and said I could try. I wrote to him, paid him two more calls, which also terminated at the doorstep, and then a final visit when he asked my colleague, Sam Collyns and myself in and, after much discussion, finally agreed to an interview. Although he was not strong and he sometimes had difficulty in drawing breath, his mind and recollection were still razor sharp. He made no attempt to rewrite his own history or his attitude towards civil rights. Craig had always been admired by his loyalist supporters for his direct, no-nonsense approach, and it soon became clear that nothing had changed.

To me it was the beginning of a republican campaign organized entirely by the IRA and it was much more significant than any previous campaign. It was a deliberate effort by the IRA to play a bigger part in the politics of Northern Ireland and the Irish Republic. Of course, it would exploit and use local figureheads where it could, but I would have said quite categorically that it was the guiding hand.

Did you know that the IRA was involved when you were Minister for Home Affairs?

Yes, within two or three weeks of joining the Ministry I started reading up on this new campaign to exploit civil rights and I've a very clear recollection of the astonishment that I felt at the time. In fact I was a little suspicious of the authenticity of the earlier reports I had received. Some were from Special Branch and others from political observers. But when one related it to things on the ground, I became quite satisfied that it was authentic and would end in violence.

Although the IRA was involved in the civil rights movement, did not the movement itself have a justified grievance?

Justified in the sense of a republican nationalist community that wanted to exert its weight, but it did not merit the attention it subsequently got because of the violence.

Did you see the civil rights movement as a threat to the state?

Anything involving the IRA always was a threat to the state. The mistake I think we probably made was not taking enough notice of it then. No early preparations were made to deal with civil disorder.

The civil rights movement exploded into violence on 5 October 1968. NICRA had planned a march in Derry, the city that to nationalists had long been the symbol of Protestant supremacy. The marchers planned to challenge it by assembling on the largely Protestant east bank of the River Foyle that divides the city and marching across the Craigavon Bridge and into the Diamond, the Protestant heart of the city, which lies within its ancient walls. By so doing, they would assert their right to equal treatment or, in the republican language of today, 'parity of esteem'. To Protestants, such a route would be an assault on their inner sanctum and tantamount to breaking the siege. In response, the Apprentice Boys of Derry announced that they were going to march on the same day, thus virtually guaranteeing trouble. In response, Craig ruled that no parade could be held on the east bank or within the city walls. His ruling in effect was a ban on the civil rights demonstration. Nevertheless the marchers assembled, and in the resulting confrontation with the police, who were enforcing the Minister's order, unprecedented violence erupted and was captured by the world's media whose camera teams had flocked to Derry in anticipation of dramatic pictures. They were not disappointed, and viewers, most of whom were unaware of what was happening in Northern Ireland, watched in horror as policemen laid into marchers and beat them to the ground with their batons. Even today, William Craig has no regrets.

I was quite pleased with the way the RUC reacted. Maybe we'd made a mistake and we should have strengthened the RUC. The mistake that was made by the RUC was to amend the original plans they had for coping with the disorder. It was approached with a virtually certain knowledge that it would end in disorder.
How did you react to the scenes of policemen beating demonstrators over the head?
They were a few that caught the attention of the media. I didn't see anything wrong with it.
You didn't see anything wrong with policemen batoning marchers?
People were involved in violence, they weren't marching.

Most loyalists would have agreed with Craig that the violence in Derry was caused not by the police, who were acting under acute provocation, but by republicans who were bent on fomenting civil disorder. Whoever was to blame, disorder was the result and it did not stop at Derry but soon spread throughout the province. Loyalists in general and Paisley's Ulster Protestant Volunteers in particular were determined to see that the civil rights marchers did not have their way again. If Prime Minister O'Neill, whom they continued to assail as a 'Lundy', would not stand up to the marchers, Ian Paisley and his UPV made it clear that they would.

The next confrontation came almost two months later in Armagh on 30 November 1968, by which time the UPV and its umbrella organization, the Ulster Constitution Defence Committee (UCDC), had their plans in place. Paisley was still chairman of the UCDC but Noel Docherty was no longer its secretary as he had gone to gaol after getting involved with explosives and the UVF. Nevertheless, despite Docherty's absence, the UPV was ready for action. Docherty had set it up with precisely such circumstances in mind. When Armagh's local civil rights committee announced a march for 30 November 1968, Paisley's organizations were determined to confront it, not least because they would be directly standing up to the enemy as several prominent local republicans were members of the Armagh civil rights committee and some of them were actually members of the IRA.[6]

Eleven days before the march, Paisley had a meeting with the local police and metaphorically laid down the law, telling them that they could not contemplate letting such a march go ahead, as recent events in Londonderry clearly showed that O'Neill's Government had lost control of the situation. He said that his Ulster Constitution Defence Committee had made their plans for 'appropriate action'. According to the subsequent government report, Paisley's attitude to the local constabulary was 'aggressive and threatening'.[7] It was the tactic Paisley had used in 1964, threatening to take action to get the Irish Tricolour removed from the Sinn Fein election office if the police did not do it themselves. In Divis Street, the RUC obliged. In Armagh they did not. The march was to be allowed to go ahead. Traditionally the city, which is the seat of both the Anglican and Roman Catholic churches in Ireland, had experienced little sectarian trouble, as each community generally tolerated the traditions and parades of the other. As the police had no reason to believe that this march was going to be any different, they were not in the mood to ban it and give in to Paisley's bluster. Here Paisley could argue he was not an outsider, as Armagh was the city where he was born, in a two-storey terrace house on 6 April 1926.[8]

Over the next few days, red printed notices were pushed through the letter boxes of many of Armagh's shops, a 'Friendly Warning' from 'Ulster's Defenders'. 'Board up your windows,' they said. 'Remove all women and children from the city on Saturday 30 November. O'Neill must go.' Despite impressions to the contrary, Armagh was expecting a peaceful civil rights march not Armageddon. Then, as the day of the march approached, posters suddenly appeared in the city. 'For God and Ulster. SOS,' they read. 'To all Protestant religions. Don't let Republicans, IRA and CRA [Civil Rights Association] make Armagh another Londonderry. Assemble in Armagh on Saturday 30 November.' This time there was no doubt whose hand was behind it. It was signed UCDC – the Ulster Constitution Defence Committee. The police took many of the offending posters down. But Paisley was not to be thwarted.

In the early hours of the morning of the march, Paisley and twenty to thirty cars of his supporters drove into the area where the march was planned to climax. When the police inquired what Paisley was up to, he replied that he was going to hold a religious meeting and did not plan to interfere with anyone. The police were not taken in, especially as they had set up roadblocks around the city and intercepted hundreds of Paisley's supporters who were pouring into Armagh. Among them, they had uncovered two revolvers and 220 other weapons including bill-hooks, pipes hammered to a point, and scythes.[9] The police managed to avoid a potentially violent confrontation by placing a seventy-five-yard *cordon sanitaire* between 5,000 incoming civil rights marchers and 2,000 hymn-singing Paisley supporters. Many of the Paisleyites, presumably members of the UPV, were carrying cudgels, some of which were studded with nails. There was no evidence that the civil rights demonstrators were carrying weapons of any kind.[10] Thanks to the firm handling of the situation by the police and their refusal to be intimidated by Paisley and the UPV, the day passed off relatively peacefully, despite a few minor skirmishes as marchers and counter-demonstrators prepared to return home.

By the end of 1968 as the season of goodwill approached, it seemed for a moment that the forces of law and order and good sense might be winning. O'Neill introduced some reforms, although they fell far short of what NICRA was demanding, and sacked his Home Affairs Minister, William Craig, who was advocating not reform but a much tougher line. O'Neill was also about to see his fiercest critic, Ian Paisley, appear before Armagh magistrates charged with 'unlawful assembly' in the city. But O'Neill's actions and the prospect of Paisley's incarceration only raised not lowered the temperature. The marchers were now even more resolved to push their point home and the UPV was even more determined to resist. Such pressures made violence seem almost inevitable. O'Neill was fully aware of the dangers when, in a famous television broadcast on 9 December 1968, he told viewers in Northern Ireland that 'Ulster stands at the crossroads', and warned that 'as matters stand today, we are on the brink of chaos where neighbour could be set against neighbour'. In a peroration that was both moving and prophetic, he outlined the choice the province faced.

> What kind of Ulster do you want? A happy and respected province in good standing with the rest of the United Kingdom? Or a place continually torn apart by riots and demonstrations and regarded by the rest of Britain as a political outcast?[11]

It was two days later that O'Neill sacked Craig from his Cabinet. Perhaps he thought he was winning.

But the most violent clash of all was still to come. The civil rights campaign had gained more young blood and impetus from a group known as 'People's Democracy', formed by left-wing students from Queens University, Belfast. They proposed to use different tactics from NICRA and make their point province-wide by marching the eighty miles from Belfast to Derry, taking their cue from America and Martin Luther King's great civil rights march from Selma to Montgomery, Alabama in 1965. In so doing, they also deliberately planned to stretch the police to the limit. Naively, the organizers had expected only token resistance in which loyalists would simply say 'Boo!' and 'Go Home!'[12] They had no idea what lay in store.

The march left Belfast on 1 January 1969 with around eighty students prepared to make the eighty-mile trek. The beginning was good humoured, with one of Paisley's right-hand men, Major Ronald Bunting, taunting the procession with a Union Jack. Bunting was a former regular army officer who had become one of the leaders of the Ulster Protestant Volunteers. He had been a prominent figure at Paisley's side in Armagh and was about to appear before Armagh magistrates with him.[13] Bunting then went ahead of the march and met Paisley in Derry as the marchers approached the city three days later. A riot broke out outside the Guildhall that evening following a religious meeting held by Paisley, alcohol and sectarianism proving a potent mix. Major Bunting, whose car was burned, inaccurately blamed the riot on 'a civil rights mob' and urged loyalists to join the Ulster Protestant Volunteers and assemble next morning near Burntollet Bridge, a few miles outside Derry, 'to see the marchers on their way'.[14]

The following morning, 4 January 1969, the marchers were warned by the police that they continued the last stage of their journey at their peril, given the violent disturbances and threats the previous night in Derry. But the marchers ignored the warnings and embarked on the last leg, with its leaders, in the words of the Cameron Report, calculating that 'martyrdom' would further radicalize the civil rights movement.[15] If indeed that was their intention, they were not disappointed. At Burntollet Bridge the marchers were ambushed by around 200 loyalists, many of them members of the UPV and off-duty 'B' Specials, hurling stones and armed with cudgels and clubs. The police, who numbered around eighty, were unable to protect the marchers, several of whom were taken to hospital. As the television cameras captured more images of peaceful marchers with bleeding skulls assaulted by Protestant bigots, martyrdom was assured and with it the calculated perception of the repressive sectarian state. In its damning conclusion, the Cameron Commission had no doubt where blame lay, not just for Burntollet but for the loyalist counter-demonstrations that had turned peaceful protest into violent confrontation.

> It is our considered opinion that these counter-demonstrations were organized under the auspices of the Ulster Constitution Defence Committee and the Ulster Protestant Volunteers . . . That the use of force was contemplated or expected both in Armagh on 30 November and Londonderry [Burntollet] on 4 January, is amply proved by evidence of the weapons and missiles seen by the police and others to be carried and used by those concerned in the counter-demonstrations in Armagh and at Burntollet Bridge.
>
> Dr Paisley and Major Bunting . . . and the organizations with which they are so closely and authoritatively concerned, must, in our opinion, bear a heavy share of direct responsibility for the disorders in Armagh and at Burntollet Bridge and also for inflaming passions and engineering opposition to lawful and what would in all probability otherwise have been peaceful demonstrations . . .[16]

For both sides, Burntollet became a legend. To loyalists it represented Protestant Ulster fighting back, while to republicans it was proof that if the nationalist people were to be defended, there had to be an armed IRA to do it. Burntollet set the scene for the conflict to come.

Chapter Five

Explosion

O'Neill's new-found confidence barely survived Burntollet and the New Year. On 30 January 1969, William Craig and John Taylor along with ten other Stormont Unionist MPs called for O'Neill's resignation. They believed that his 'moderate' policies were capitulation to those prepared to use violence and an incentive for the demonstrators to go further to extract still more concessions from the unionist government. William Craig, who had been sacked by O'Neill on 11 December 1968, had no time for O'Neill and believed that his policies were leading Ulster to disaster.

> I could not go along with his appeasement of violence. I think that was the mistake that was made all around at that time. He compromised the rule of law and offered reward, albeit minor reward, to those who were engaged in violence. I called for his resignation because I think he lacked the resolution to cope with the situation and he was far too easily pressurized.
>
> **What do you think the Stormont Government at the time should have done and could have done – but didn't do?**
>
> Well, I don't think the situation ever would have become serious if the police had been trained and equipped to deal with riots. It really was an impossible situation to ask a small police force without proper equipment to take on the situation they had to. But there was no alternative at the end of the day.

Four days later, O'Neill dissolved the Stormont parliament and called a general election in the hope of ending the uncertainty and silencing his critics. But his fiercest critic was not to be silenced. Paisley and Major Bunting had appeared before Armagh magistrates only the week before on 27 January 1968 and been sentenced to three months' imprisonment for 'unlawful assembly'. But it was far too crucial a time for Paisley to be languishing at Her Majesty's pleasure. Within three days of the cell door being closed, he had obtained a 'get out of gaol free' card by signing a bail bond, leaving Bunting inside to serve out his sentence. The elders of his Free Presbyterian church had decided that their Minister was too valuable an asset to languish in gaol.[1]

Now a free man and a martyr, Paisley announced that he would stand against O'Neill in the Bannside constituency. His freedom, however, was to be short-lived as he returned to gaol after the election to serve another five weeks. For O'Neill, it was a bruising campaign, with Paisley marching through towns and fields at the head of the Ulster Protestant Volunteers to the sound of flute bands and the roar of Lambeg drums.[2] The 'Big Man's' oratory was at its magnificent best as he fired up a packed Ulster Hall with words and sentiments that were to become increasingly familiar as the years went by. 'There is a grave crisis in our province,' he boomed. 'But the marching feet of the Protestants today will cause the traitor to tremble.' The hall erupted to the sound of wild cheering and the stamping of feet, as the cadences rolled round the great hall. On election day, 26 February 1969, O'Neill kept his seat with a majority that was less than overwhelming. Paisley was only 1,414 votes behind; but O'Neill was still not ready to fall on his sword. More sinister forces were about to give him the final push.

The collusion between the Ulster Protestant Volunteers and the Ulster Volunteer Force, which had begun when Noel Doherty had helped provide the Shankill UVF with explosives, now grew even closer, although it would be a mistake to think that the shadowy world of Ulster's early paramilitaries was neatly organized into separate compartments. Many of those who were prepared to use violence were ready to do so as members of more than one body, so that a member of the UPV might also be a member of the UVF (which had been made illegal two days after the killing of Peter Ward) or Tara, another equally shadowy Protestant organization run by a Protestant homosexual called William McGrath,[3] or the Shankill Defence Association (SDA) run by John McKeague, another homosexual and Protestant bigot. McKeague himself was also a member of the UPV.[4] Together, these organizations, with the UPV and UVF at their heart, conspired to get rid of O'Neill. If political pressure would not force him to stand down, then a few well-placed explosions might, especially if the IRA was thought to be behind them. They also thought it would help get Paisley out of gaol now that he was back inside. Two of the loyalists involved in the plot were Samuel Stevenson, a former 'B' Special and member of the Ulster Protestant Volunteers, and Thomas McDowell, a member of the UPV and Paisley's Free Presbyterian church as well as the UVF. A decision was made to attack Belfast's electricity and water supply causing maximum alarm to its citizens and maximum political embarrass-ment to O'Neill who would, it was reasoned, be unlikely to survive the public outcry if the finger appeared to point at the IRA. The first target was Castlereagh electricity substation, which provided South and East Belfast with much of their power. The attack was planned for Sunday 30 March 1969, the eve of a critical meeting of the Ulster Unionist Council at which a vote of confidence was being sought for O'Neill. Thomas McDowell, another quarryman, was to provide the gelignite and Samuel Stevenson was to provide the safe house.

That Sunday evening, McDowell and three other men went to Stevenson's home in Hartington Street near the UCDC headquarters in Belfast's Shaftesbury Square. The gelignite and other necessary materials had previously been brought to the house in a sack and placed in a shed in the back yard. Stevenson and his accomplices went out in the early evening, returned after midnight and made some tea. Stevenson's wife, Eileen, came downstairs worried about what they were doing and over-heard them saying, 'It will go off any minute now!' She asked what they were talking about, but none would say. They all then went out into the back yard and looked up at a yellow glow in the sky rising from the place where the bomb had exploded. Castlereagh electricity substation had been put out of action and much of Belfast was plunged into darkness. The cost of the damage was estimated to be around £500,000.[5]

The following day, after surviving the vote of confidence, O'Neill mobilized a thousand 'B' Specials to guard the province's sensitive installations. Suspicion immediately fell on the IRA. In its edition the following week, Paisley's newspaper, the *Protestant Telegraph*, told its readers there was no doubt who was to blame.

> This is the first act of sabotage perpetrated by the IRA since the murderous campaign of 1956 . . . the sheer professionalism of the act indicates the work of the well-equipped IRA. This latest act of terrorism is an ominous indication of what lies ahead for Ulster . . . Loyalists must now appreciate the struggle that lies ahead and the supreme sacrifice that will have to be made in order that Ulster will remain Protestant.[6]

Stevenson, McDowell and their co-conspirators now changed target and, confident that the IRA was the main suspect, hit Belfast's water supply to intensify the pressure on O'Neill. On 4 April, a bomb wrecked Belfast's main water-supply pipe at Dunadry, County Antrim; on 20 April, another explosion destroyed the pipeline between the Silent Valley reservoir in the Mourne Mountains and Belfast; four days later, on 24 April, there was an attack on the pipeline carrying water supplies from Lough Neagh to the city; and two days after that, on 26 April, a further explosion wrecked another of Belfast's main supply pipes. Much of the city was now without water and stand pipes were set up as wagons trundled round the streets dishing out emergency water supplies to those who could not get to the stand pipes. That day, a meteorite swept over the province, broke up and crashed through the roof of the RUC's armoury. It did not seem like a good omen. O'Neill knew he could no longer survive and resigned four days later, having just narrowly persuaded his Unionist parliamentary party to accept the principle of 'one man, one vote' for local government elections, which had been the main demand of the civil rights campaign. O'Neill later said the explosions 'literally blew me out of office'. In the struggle for the succession, Major James Chichester-Clark defeated the hardliner, Brian Faulkner, by just one vote, thereby ensuring that the office of Northern Ireland Prime Minister was kept in the 'Big House' (the gentry's) hands. O'Neill and Chichester-Clark were 'old money' with Eton and the Guards in common. Faulkner was a businessman and 'new money'. One of Chichester Clark's first acts was to declare a political amnesty. Paisley was now released from gaol.

Noel Docherty's purpose in setting up secret cells within the UPV had been to defend Ulster, and no doubt removing Captain O'Neill would have fallen into that category. I asked Gusty Spence about the explosions since he would have been well informed about what was going on although he was in prison:

> The plan when the electricity and water supplies were blown up was simply to give the impression that O'Neill with all his liberality was perhaps responsible for the IRA taking liberties. It was carefully planned to bring down O'Neill so that a new leadership would take over. It was put about that the IRA were involved but it was a conglomerate. There were UVF men involved and there were members of the UPV and the UCDC involved.

The plot came to light when Samuel Stevenson was arrested along with five other men, four of whom were members of the UPV or UCDC. The fifth was the circulation manager of Paisley's *Protestant Telegraph*. Stevenson turned Queen's evidence and implicated his colleagues in a statement to the police. He also named James Murdock, to whose farmhouse Paisley had driven Noel Docherty and Billy Mitchell in 1966, in connection with one of the explosions. Murdock had been cleared of explosives charges in 1966 when Noel Docherty was sentenced to two years. Murdock was cleared again when the case came to trial, it was Stevenson's word against theirs, but Stevenson was discredited as a witness when he admitted previous convictions for larceny, fraud and breaking and entering.[7] Stevenson was sentenced to twelve years and his co-accused were released amid scenes of great jubilation.

But what of Stevenson's co-conspirator, Thomas McDowell? There is no doubt that he would have been in court with Stevenson and the others had he not been killed while trying to blow up a hydroelectric power station across the border near Ballyshannon. McDowell's body was discovered on 19 October 1969 lying on top of a transformer with, according to one eyewitness, 'flames' coming from it. A passer-by described 'a flash like lightning' that lit up the sky. At first, the Electricity Supply Board engineers who rushed to the scene thought it was a swan dangling from the high-tension cable. Then the body fell to the ground and they realized it was a man. McDowell had been electrocuted by 5,600 volts; all his clothes had been burned off. On the ground close by were 181 pounds of gelignite, a loaded Belgian-made .32 revolver and a coat with a UVF armband in the pocket.[8] McDowell was still alive when he was found although very seriously burned. He died in hospital two days later and was buried in the graveyard of the newly built Mourne Free Presbyterian church to which he belonged. Among the dozens of tributes were wreaths from the Ulster Protestant Volunteers and the Ulster Constitution Defence Committee.[9]

A few days later, the UVF issued a statement: 'We wish to state that an active service unit from Northern Ireland was dispatched to undertake this task . . . So long as the threats from Eire continue, so long will the Volunteers of Ulster's people's army strike at targets in Southern Ireland.'[10] Thomas McDowell's name heads the UVF's Roll of Honour. Ironically, it was his death that led the police to Samuel Stevenson and the other UPV members who were subsequently charged.

The question uppermost in many people's minds at the time was how much did Paisley know of what was going on? When asked this question during his interview with the police following his arrest, Stevenson alleged the following exchange with one of Paisley's associates, who was also one of his co-accused. 'During my meetings with him [the co-accused] . . . he was always telling me to be very careful, that nothing must leak out that Dr Paisley had anything to do with any of the explosions or had any previous knowledge of them. I wanted to know if Dr Paisley was doing these jobs . . . He said, "Certainly he does. You have to tell him and you haven't. He knows and he doesn't know." ' The cryptic reply was not unlike the answer that Noel Docherty gave me in answer to the same question – although Docherty had never told me that Paisley *did* know. I questioned Dr Paisley about the explosions and the involvement in them of Samuel Stevenson and Thomas McDowell, both of whom were members of the Ulster Protestant Volunteers and one of whom, McDowell, was a member of his church.

Did you have any idea who was behind those explosions?

No, I didn't have any idea. I knew certain people who were lifted but I must say these people were not found guilty, the people who were charged.

Samuel Stevenson was a member of the UPV.

He was a member of the UPV, yes.

Thomas McDowell was also a member of your church and also a member of the UPV. Here are people closely connected with you and your organization who were involved in terrorist activity.

Yes, well, I don't know whether you can say that they were closely involved with me or not, but they were in organizations that I was leading. I can't be responsible for everybody who is a member of a church that I pastor, or an organization that I lead. To say that I am responsible for those things would be trying to find accusations against me when those accusations are not proved or are not founded on fact.

But some of the people who were involved believed that they were doing what they did in your name. That's what they thought. That's what went through their heads.

Well, they may have thought that to give themselves a cover, but that was not true and that has been proved to be untrue.

To this day, Dr Paisley insists he did not know what his associates were doing when Noel Docherty was involved with explosives in 1966 or Stevenson and McDowell were involved with bombings in 1969. But whatever the case, there is no doubt that the emotions Paisley stirred contributed to the climate of fear and sectarian hatred that led to the final explosion in August 1969.

The Apprentice Boys' parade in Derry is the climax of the Protestant marching season, marking as it does the ending of the epic siege of the city on 12 August 1689. The gathering of thousands of Apprentice Boys and their supporters in Derry on that day in August 1969 was bound to provoke trouble given all that happened in the months before. It was also the 300th anniversary of the lifting of the siege. There had been serious rioting following the Orange parades on 12 July and tension in the city was still high. Memories on the nationalist side were also still fresh of how, in the week before O'Neill's resignation, the police had pursued rioters into the Bogside and savagely beaten a forty-two-year-old taxi driver, Samuel Devenney, who later died from his injuries. Thirty thousand people came to his funeral in silent protest at what they called 'police brutality'. An inquiry into his death was conducted by Sir Arthur Young, the Chief Constable of the City of London police, who regretted that he could not identify those responsible because of what he called 'a conspiracy of silence' among the police.[11]

Given that the parade was an explosion waiting to happen, it is astonishing that it was not banned and the situation defused. The Stormont Government had the power to do so, but was reluctant to use it lest it be seen as yet another sign of weakness, and the new Prime Minister, Major James Chichester-Clark, had no wish to go the same way as his predecessor. Harold Wilson's Labour Government could have saved Stormont the embarrassment by banning the march itself but the Home Secretary, Jim Callaghan, was not inclined to do so. 'I'm a libertarian,' he said. 'I don't like banning marches.' Under the circumstances it would have been remarkable if Derry had not exploded on that day, Tuesday 12 August 1969. The 15,000 Protestants who marched round the walls now felt that the siege was real, while the Catholics of the Bogside who watched resentfully below saw them and the police who protected them as their oppressors. Both sides had good reason to feel as they did. Before the parade began, a few Apprentice Boys disdainfully tossed some coins from the walls down into the Bogside below, an action that was hardly designed to relieve the tension. With the march under way, a handful of nails was thrown at the police from the Catholic side of one of the barricades the RUC had erected to keep the two sides apart. Soon the Apprentice Boys themselves were attacked, and the two days and two nights of ferocious rioting that became known as the 'Battle of the Bogside' began. As the police pursued the rioters into the Bogside once more, they ran into a hail of petrol bombs hurled from the ground and from the roof of Rossville Flats that overlooked the entrance to the area. This time the Bogsiders were ready. The police were not. Despite the introduction of water cannon and CS gas, now used for the first time in the United Kingdom, the riot continued unabated. In frustration, the police started to throw the stones back. Gregory Campbell, who was then a young shop assistant in the city centre, remembers feeling a mixture of horror and anger.

I had a grandstand view of all this and I can recall making excuses to leave the shop to go to the 'Free Derry' corner to help the police. If there was a turning point for me, it was probably when I saw the violence up front, right there within yards of me. What I saw was an insurrection. I saw groups of people defying law and order, trying to destroy Northern Ireland, and the police were the bulwark against them. The police were coming under severe pressure because at that time I think there had been rioting for about three days and nights and they had been on duty twenty-four hours a day for all that time. They were fatigued and it was difficult for them to hold the line. I felt then that they needed all the help they could get. They needed to cope with and repel the rioters and I felt what I was doing was helping them and a lot of others felt likewise.

What was going through your mind when you were throwing stones behind the police?

I suppose it was righteous indignation working its way out in a physical way. I felt these people are trying to destroy Northern Ireland. They are marching for rights that I don't have. They're saying that I'm preventing them from getting the rights and now they're trying to destroy the country. I felt I had to do something and it was all that I could do at that stage and it was just about bordering on what was morally acceptable for me to do.

I asked Gregory Campbell why he had not gone on to join the loyalist paramilitaries as so many of his contemporaries had done. 'I just felt that if I joined a paramilitary organization, I may well end up doing what the IRA were doing,' he said. 'I took a conscious decision not to on moral grounds.'

After hours of rioting, the police, who were not equipped or trained to cope with civil disturbance on such a scale, were exhausted and their reinforcements took heavy casualties. One unit of fifty-nine police officers brought in from rural County Down lost two-thirds of its number through injuries.[12] Finally, Stormont authorized the mobilization of the 'B' Specials, having been reluctant to do so before knowing the likely effect of their introduction. The message went out over the radio, calling on all special constables to report for duty. The effect, of course, was that the Bogsiders knew they were coming. Sixty Specials were deployed, armed with batons and pick-axe handles.[13] Their introduction had the predictable result, and the violence intensified as the Catholics of the Bogside now had their most hated enemy in their sights. Shortly afterwards, the army arrived on the scene to 'assist the civil power' as clearly the civil power was unable to cope. But the arrival of a company of soldiers from the First Battalion of the Prince of Wales did not represent at this stage the mobilization of troops from England as they were part of the resident battalion in Belfast who had been moved to Derry to be on standby. According to the Scarman Report, the Government's official inquiry into the dramatic events of that week, the arrival of the soldiers in Derry in the middle of the riot had an instant effect. 'Whatever and wherever the soldiers appeared, rioting ended. It is true to say their arrival was welcomed. The city was tired and the army presence afforded a sound reason for going home.'[14]

Meanwhile, on the evening of Tuesday 13 August, the rioting had begun to spread to Belfast. There had always been a fear that, if it erupted in the city, it would ignite sectarian tensions along the 'Orange–Green' line where the

Protestant Shankill Road meets the Catholic Ardoyne on one side and the Catholic Falls Road on the other. Protestants on the Shankill felt themselves to be the meat in the sandwich. Although there was a certain inevitability to what eventually happened, the violence in Belfast was in fact triggered by nationalists and was not sectarian but initially directed against the police. It happened after the call had gone out from republicans in Derry to their NICRA comrades elsewhere to hold meetings in other parts of the province to stretch police resources and take the heat off the besieged Bogsiders. To be fair, NICRA made a decision not to do so in Belfast because of the potential danger of igniting the sectarian powder-keg. Nevertheless some elements ignored the advice and on the evening of Wednesday 13 August held a meeting in the vicinity of Divis Flats to protest against 'police brutality' in Derry.[15] Shortly afterwards, the Irish Prime Minister, Jack Lynch, made a television broadcast that did anything but calm the situation. The Taoisach's words only confirmed loyalists' worst fears that their community was faced with an insurrection backed by Dublin.

> The Stormont Government is evidently no longer in control of the situation. Indeed the present situation is the inevitable outcome of the policies pursued for decades by successive Stormont Governments. It is clear that the Irish Government can no longer stand by and see innocent people injured and perhaps worse . . .
>
> Recognizing, however, that the reunification of the national territory can provide the only permanent solution for the problem, it is our intention to request the British Government to enter into early negotiations with the Irish Government to review the present constitutional position of the Six Counties of Northern Ireland.[16]

Lynch's words were tantamount to pouring petrol on the flames. He also announced that he was sending 'field hospitals' to the border to treat casualties from Derry and elsewhere. To loyalists, this was nothing less than a cover for using the Irish army as a prelude to an invasion.

After Lynch's broadcast, the crowd that had gathered at Divis Flats marched to Springfield Road police station to make their protest against 'police brutality'. Missiles were thrown at the corrugated-iron hoarding protecting the front of the new station and there was the sound of breaking glass.[17] The crowd then proceeded down to Hastings Street police station where three RUC constables were standing outside ready to receive their petition. But certain elements were clearly no longer interested in petitions but bent on attacking the police and hurled 'pieces of grating, stones and petrol bombs' at the officers, who made a hasty retreat inside the station. Armoured vehicles, designed for use along the border and not urban riot control, were ordered to disperse the increasingly volatile gathering. Predictably, the vehicles were pelted with stones and petrol bombs. Then, ominously, shots rang out as the IRA brought out the few old guns it had and opened up on the police and their vehicles. It was the first shooting incident of the week in Belfast. The violence escalated as a car showroom on the Falls Road was looted and set on fire. One Catholic eyewitness described the scene as 'a mob out of control'.[18] In response to the growing violence, the police deployed Shorland armoured cars and a full-blown confrontation developed, in which both the IRA and the police opened fire. At this stage, as the Scarman Report acknowledges, the rioting 'involved the activities of Catholic crowds in Catholic areas', and there was no evidence of any sectarian clash on that first night of violence in Belfast.[19]

Loyalists, already incensed by Jack Lynch's television address, looked on late that Wednesday evening with increasing anxiety as the rioting and shooting raged in the nationalist communities on both sides of the Shankill Road. The scenes left a lasting impression on young loyalists like Eddie Kinner. 'I can remember there was a lot of rioting going on up in Derry and there were rumours that there were going to be riots in Belfast in order to weaken the police, and the next minute the car showrooms were burned out in Conway Street. Loyalists were waiting patiently and said, "Well, we'll make them pay for anything that they do."' Eddie Kinner came from a family steeped in the UVF tradition and later went on to join the organization himself. He subsequently served a life sentence for murder. William 'Plum' Smith was also a young teenager on the Shankill Road at the time and watched his community prepare for the anticipated nationalist attack.

In those days it was the word of the jungle where rumours spread very quickly. People were under the impression that the Protestant parts of the Shankill had been attacked on the Wednesday night and that more was to follow. I remember Protestants at that time making petrol bombs and getting ready for an attack that they believed would come on the Thursday night from the Falls. We were kids and we were watching the older ones and everybody seemed to be excited. Everybody was involved – the whole community. Basins of water were set out and doors left open for people to run into. Everybody was bracing themselves for what they believed was going to be a massive attack from nationalists on the Falls Road in order for them to spread the violence and therefore help other nationalists in the Bogside.

The showdown came on Thursday evening as nationalist and loyalist crowds faced each other at opposite ends of Dover Street and Percy Street, the narrow roads of terrace houses which run directly from the Shankill to the Falls. Catholics lived at one end and Protestants at the other. Any move

by one crowd, whatever its intention, was seen as a threat by the other.
The Shankill was soon swelled by loyalist football supporters fired up from
supporting their team, Linfield, at an away match in Newtownards. By
now, both sides were spoiling for a fight.[20] Inevitably, given the circumstances, the crowds clashed. Catholics thought Protestants were invading
the Falls, and a handful of IRA men, with guns still warm from the
previous night, opened up to repel the invaders.[21] The police responded to
silence the gunmen but with much heavier fire, including rounds from .30
Browning machine-guns mounted on top of the RUC's Shorland armoured cars. The Browning has a rate of fire of 500 rounds a minute. In
the confusion and the exchange of gunfire that night, seven people died.
One of them was a nine-year-old Catholic boy, Patrick Rooney, shot
through the head by a stray round from one of the Brownings while asleep
in his bed in Divis Flats. Of the other six, Hugh McCabe (20) was a soldier
home on leave in Divis Flats; three were Catholics – Samuel McLarnon
(47), Michael Lynch (28) and Gerald McAuley (15), who was a member of
Na Fianna Eireann, the junior wing of the IRA;[22] and two were
Protestants – Herbert Roy (26) and David Linton (48). Four were shot
in the Divis Street–Falls Road area and three in the vicinity of the Crumlin
Road–Ardoyne area on the other side of the Shankill where there was
simultaneous rioting and shooting. Eddie Kinner has vivid recollections of
the night and the small part he played in it.

> We gathered up the bottles and then went and got the petrol and
> sugar and we made up petrol bombs to be used that night. How did
> we make it? We put in a level of sugar, petrol, put in a slip of rag with
> petrol and tied it round the top of the bottle.
> **Had you ever made a petrol bomb before?**
> No. I mean I did it for the first time.
> **Did you throw them?**
> No, we weren't allowed to throw them. Whenever they were
> being used, we would have been well out of the road.

Eddie also remembers the trauma of almost losing his father and sister to an
IRA bullet.

> I can remember standing on the corner of Dover Street watching the
> tracer bullets flying up the street feeling totally terrified – and my
> mother pulling me in and putting me into the house. Then my sister
> came in in hysterics. She had been down at the bottom of the street
> with my father and they'd been standing alongside 'Herbie' Roy
> when he was shot dead. My sister had seen that. She had turned away

for a second and then turned round again and 'Herbie' Roy was gone. At first, she thought it was my father who had been shot. She was in complete hysterics and it took a number of days for her to recover.

Protestant crowds, believing with some justification that they were now under IRA attack, surged into the Catholic areas of the streets that run between the Shankill and the Falls, setting fire to Catholic homes as they went. In Conway Street, forty-eight houses were burned to the ground and in Bombay Street, further up the Falls Road, 60 per cent of houses were destroyed by fire. The night entered nationalist folklore as the loyalist pogrom. But loyalists did not see it like that. They believed they were defending their area and responding to the IRA attack. William 'Plum' Smith remembers watching Bombay Street burn.

Bombay Street exploded when the two sides started throwing stones at each other. As far as I can remember there were a few petrol bombs thrown at the first couple of houses and they spread right up the whole street because of the way they were built with two houses sharing the same 'loo' space [in the back yard]. Protestants threw petrol bombs over the yard walls and the flames spread up the whole street. Shots were fired and I remember two Protestants getting hit by shotgun pellets and the situation developed from there. But at no time did Protestants actually have weapons in Bombay Street.

By this time, with Belfast ablaze, a decision had been made to call in the British army to prevent what looked like becoming a civil war in a part of the United Kingdom. The Stormont Prime Minister, Major James Chichester-Clark, who had fondly hoped that things would get better when he took over, had already made the historic phone call to the British Home Secretary, James Callaghan, to seek authorization to use the resident Belfast Battalion to come to the aid of the police in Derry. He might not have envisaged they would soon have to be used in Belfast too.

My recollection, as far as I can remember, was that I rang up Jim Callaghan and said that we felt we needed help and we needed some troops. I think he had indicated to me that troops would probably be available if the worst happened. Anyway, the next thing was he rang me back after some time and said that he had just got permission for me to use the troops from Harold Wilson. He said, 'I'm actually in an aeroplane coming from the islands of Scilly.' Harold Wilson was on holiday in the Scilly islands at the time.

Did you think it was a situation that could be contained?

I thought that initially it would probably blow over but when we had a sort of 'second calling' of the troops into Belfast, I was beginning to wonder just a little bit where we were really going and whether we would really be able to solve all the problems.

On Friday, British troops flown in from the rest of the United Kingdom, marched into Belfast and took up positions on the Falls and the Shankill. Loyalists had mixed feelings about their arrival and Eddie Kinner, for one, was confused.

I can remember the troops marching down Dover Street with fixed bayonets and steel helmets. My ma came and pulled me in by the ear. She was terrified. It was like an invasion. This was our own army coming in and it felt as though we were being invaded by them. They were fairly abusive towards us because they looked at the damage that had been done to the nationalist or Catholic community.

There is no doubt that at the time, surveying the smouldering ruins of what were once Catholic homes, most soldiers thought the Protestants were the villains because they inflicted all the damage. Not surprisingly, resentment on the loyalist side grew when they saw Catholics welcoming the soldiers as their saviours. 'Plum' Smith, however, knew it was not that simple.

People very fearful. There were a lot of people burned out on both sides of the community. There were Protestant families that were burned out of their homes as well. Law and order had just completely broken down and if the British army hadn't have come in at the time, I fear it would have been far, far worse and more people would have been killed.

At the end of that nightmare week in August 1969, the British Government had become directly involved in Northern Ireland for the first time since partition because Stormont could not cope. At the time, there were those who advocated that Westminster should assume political as well as military responsibility for the province and abolish Stormont altogether. The proposal, which, with hindsight, should have been glaringly obvious at the time, was rejected. Harold Wilson had no wish to become embroiled in the Irish Question as his predecessors Gladstone, Asquith and Lloyd George had done, or to further antagonize unionists who would have been bitterly opposed to the idea of surrendering the parliament that was the cornerstone of their state. The price that was subsequently paid for not abolishing Stormont was heavy as loyalists now began to wonder about Britain's long-term intentions for their province.

Chapter Six

Defence

The following month, loyalist fears were confirmed when the British Government announced that the RUC was to be disarmed and the 'B' Specials disbanded. Through Orange vision, not only had the Government sent in the troops to support the nationalists – why else would the women of the Falls fill up the soldiers with endless tea and buns? – but it was now depriving the Protestant community of its own defence against the IRA. The anger loyalists felt was deep. On 10 October 1969, as part of its package of reforms, the Government published the findings of the Hunt Report into policing in Northern Ireland and tried hard to sugar the pill by announcing that a new force would be created, to be known as the Ulster Defence Regiment (UDR), which would come under the control of the British army and not the RUC. It also paid tribute to the 'gallant service' that the current 'B' Specials and their predecessors had given 'to the cause of Ulster'. But the words sounded hollow. Chichester-Clark had gone to London and argued forcefully against it but found that his words fell on Home Secretary Callaghan's deaf ears. 'I felt very badly about it in lots of ways,' he told me.

> What happened was that Jim Callaghan and I were having a conversation rather late at night and we discussed the 'B' Specials. I remember saying to him that we didn't think we could face up to the population if we had to get rid of them and he said, 'Well, for goodness' sake do it because we won't give you the UDR in exchange unless you do.' I had called a Cabinet meeting the following morning and I let everybody say their own piece as to what they thought ought to be done and with one accord everybody said the only thing to do was to go for the UDR – which we did.
> **You didn't have a lot of choice, did you?**
> We didn't have any.
> **Why were feelings so intense?**
> I think they were very intense because the 'B' Specials were very

well thought of and I myself would say they were really on the whole a pretty good lot. But, of course, there are bad eggs in everything and there were bad eggs in the 'B' Specials. I don't think very many but I think on the whole they did a pretty good job.

That night there was fearful rioting on the Shankill after a loyalist parade was attacked on the way home by nationalist youths throwing stones from the Catholic Unity Flats, the nationalist flashpoint at the bottom of the Shankill Road. The RUC came under a hail of petrol bombs and the army moved in to their aid. The UVF opened fire and the soldiers returned it, shooting dead two Protestants, George Dickie (25) and Herbert Hawe (32), whom the army said were petrol bombers. The rioting lasted for almost two days. Billy Hutchinson was on the Shankill for most of the time.

I was involved in riots then and also on the next day. I think that was my initiation and I was involved in most of the riots from then up until the early seventies. People started putting cars across the road to act as barricades and going to Kelly's car showroom, taking the cars out and putting them across the road. I remember that night the water cannons coming up and dispersing everybody with shooting the water. It was the first time that I had seen this. I had seen it on television whenever the student riots were going on in Paris and it was quite strange to have watched it on television and then to find yourself in the middle of this.

In the confusion and violence of that night which saw loyalists ranged against the security forces of the country to which they professed to be loyal, a policeman, Constable Victor Arbuckle (29), was shot dead. He was the first police officer to be killed in the current conflict and, ironically, he was killed by a loyalist gunman, not the IRA. Neither the irony nor the significance was lost on unionist politicians. John Taylor remembers it well.

It was very confusing for me, and for our unionist people generally, to see a member of the Royal Ulster Constabulary killed by Protestants. One always assumed that Protestants were law-abiding and would never attack the police force, which many of them perceived to be their own police force. It was a tremendous shock but it did reflect the irritation and the anger of the unionist people in Northern Ireland at the loss of the 'B' Specials because they became scared that there was going to be a further diminution of the union between Great Britain and Northern Ireland.

What no one knew at the time was that the dramatic events of 1969 would give birth to what was to become the Provisional IRA.[1]

The inter-communal violence of the nights of 13 and 14 August that had left nationalist streets ablaze and seen a mass exodus of Catholics from Belfast, many of them fleeing south to Dublin, was viewed very differently on the Falls Road from the way it was perceived on the Shankill. Nationalists saw the invasion of their streets by loyalist mobs from the Shankill as ethnic cleansing, although the phrase had not yet been coined. 'Pogrom' was the term they used. Traditionally, the role of the IRA in Belfast had been to protect nationalist areas from such attacks, which had happened before in the twenties and thirties and lived on in nationalist folk memory. But in August 1969 the IRA, still riven by the ideological splits that had followed the Army Council's decision to call off its military campaign in 1962, was ill-prepared to come to its community's defence. Despite the misgivings of some of the old guard in Belfast, the IRA's energies had been directed towards involvement in the civil rights campaign, instead of towards trying to get the British out of the North at the point of a gun. When rioting broke out in Belfast, IRA veterans got hold of what few guns they had and opened up on the police and what they saw as the invading loyalist mobs. Brendan Hughes, who later became Commander of the Provisionals' Belfast Brigade and a republican folk hero, remembers seeing the IRA in action for the first time.

My old school [St Comgall's] was being attacked by loyalist crowds with petrol bombs. One of the IRA men who was there at the time had a Thompson submachine-gun and asked if anybody knew the layout of the school. I did and I went with this fella. Petrol bombs [from the loyalists] were coming in all over. There was a man on the roof of the school and people were shouting at him to fire into the crowd and he shouted back that he was under orders to fire over their heads. That's exactly what he did. He fired a Thompson submachine-gun over the heads of the crowd and it stopped the school from being burned down.[2]

The general unreadiness of the IRA to respond to these loyalist attacks led to bitter recrimination within its ranks and hostility from sections of the nationalist community, who felt that the IRA had let it down. 'IRA – I Ran Away' began to appear on walls. Billy McKee, who shortly afterwards became the Provisionals' first Belfast Commander, told me how he had left the IRA leadership in no doubt as to how he and others felt about the dereliction of its traditional duty.

I told them they had failed the people, the nationalist people of the North. I told them they had used the money that they had got from subscriptions for their own political ends, not for weapons to defend the people. I also told them over the three years previous, the writing was on the wall. The dogs were barking in the streets that there was going to be sectarian trouble in Belfast. Paisley was stirring it up. But it was like hitting your head against a stone wall . . .

We weren't so much wanting to take over the IRA as determined to break from Dublin . . . So the Northern lads got together and we told them that we wouldn't have any more truck with the South and with the Dublin leadership.

McKee and Belfast IRA veterans like Joe Cahill started to gather around them others of like mind, including some who had previously left the IRA because they felt its abandonment of 'armed struggle' was a betrayal of its historical mission. Martin Meehan, another future republican legend, had left the IRA in disgust at what he saw as the fiasco of August '69, but was now persuaded by Billy McKee to rejoin.

He outlined what his plans were. He guaranteed first and foremost that the nationalist areas would be defended at all costs and that what happened in 1969 would never happen again.

What did he tell you about the policy towards British soldiers?

He didn't indicate that there was going to be an immediate offensive against the British army. He said, 'These things take time. People have to be trained. People have to be motivated. People have to be equipped. All this won't happen overnight.' But the intention was there and it sounded good to me.[3]

A few months later at a specially convened Army Convention held just before Christmas 1969, the IRA split. On 28 December 1969, the new 'Provisional' Army Council issued its first public statement in which it said the split was:

. . . the logical outcome of an obsession in recent years with parliamentary politics, with the consequent undermining of the basic military role of the Irish Republican Army. The failure to provide the maximum defence possible of our people in Belfast and other parts of the Six Counties against the forces of British Imperialism [the IRA's way of referring to loyalists] last August is ample evidence of this neglect.[4]

On 11 January 1970, Sinn Fein followed suit at its Ard Fheis (annual conference) held at Dublin's Intercontinental Hotel. The Republican Movement – the IRA and Sinn Fein – was now irrevocably split into two wings: the 'Provisionals', who wanted the IRA to revert to its traditional military role, and the 'Officials', who remained loyal to the old Dublin leadership.[5]

At the time, loyalists would have known little about these Byzantine manoeuvrings or about what was going on behind the barricades that had been erected throughout nationalist areas. Nevertheless, they would have had their suspicions, not least that Dublin was ready to fish in the troubled waters. The Irish Prime Minister Jack Lynch's speech could not have made it plainer that his Fianna Fail Government was ready to act and the words – and subsequently the deeds – of some of his Cabinet ministers confirmed that the assistance amounted to far more than words.[6] Neil Blaney, who was then Minister for Agriculture and proud to parade his republican credentials, told me how he saw the situation in the North when Lynch announced he was sending troops to the border.

I was convinced that really this was the final break-up of the entity that is Northern Ireland and therefore would have brought about the situation wherein we could have ended the division of our country . . . I'd have looked on it as the home army entering home territory. I remember arguing at a meeting that we had the same right to protect any citizen of the Six Counties as we would have had it happened in Cork. I mentioned Cork deliberately because Jack Lynch came from Cork.[7]

The Irish army did get as far as the border but no farther. The assistance that the Dublin Government was to lend to its beleaguered fellow nationalists in the North was strictly covert. Government money was channelled through various bank accounts and ended up largely, but not exclusively, in the hands of the IRA in Belfast. Most of the recipients were members of the newly emergent Provisional IRA. This was no accident as the Dublin Government was thought to favour the more traditional 'nationalist' IRA, the Provisionals, over the Officials, whom ministers regarded as dangerous Marxists who would be as eager to overthrow the Southern state as they were Northern Ireland.

Ostensibly the money was to be used for 'Relief of Distress in the North' but once it had crossed the border and the barricades, there was no check on where it went. Between 20 August 1969 and 24 March 1970, £100,000 of public money passed through the chain of bank accounts in Dublin and the border town of Clones to bank accounts in Belfast.

According to a subsequent investigation launched by the Dublin Government's Public Accounts Committee, the payments were 'individually
authorized either in writing or orally . . . by the then Minister for Finance,
Deputy Charles J. Haughey, personally'.[8] But government money was also
going in a different direction to be used for a different purpose. An account
was set up under the name of 'George Dixon' at the Munster and Leinster
bank in Lower Baggot Street in Dublin and £32,500 was withdrawn from
it for the sole purpose of buying arms for the IRA in the North. The IRA's
chief arms purchaser at the time was the Belfast Provisional, John Kelly,
who travelled to Europe and America to buy guns. 'We'd been told by the
Irish Government that money was available for the procurement of arms,'
he told me.[9] In the end, in what became an embarrassing fiasco, Kelly and
his colleagues purchased arms in Europe with Dublin Government money,
which were then seized as they arrived at Dublin airport. As a result, three
Government ministers were sacked – Neil Blaney, Kevin Boland and
Charles Haughey – and put on trial on 7 October 1970 with John Kelly
and his associates. All were charged with the illegal importation of arms. In
a sensational verdict, all were acquitted, not because they were innocent of
importing arms but because the Minister of Defence had authorized the
operation; hence the importation was not 'illegal'. The trial was a clear
indication to loyalists that the Dublin Government had helped set up and
finance the Provisional IRA to whom much of the money had gone. I
asked Neil Blaney whether he accepted that by his actions he had helped
create the Provisional IRA. He sucked on his pipe, then went through the
ritual of stoking it and prodding it with a match before he answered. 'We
didn't help to create them [because that was the result of the IRA's own
internal dynamics], but we certainly would have accelerated, by what
assistance we could have given, their emergence as a force.' It was an
admission of partial responsibility. But loyalists and their politicians had no
doubt who was to blame. I asked John Taylor if the revelation that Irish
Cabinet ministers had been involved in gun-running had come as a
surprise.

> Well, it wasn't a major surprise. The average unionist in Northern
> Ireland would have expected nothing less, you know. They don't
> trust Dublin Cabinet ministers and they kind of assume that people
> who are in the Cabinet in Dublin would be involved in some way
> with republican terrorism. So when this actually came out to be a
> reality, people weren't as shocked as you would imagine.

As 1970 began, both republicans and loyalists were organized into wha
were primarily defensive groups, with each protecting its own communit

against the other. With British troops standing in the middle, however confused they initially were as to which side was which and who was doing what to whom, there was little opportunity or inclination on the part of loyalists or republicans to take offensive action against each other. By and large most of the participants, including the British Government, thought that the emergency would be over by Christmas and few, with the possible exception of the Provisional IRA who had longer-term plans, really imagined that the troops would be staying well into the new year, let alone for almost the next thirty years.

On the loyalist side, the UVF was now largely inactive as, following the murder of Peter Ward, its leadership had been identified and, with Gusty Spence in gaol, largely neutralized – at least for the time being. With the exception of the UVF, which had proved its capacity for killing, loyalist groupings in those early days did not merit the description 'paramilitaries'. Those who were involved were members of what became known as 'defence associations', the largest and most active of which was the Shankill Defence Association (SDA), whose chairman was the extreme loyalist, John McKeague. McKeague had also been a member of the Ulster Protestant Volunteers until Paisley kicked him out following McKeague's court appearance in connection with the UVF/UPV's bombing of Belfast's electricity and water supply the previous year. McKeague said that Paisley had 'dropped him like a hot cake'.[10] Noel Docherty had suffered the same fate a few years earlier. By this time, McKeague was already notorious because of the role he had played during the rioting of August 1969 when he had become a familiar figure on the Shankill, helmet on head and stick in hand, offering the services of his 2,000 cohorts in the Shankill Defence Association to provide the protection for Protestants that he said the forces of law and order could not. He was soon boasting that the SDA had 'hundreds of guns' and friends with deep pockets if they needed more. 'We will see the battle through to the end,' he threatened. 'What they [the nationalists] started, we, the Protestants, will finish.' Major Bunting, Paisley's former trouble-stirring lieutenant, who had since broken ranks with his leader, had thrown in his lot with McKeague and warned, 'The Protestant dog can bark, the Protestant dog has teeth and the Protestant dog will bite if need be.'[11] These defence associations were replicated all over Belfast as good Protestant citizens believed it was their duty to protect their community and willingly did their night's tour of duty as vigilantes on patrol. In those days, there was nothing particularly sinister about family men patrolling their neighbourhoods to protect their hearth and home. Forming vigilante groups, as Andy Tyrie remembers, gave 'the security people a free hand', releasing them to deal with trouble elsewhere while Protestants looked after their own areas. The loyalist paramilitaries grew from these relatively innocuous beginnings.

Martin Snodden, who subsequently joined the UVF and was sentenced to life for murder, served his apprenticeship as a young vigilante as the seventies began. He lived in a Protestant enclave of Suffolk at the foot of the strongly nationalist Lenadoon Avenue on the western fringe of the IRA stronghold of Andersonstown. In the territorial wars that were to bring about the end of most mixed areas in Belfast and divide the city into opposing sectarian camps, Protestants living at the bottom of a Catholic area were not welcome. Martin Snodden remembers the intimidation loyalists on his estate suffered at the time.

There were daily attacks on Protestant families in the area ranging from stonings, riot situations and shootings. The reality was that as there was no security force presence evident on the ground, then it really lay with the adult male members of the area to try and form some form of defence. During that whole period of the early seventies there was a siren system that was set up and whenever the area came under attack, the siren was sounded and every man came out of their home in defence of the area. I participated in whatever way I could at that particular time and that ranged from walking round the estate at night – being a sort of warning system – through to physical violence, rioting and fighting on the streets.

How old were you when you first held a gun?

I was handed a gun in Lenadoon Avenue in 1970 when I was sixteen years old and the man that handed me it nearly got shot as a result. As far as I was concerned, guns were seen on television and you sort of pointed it and pulled the trigger and that was it. Unfortunately whenever he handed it to me I was pointing it at him and he wasn't too amused.

Do you remember holding a gun for the first time?

For the first time my recollection of holding a real gun was the weight of it. It was quite heavy. It wasn't the plastic thing that I had been carrying about as a child in a holster. Guns that I had previously held had fired caps. That was quite frightening with regards to the potential of the weapon itself, what it could do. What I felt at that particular time was a combination of fear and love. Fear for what could happen and what was happening in the area at the time but also a wider sense of love for my whole tradition and the country that I had grown up in.

When the young Martin Snodden held a real gun for the first time in 1970 as a member of a loyalist vigilante group, he would have been the exception and not the rule. It was only when the situation started to get serious and the shooting and the killing began that Protestants realized they were faced with the choice of going back indoors or of doing things they would never have contemplated before. Escalating violence soon blurred the distinction between defence associations and paramilitary groups.

After the trauma of August 1969, it was to be almost another year before the battle lines were drawn once again and inter-communal violence turned into shooting. Again, as with the Apprentice Boys' parade in Derry, it was a loyalist march that sparked the violence. It began with stoning but this time ended with dead bodies on both sides. There had been sporadic trouble during the preceding months but at least it had been confined to missiles and petrol bombs.[12] On 27 June 1970, with a new Conservative Government in office only a few days, Orangemen in Belfast polished their fifes and tightened their drums in preparation for a series of marches that were traditionally a warm-up for the huge loyalist parades on 12 July. The route one of the Orange parades was to take skirted two of the most sensitive nationalist areas in West Belfast, the Springfield Road and the Clonard area, which had been the scene of much of the rioting and burning the previous August. Bombay Street in the Clonard, which had been torched by a loyalist mob, was still a charred row of empty terrace houses and a reminder to nationalists of how the 'Orangies' had laid waste to their community. They were in no mood to have an Orange parade, with all the trappings and tunes that proclaimed Protestant supremacy, marching through their territory. Inevitably fierce rioting broke out which soon spread to the rest of the city.

The following day another Orange parade marching down the Crumlin Road, the explosive interface between the Protestant Shankill and Catholic Ardoyne, provoked an even more serious disturbance in which, ominously, the newly formed Provisional IRA brought out its guns and shot dead three Protestants – William Kincaid (28), Daniel Loughins (32) and Alexander Gould (18). The IRA commander in Ardoyne at that time, Martin Meehan, told me that the loyalists fired first. 'The Orange march took people unawares and a serious riot followed. I know for a fact that four shots were fired from the loyalists side of the Crumlin Road and the shots were returned by the IRA.' In the confusion, it is impossible to tell who fired first as both sides inevitably blame the other. That same evening there was another fierce gun battle in East Belfast around St Matthew's Catholic church, which stands where the nationalist enclave of Short Strand meets the heartland of Protestant East Belfast. The widely received view of this violent encounter, which I reflected in my account in *Provos*, is that loyalist mobs attacked the church with petrol bombs until the Provisional IRA came to the rescue and made a stand in its grounds. In the gun battle, the Provisionals shot dead two Protestants, Robert Neill (38) and James McCurrie. The IRA also lost one of its auxiliaries, Henry McIlhone (33), who was defending the church with the Provisionals' Belfast Commander, Billy McKee. Subsequently when I was in East Belfast researching *Loyalists*, I was taken to task by angry local residents who said that I had got the story wrong and fallen for IRA propaganda. They insisted that loyalists in the area had come under attack from nationalists and were only defending themselves. The depth of feeling concerning an event that happened so many years ago suggested that there might be some truth in what they said. Whatever the truth – and nothing will change each community's perception of it – that violent weekend marked a turning point in the conflict. The Provisionals claimed that they had defended the nationalist people of Short Strand by their actions at St Matthew's church, while loyalists claimed that, with five Protestants dead, they were now the victims of an IRA murder campaign and had to do something about it.

At this point, the UVF was still in disarray following Gusty Spence's arrest, and there was a limit to what the scattered and as yet uncoordinated defence associations could do. William 'Plum' Smith, and a number of his friends who had been members of the same Shankill Defence Association platoon, decided to set up their own organization, called 'The Red Hand Commando'. John McKeague was also associated with its formation although he always denied it. The 'Red Hand', as it became known, was closely linked with the UVF. 'We believed that the Protestant community not only needed to defend themselves but needed to play a proactive role in the war,' Smith told me. 'We believed that if loyalists didn't take on that role, then eventually the Provos would have their way because the British Government would just bow to the pressure.' I asked him where such an organization, starting from scratch, got its guns.

> From all over the country. People had obviously buried them way back in 1912 [when they were smuggled in to arm Carson's UVF]. We were getting all sorts and you'd actually need to be a professor to be a paramilitary at that particular time because there was such a big selection of guns, all different calibre and all different makes. We had no big routes to bring loads of guns in. So initially it was just a hotch-potch of whatever weapons were lying about. You took whatever you could get your hands on because you're starting off with nothing.

By the end of 1970, the Provisionals had begun their bombing campaign against what they claimed were 'economic' targets that were invariably Protestant-owned businesses and premises; then, at the beginning of 1971, they started to shoot soldiers and policemen. By this time, loyalists had recognized that there had to be a more coordinated response to the IRA's offensive. Many Protestants did join the RUC and the newly formed Ulster Defence Regiment to defend their province by wearing the Queen's uniform, but many more opted to join the paramilitaries whose hands they believed were not tied in the way that those of the security forces were. One incident in particular confirmed loyalists in their belief that the IRA had to be stopped. On 6 February 1971, the Provisionals had shot dead Gunner Robert Curtis, the first British soldier to die on duty in Ireland since 1921, but it was the killing of three more soldiers the following month that had a far greater impact. They were Scottish and died in a particularly horrific way. The three young soldiers, aged seventeen, eighteen and twenty-three, were off duty and drinking in a Belfast city pub, when they were picked up and driven away, presumably thinking they were being taken to a party for a good time. At this period the IRA had not yet declared that off-duty soldiers were targets. They were driven into the hills above Belfast and as they got out of the car to relieve themselves, they were shot in the back of the head. One of them was said to have been found propped up with his half-empty beer glass still in his hand.[13] An IRA unit from Ardoyne was thought to have been responsible but no one was ever charged. The province was stunned by the callousness of the killings and the age of the young victims. As a result, the army changed its rules so that no soldier under the age of eighteen would be allowed to serve in Northern Ireland.

The killings had another effect. In memory of the Scottish soldiers, young loyalists on the Shankill and elsewhere set up 'Tartan' gangs whose purpose was to cause Catholics as much grief as possible because they saw them as supporting those responsible for the soldiers' deaths – not least those in Ardoyne. The 'Tartans' became a familiar sight in Belfast, with their knee-length blue jeans and 'bovver' boots, marching with their tartan scarves alongside the loyalist bands. They were the seventies equivalent of today's serious football hooligans, and where there were Tartans there was likely to be trouble. The gangs provided ready recruits for the paramilitaries whose numbers were now growing since most of their members were only too eager to graduate from sticks and stones to guns and bombs. Eddie Kinner used to travel to school at the time with a rucksack bearing the initials SYT, YCV and UVF. I asked him what they stood for. 'Shankill Young Tartan, Young Citizens Volunteers [the junior wing of the UVF] and Ulster Volunteer Force. I think that was the route I travelled,' he said. So did hundreds of other young loyalists. Most of the Shankill Young Tartans won their sectarian spurs when they returned from watching Linfield play football and hurled abuse and missiles at the Catholics of Unity Flats. Billy Hutchinson travelled much the same route. 'We would have stopped outside Unity Flats and sung the national anthem. That would have really wound the Catholics up. We would have done it on a regular basis, particularly in the football season, and maybe sometimes twice a week.' Hutchinson actually set up the Young Citizens Volunteers and recruited many of its young members, a good number of whom went on to join the UVF. Martin Snodden was now ready to graduate from his defence association and decided to join the YCV.

> I joined the YCV because they were an organization that was taking the war to the enemy and that's where I felt it had to be taken.
> **Do you remember being sworn in?**
> It's something that you're unlikely to forget. As far as I was concerned if they'd have said to me 'Cut your wrist and write it down in blood', I would have done that, just like in the days of the Covenant. That was the type of young person I was at that stage in my life. I took an oath of allegiance and was quite proud to be taking it. It was a sacrifice that I was prepared to make.
> **Did you fully understand the consequences of what you were doing when you joined, what might happen to you?**
> Well, I knew that there was a war raging. I knew that the likelihood of being caught and imprisoned was there. I knew that the likelihood of being shot or captured in some other way by the security forces was there. I knew that the likelihood of being targeted by the IRA was there. But I also knew that even if I wasn't a member of the organization, the likelihood of being targeted by the IRA was still there because I was a member of the Protestant community.

Martin Snodden's grandfather had been a 'B' Special and his father had joined the Ulster Defence Regiment, so why had Martin not done the same if he wished to defend his country?

> If the security forces *had* been defending Ulster, then I may well have joined the security forces. But, as I say, in the area where I lived, there wasn't any evidence of the security forces defending my community. So the security forces didn't appear at that stage to be a viable option.

By the spring of 1971, following the deaths of Gunner Curtis and the three Scottish soldiers, it was clear that the IRA was now embarked on a full-blown campaign to complete what it regarded as the unfinished business of 1921 and force Britain to withdraw from Northern Ireland. Protestants were horrified as the death toll rose in those early months and the security forces seemed powerless to stop it. By the beginning of May, the

Provisional IRA had killed thirteen people, five of them soldiers, two policemen and three Protestant civilians blown up by an IRA landmine. On 15 May 1971, around 300 representatives of defence associations from all over Belfast gathered in the dining hall of North Howard Street school to discuss amalgamating the different groups into one umbrella organization not just in Belfast but all over the province. Members of the UVF and other paramilitary groups such as Tara were also there. The organization that emerged became known as the Ulster Defence Association (UDA) and was to become the largest of all the paramilitary groups, at its height in the early seventies commanding over 50,000 members. The organization was structured along British army lines, as were both the IRA and the UVF in a compliment to their opponents. The country was divided up into seven 'brigade' areas: North Belfast, East Belfast, South Belfast and West Belfast, South-East Antrim, Londonderry and the Border Counties. They were then organized into battalions, companies, platoons and sections. A steering committee was set up at the top known as the 'Inner Council', consisting of the 'brigadiers' from each of the areas and their 'staffs'. It was the equivalent of the IRA's 'Army Council'. At one stage the Inner Council consisted of over fifty people until the composition and structure of what had become a hugely unwieldy organization was finally streamlined. One of the UDA's early recruits was a young man called Andy Tyrie, who later became the UDA's Chairman and then its Supreme Commander, a position he held for fourteen years, an astonishing length of time in an organization racked with personality clashes, suspicions and feuds.

Tyrie's journey into the UDA was typical of many. He was brought up in the Upper Springfield Road, which, because of its proximity to the nationalist areas of West Belfast, was the scene of frequent rioting and population change as Catholics moved into the area and Protestants moved out in the pattern repeated all over Belfast. The hint to move was not always that subtle. One loyalist told me of how he had returned home one day to find his house blackened by fire and the family furniture on the front lawn. Tyrie says that at one time his neighbourhood became like 'a transit camp'.

> Protestants would go and Catholics would come. The population was on the move all the time because of the riots and people were looking for somewhere to stay. We actually set up a peace group between Catholics and Protestants up there in a church on Springfield Road. The aim was to try and control the people who were coming into the area. That was pretty successful for a while but then the old suspicion came in, that more Catholics were getting houses than Protestants and they were saying more Protestants were getting houses than Catholics.

So we became very suspicious of each other and gradually we went our own way. I finished up joining Woodvale Defence Association because I felt that Protestants in these areas were in danger and they needed all the help they could possibly get. Most areas were not mentally or physically equipped to deal with the resurgence of the IRA.

Despite the atmosphere of the time, recruiting for an organization with overt military pretensions, whose brigadiers and colonels wore combat uniforms and bush hats, was not always easy. Sammy Duddy, who became Andy Tyrie's faithful follower and court jester, recalls his first meeting.

I remember one night the recruiting sergeant for the UDA came up and we all met in a little community centre. He walked in in full combat uniform, put a Union Jack on the table, a Bible on top of it and a Sterling submachine-gun in the middle of the lot. He says, 'Right, we're all here to join.' I was nearly killed in the queue to get out. There was a mad rush for the door. And out of, I would say, fifty people present, fourteen stayed and joined the UDA. I was one of them. I remember feeling a bit derisory towards those who had bolted.

Why did you stay and join?

Well, we had been part of a vigilante system, armed with cudgels and baseball bats guarding our own area, our own housing estate. I thought, 'Well, here's a bit of authority coming on the scene.' We were promised there'd be guns and all for our protection. I mean you can't use a baseball bat against a gun. And I fell for the pitch. I thought it was pretty good.

And did the guns come in? Were the promises kept?

Yes indeed.

The guns came in the following year, 1972, when it became clear to the UDA leadership that its men had to be armed with more than baseball bats and clubs.

Chapter Seven

Tit for Tat

In the furore that followed the brutal killing of the three Scottish soldiers, Prime Minister Chichester-Clark asked the British Government for more troops to combat the growing IRA threat but received what he regarded as merely a token gesture in the form of 1,300 extra men. At the time, the Conservative Government was not inclined to alienate the nationalist population by saturating their areas with an even heavier army presence. Less than a fortnight later, Chichester-Clark resigned. In the battle for the succession, it was one hard-liner versus another. William Craig stood against the ambitious Brian Faulkner but was heavily defeated by twenty-six votes to four in the election held by Unionist MPs. Faulkner had campaigned on a law and order platform and had every intention of seeing that as Prime Minister there would be substance to his words. After his election, he addressed the media from notes he had jotted down on the back of an envelope the previous night before going to bed. 'Obviously the kernel of our immediate problem is the law and order question,' he said. 'I am convinced that what we need on this front are not new principles but practical results on the ground in the elimination not only of terrorism but of riots and disorder.'[1] Here at last, loyalists thought with relief, was a Prime Minister who was going to get tough with the IRA and return stability to the province.

Faulkner was as good as his word. On 9 August 1971 he introduced internment after finally persuading the Conservative Government and an even more reluctant British military establishment that locking up suspects without trial, however undesirable, was a necessity as the violence grew worse. By the beginning of that month, five more soldiers had been killed, four of them by snipers and one by a time bomb left inside an army base. But statistics give a grimmer indication of the general mayhem that unionists saw now engulfing the province. Since the beginning of the year, there had been over 300 explosions, 320 shooting incidents and more than 600 people had received hospital treatment for injuries.[2] In the light of these figures that seemed to be increasing by the day, Faulkner was given the green light for internment by a Westminster Government that, if not convinced of the security advantages, recognized the political difficulties he would face were Faulkner's request refused. Yet another change of Northern Ireland's Prime Minister was the last thing the Government wanted. Three PMs in just over a year were quite enough.

At 4.15 on the morning of 9 August 1971, 3,000 troops swooped on sleeping cities, towns and villages and arrested over 300 republican suspects. The problem was that most of the key IRA 'players' were elsewhere, in many cases across the border, not sleeping soundly in their beds. (The Dublin Government, which had interned IRA suspects simultaneously in the 1956–62 campaign, thereby crippling the organization, refused to reciprocate now. In loyalists' eyes, the Irish Republic was the terrorists' 'safe haven'.) The IRA's Army Council had received a tip-off, allegedly from a 'mole' inside army headquarters, that 'Operation Demetrius' – internment – was coming and had ordered its Volunteers to get 'offside'. The operation was a military and political disaster, carried out on the basis of out-of-date Special Branch files. As one veteran told a bemused British officer, 'I'm delighted to think that I'm still a trouble to the British Government but I have to tell you I have not been active since the Easter Rising!'[3] Some of those arrested were severely maltreated during inter-rogation – the word 'torture' was never officially recognized – fuelling the resentment the nationalists already felt at the way their community had been singled out and dealt with. The fact that not one Protestant was arrested did not come as any surprise to most members of the majority community since to them it was Protestants who were being killed and not doing the killing. Although the IRA constantly maintained when they killed a policeman or member of the UDR that they were attacking the 'uniform' and not the person, Protestants saw it as an attack on their community as 99 per cent of the police and locally recruited security forces were Protestants. Since the UVF had shot dead Constable William Arbuckle during the Shankill Road riots in October 1969, loyalists had killed only two people. The IRA had killed thirty-three.[4]

No attempt was made to present internment as anything other than it was: a very public demonstration that the new Unionist Government was getting tough with terrorism and that Faulkner was a man of his word. Loyalists were delighted, but their celebrations were short-lived. Far from curbing the violence, internment only made it worse with the increasingly alienated nationalist community now extending a support for the IRA many would have withheld before. In the following two days, seventeen people were killed, most of them shot dead by the army in the gun battles that raged across the province. Only one of the victims was a member of the Provisional IRA.

The month after internment, the IRA, now under the uncompromising leadership of its new Chief of Staff, Seán MacStiofáin, introduced a new and bloody dimension that was to have dreadful repercussions. Hitherto, most of its targets had been what it called 'economic' or members of the security forces. On the evening of 29 September 1971, all that changed. Billy Hutchinson was returning from a Wednesday evening football match and walking up the lower end of the Shankill Road when he heard an ear-shattering explosion further up where the Shankill meets Ainsworth Avenue. It was just after half past ten and the pubs on the Shankill were full. In one of them, the Four Step Inn, the 'singing lounge' was crowded with people watching a television programme about 12 July. A bomb of between fifty and a hundred pounds of explosives had been planted against the wall in the hallway. The explosion reduced the concrete blocks to dust, collapsing the roof of the bar and injuring twenty-seven people. Two were killed, Alexander Andrews (60) and Ernest Bates (38). Mr Andrews' son was able to identify his father in the mortuary only by his clothes and shoes, so badly had he been disfigured by flying glass.[5] Billy Hutchinson and his friends were on the scene in minutes.

> We all rushed up. I remember getting there and the dust was everywhere. People were covered in it and they were pulling the bodies out of the rubble. I remember the two people who were killed, they were well known in the area and they were two characters. I think that had a devastating effect on me. Here again the IRA had come into the Protestant community and planted a bomb which was indiscriminate and was killing Protestants. The security forces had done nothing to prevent it and weren't seen to be doing anything to actually apprehend the people who did it.

The attack was seen as nakedly sectarian, and Belfast had never witnessed anything like it before. Four months earlier, a bomb had been thrown at the Mountain View Tavern, a bar close by, injuring several people but no one had been killed. The Four Step Inn was different – and the Shankill never forgot it. The Northern Ireland Civil Rights Association was uncompromising in its condemnation, describing the attack as 'the work of politically bankrupt madmen'. 'This cold-blooded act was an obvious attempt to stir up more bitter sectarian hatred in our community and to further divide the working people of Belfast. No organization can ever hope to build any kind of decent society on the bodies of slaughtered innocent people.' The following day, the Reverend Ian Paisley addressed a crowd outside the ruins of the bar and announced that he had formed a new political party to 'shift this Government' and restore law and order.

Paisley's Democratic Unionist Party (DUP) rose from the rubble of the Four Step Inn. The funerals of Mr Andrews and Mr Bates were the largest Belfast had seen, their coffins flanked by large contingents of the Orange Order and followed by a lorry bearing more than a hundred wreaths.[6] Tragically, the sight was to become all too familiar in the months and years ahead. There were pleas for no retaliation, but in vain. On 4 December 1971, the UVF hit back with a devastating attack on McGurk's Bar, a Catholic-owned pub in Belfast city centre. It was the sort of quiet place where the older generation went to talk about horse-racing and the pools over a pint; it had no IRA or republican connections. The owner, Patrick McGurk, who lived above the bar with his family, was known to ask those who used bad language to leave.[7] At a quarter to nine on Saturday evening when the bar was just getting busy, a car with three men inside drove up. One got out and planted a fifty-pound bomb in the doorway. The explosion collapsed the pub and the family flat above it like a house of cards. Fifteen people were killed in the explosion, the biggest loss of life in Belfast in one incident in the whole of the current conflict. Patrick McGurk was serving at the bar at the time and miraculously survived.

> I saw a flash, and a very short time after that, the bar went up in the air. It just collapsed around me and I was buried underneath amidst the rubble and glassware. I just said, 'What have I done to suffer this?' I was stranded there. Then I heard some people talking in the snug behind me and a person answered them saying, 'You're all right, we'll get you out.' A short time after – and I don't know how long I was actually underneath there – this person who was trying to help people out spoke again. And so I shouted up and said, 'I'm down here.' And he said, 'We'll get you out all right.' Then somebody eventually pulled me out. I don't know who he was.

It was only when Patrick was lying in the Royal Victoria hospital that he heard the worst news of all, that his wife, Philomena, and fourteen-year-old daughter, Marie, had been killed in the blast. He knew they had gone over to church but was not aware that they had returned. Marie had been due to go to an away hockey match that Saturday which had been cancelled because of the rain. Had she played, she would have lived. 'It was devastating all right,' Patrick told me. 'It's just one of those things that just hits you like a ton of bricks. It was a difficult thing to get over. You just have to get resigned to it. It's your opportunity for praying more than you prayed before. I think if you walked along Royal Avenue [Belfast's main street] today and asked people there if they remembered McGurk's Bar, I don't think they'd know what you're talking about.' I asked Patrick if he felt bitter at the loss he had suffered. I suspected before I asked him that bitterness was an emotion he was incapable of feeling. 'It does come into your mind periodically,' he said with a barely audible sigh. 'But of course then you have to control it because it's no use keeping it in your mind because you'll only start getting vindictive then and that'll not serve any useful purpose.'

Initially, the UVF did not claim responsibility, so great was the slaughter and so deep the public outrage. At first it was thought that the IRA was responsible, while its Chief of Staff, Seán MacStiofáin, fancifully believed it the work of 'British undercover elements trying to bring about a limited sectarian confrontation in Belfast', its purpose being, he surmised, to draw out the Belfast IRA so the British army could engage them openly in battle.[8] The following day, the bombing was claimed by a group describing themselves as 'Empire Loyalists'. The name was a fiction. It was to be almost seven years before Robert James Campbell was charged with the outrage and given sixteen life sentences for the fifteen murders. Campbell, who had joined the UVF earlier in 1971, had driven the car but not actually planted the bomb; the bomber himself was never caught. In his statement to police, Campbell said, 'I have worried about this ever since and I am glad I am going to gaol and try and get it out of my mind.'[9] I asked Billy Hutchinson how he regarded the UVF's bombing of McGurk's Bar, which was every bit as indiscriminate as the IRA's bombing of the Four Step Inn, about which he had been so incensed.

I think that this was always the problem with Northern Ireland – that people always copied each other in terms of what would be done or wouldn't be done. I think that with the IRA campaign against the Protestant community it was inevitable that Protestants or loyalists were going to move towards a similar state of play. That was always a difficulty.

But the IRA was targeting, it would say, the uniform, it was targeting soldiers in uniform, policemen in uniform, UDR men in uniform, it would deny that it deliberately attacked civilian targets and killed civilians.

I think there's a number of civilian targets that we could point to that the IRA attacked. I think what we'd have to be careful about is when it's a 'civilian' soldier [like part-time members of the Ulster Defence Regiment]. Quite a lot of these people were attacked when they were delivering their mail, or attending animals on farms. They were actually vets but they were being attacked by IRA men who were saying that they were part-time soldiers. We get into the whole argument about legitimate targets and I think that the IRA have used that one to hide their sectarianism for quite some time. But in terms of uniforms, it was much easier for the IRA to identify people in uniform that it was for the UVF or any other loyalist organization actually to identify IRA men.

Exactly one week later, on 11 December 1971, the IRA took revenge for the outrage of McGurk's Bar by bombing the Balmoral Furnishing Company in the heart of the Shankill Road. Again, as with the bombing of the Four Step Inn and McGurk's, there was no warning. It was a busy Saturday and the Shankill was crowded with shoppers. Four people were killed: two adults, Hugh Bruce (70) and Harold King (29); and two babies, two-year-old Tracey Munn and one-year-old Colin Nichol. That Saturday lunchtime, Billy 'Twister' McQuiston and a friend were walking down the Shankill on their way to the city centre where they used to hang out on Saturday afternoons buying records and clothes and having a bit to eat. When they heard about the explosion, they rushed to the scene and arrived in time to see the bodies being brought out. Hundreds of people had formed human chains to dig through the rubble in search of survivors in scenes reminiscent of the London Blitz.

> Women were crying. Men were trying to dig out the rubble. Other men were hitting the walls. One person was crying beside you and the next person was shouting 'Bastards!' and things like that. I didn't actually see the babies' bodies as they had them wrapped in sheets, but the blood was just coming right through them. They were just like lumps of meat, you know, small lumps of meat. All these emotions were going through you and you wanted to help. There were people shouting at the back, 'Let's get something done about this.' To be honest with you I just stood there and cried, just totally and utterly numb. It wasn't until I got back home that I realized, this isn't a game. There's a war going on here. These people are trying to do us all in. They're trying to kill us all and they don't care who we are or what age we are. Because we're Protestants, they're going to kill us so we're going to have to do something here.

The following day, the local UDA unit in Twister's area was holding a meeting, and he and his friends went along to offer their services.

> We just put our names down to see what we could do. We were told to go away and think about it and come back in a couple of weeks' time. We talked about it among ourselves and from then on every single bullet that was fired and every single bomb that we heard about

was personal. It just felt that we had to fight back. So we went back again and enrolled in the junior wing of the UDA [Ulster Young Militants].

Do you remember being sworn in?

I remember it very well. We were brought into the room one at a time and there were three people sitting at a table. On it was an Ulster flag, a Bible and a gun. Two hooded men brought you in and stood in front of the table. You were asked, 'Why do you want to join the Ulster Defence Association?' You gave your answer and then there was an oath which you had to repeat with your hand on the Bible and your hand on the gun. I remember when I came out, my heart was swollen with pride that I was going to do something. I was going to fight back.

Fighting back in the end meant being prepared to kill people, did it?

Whatever it took to defend the people of my area to make sure no more children's bodies were getting carried out of buildings. I was prepared to, yes.

Another young loyalist who rushed to the scene was the young Eddie Kinner, who lived just round the corner from the Balmoral Furniture Company. When the bomb went off, he felt as if it had exploded right next to him. He, too, was appalled at the carnage, especially when he heard what had happened to the two babies. His reaction was even more extreme than 'Twister's'.

I was angry and wanted to do just as much damage to the community responsible for those actions. My mentality then would have been, whenever they blow up a location in the Shankill, killing one or two people, I would want to blow up somewhere in the Falls killing double. Doing twice the amount of damage that they were doing in my community.

But it wasn't the Catholic community that planted the bomb, it was the IRA that did it.

I think you're right about that, but that's not how I saw it then. I would have linked it into other events that were taking place and would have seen it as not necessarily the Catholic community carrying it out but it being done on their behalf. So they were part of it.

But very many of that community would dispute the fact that the IRA did anything on their behalf or did anything in their name. They didn't support the IRA. Most Catholics

voted for the SDLP [John Hume's moderate Social Democratic and Labour Party] **who were against violence. Did that occur to you?**

No. At that stage I wouldn't have been looking at that. I would have been reacting to what was going on in the streets.

After the bomb, what did you want to do?

On that occasion, if somebody had handed me a bomb to plant it anywhere you want in the Falls, I would have done it.

Without discriminating?

No. I mean I would have seen the attack on my community as indiscriminatory. What was the justification for killing those babies? What was the attack on the showroom? I mean as far as I was concerned, the attacks that were taking place on the Shankill were attacks on my community or attacks on me.

Some months later, after even greater IRA atrocities, Kinner was approached by a person who asked him if he would be interested in joining the junior wing of the Ulster Volunteer Force, the Young Citizens Volunteers. The approach would not have come as any surprise as his family had a long UVF history. His paternal grandfather had lied about his age in 1912 to join Carson's original Ulster Volunteer Force and his maternal grandfather had also enlisted; both fought and were wounded at the Somme. One of his uncles was a member of the modern UVF before he was killed in a car crash. Young Eddie was ready for the call and the warning that came with it. 'I was told that if I joined, if I became active, there was a strong chance that I could be killed during any operations I would engage in – or imprisoned – so I needed to be aware of that whenever I would be prepared to join.' He attended his first meeting at the age of fifteen.

> The first meeting that I went to, operations were discussed and there were requests for volunteers. People volunteered but I didn't put my hand up. When I left the meeting, the guy who had asked me to join then approached me and said, 'Why did you not volunteer?' and I said, 'Well, I expect to be trained.'

Kinner said he was trained by former British servicemen in bomb-making and the use of SLR and Belgian FN rifles and Sterling and Thompson submachine-guns. He said he had no hesitation about taking life. 'As far as I was concerned, I had joined an army and we were engaged in a war. The enemy had attacked my community and I was prepared to respond in kind.'

Before the week was out, the UVF had retaliated, bombing Murtagh's

Bar in the Springfield Road in nationalist West Belfast, killing James McCallum, a sixteen-year-old barman working in the pub. As 1971 drew to a close, there seemed to be no end to the tit-for-tat bombings. But things were to get even worse. Just as the year was ending, the Provisionals lost one of their most experienced bomb makers, Jack McCabe, an IRA veteran from County Cavan. His death was to presage a series of bombings that would lift the IRA's campaign to a new level of killing to which loyalists were now ready to respond. McCabe, who had joined the IRA in the thirties, been active in the IRA's bombing campaign in England in the forties and operational in its border campaign of the fifties, was mixing explosives known as the 'Black Stuff' on the floor of his garage in Dublin when his shovel hit the ground, caused a spark and ignited the explosives. McCabe died on 30 December 1971 and was buried with full 'military' honours. The IRA was worried that McCabe's mixture was unstable and sent word to Belfast that the consignment of 'Black Stuff' that had already been sent to Belfast was too dangerous – for IRA Volunteers, that is – to be used and should be disposed of at once. Someone put it in a car, drove it into the centre of Belfast and detonated the explosives. Thus was the car bomb born. MacStiofáin welcomed the chance discovery as it 'provided an efficient container and an efficient delivery system. It yielded far greater administrative, industrial and economic damage for a given operation. And it required fewer Volunteers to place it on target.'[10] It also killed more people. McCabe's death and his unintentional legacy were to make 1972 the bloodiest year of the Troubles with almost 500 killings. As the IRA intensified its campaign, the loyalist paramilitaries began to exact a bloody revenge.

Chapter Eight

Escalation

At the beginning of 1972, the killing escalated dramatically as the IRA sought revenge for the deaths of thirteen unarmed Catholic civilians shot dead by soldiers of the Parachute Regiment during a civil rights march in Derry on 30 January. The day went down in history as 'Bloody Sunday'.[1] Loyalists shed few tears, believing, or wishing to believe, erroneously, that all of those killed were IRA gunmen. To most sections of the Protestant community the Paras were heroes and those who harboured the IRA were getting their just deserts. By this time, many loyalists were beginning to see all Catholics and not just the IRA as the enemy. The perception, however false, was to have murderous implications. As with internment, 'Bloody Sunday' may have prompted cheers and celebrations in loyalist strongholds like the Shankill, but in nationalist areas across the province it triggered an unprecedented avalanche of recruits for both the Provisional and the Official IRA. The following month, February 1972, both wings of the IRA killed seventeen people: seven were soldiers and the rest innocent civilians, seven of whom died when the Official IRA bombed the head-quarters of the Parachute Regiment in Aldershot in revenge for 'Bloody Sunday'.

Until then politicians had been largely exempt from being made targets, either because it was IRA policy or because it was difficult to attack them because of increasingly tight security. But the targets remained too tempting and they could not be under protection all the time. On 25 February 1972, the Stormont Minister of State for Home Affairs, John Taylor, was getting into his car in his home city of Armagh. Taylor had never hidden his feelings about the IRA and those who were its supporters. As he turned the key in the ignition, he heard an 'almighty explosion' which he took to be a bomb under his car. He was mistaken as to the cause but not its purpose. Official IRA gunmen opened fire and shot him ten times, most of the bullets going through his head. Miraculously Taylor survived because his foot hit the accelerator as the bullets started flying and the car leapt forward with a roar, 'scaring off the IRA and attracting dozens and dozens of people who all came racing to the motor car'. I asked him how he had survived with most of the ten bullets in his head. 'They weren't through the brain, thank goodness,' he smiled. 'They were all down here through the jaw.' Immediately Taylor became a loyalist folk hero, seemingly blessed by the unseen hand that was Ulster's defender. Now deputy leader of the Ulster Unionist Party, the scars he still bears today are Taylor's credentials that he will never be soft on 'terrorism'.

A week after the gun attack, a bomb exploded at the Abercorn restaurant in the centre of Belfast. It was tea time on a busy Saturday afternoon when the streets were crowded with shoppers. No warning was given. Two Catholic women, Janet Bereen (21) and Anne Owens (22), were killed and over a hundred customers in the packed restaurant were injured. Two of them were sisters out shopping for a wedding dress. Both lost both of their legs. The IRA denied responsibility and blamed loyalists, but few believed the claim. To most Protestants the Abercorn bombing was the work of the Provisionals and nothing the IRA said could change that view. In the climate of the time, perceptions were more potent than the truth — whoever was responsible.

With the IRA now seemingly attacking Government ministers with impunity and bombing innocent civilians out shopping on a Saturday afternoon, loyalists looked for alternative leadership as clearly even the hard-line Prime Minister, Brian Faulkner, had proved unable to stem the IRA tide. William Craig, the former Minister for Home Affairs sacked by Terence O'Neill for his tough line on civil rights and outspoken criticism of Government reforms, was the man to whom thousands of angry and disillusioned loyalists now looked. They saw Craig, as they saw Paisley, as another Carson whom Destiny called to save Ulster. At this stage Craig and Paisley rarely shared the same platform as both were political rivals for the same loyalist constituency. The difference was that to many unionists, Craig, as a former minister, had a political credibility and, for the Protestant middle classes, a respectability that Paisley did not. The 'Big Man', whose political party, the DUP, was still in its infancy, stirred the emotions, whereas Craig's powerful intellect made people think.

In early 1972, Craig formed a movement called Ulster Vanguard to give voice and form to his ideas. 'Its purpose was to bring about a greater degree of unity amongst unionists and provide leadership that the people could respond to,' he told me. 'The Ulster Unionist Party virtually collapsed as the crisis developed and there was no real unionist leadership. Vanguard succeeded in rectifying that. It was very much a movement born out of the emergency.' What Craig may have lacked in emotional and oratorical power, Vanguard more than made up for in the numbers it attracted to the huge rallies it staged. To loyalists these vast gatherings in the early months of 1972 were an outward display of unionist unity and a collective affirmation that they would never succumb to IRA violence; to nationalists they represented, with their paramilitary trappings and the presence of the UDA, a menacing display reminiscent of Hitler's Nuremberg rallies. They were, in fact, both in tone and style modelled on the great Covenant rallies Carson had held in 1912, and the parallels were not lost on the tens of thousands who flocked to them. As with Carson's followers, Craig's supporters came from all walks of life and all classes, sharing the same fear and the same purpose, their spirits lifted by the presentation of banners, the sea of Ulster flags that increasingly supplanted the Union Jack, and the arrival of their leader flanked by motor-cycle outriders. The fact that the loyalist paramilitaries were there too, their numbers growing with each IRA attack, made Vanguard appear much more than just a political organization. Nevertheless, Vanguard was, above all, respectable. Many unionists and loyalists who were to play leading roles in the nineties learned their early political lessons in the charged atmosphere of 1972 at William Craig's side: David Trimble, Reg Empey, Joel Patton, the Reverend Roy Magee and many others. David Trimble, at the time of writing leader of the Ulster Unionist Party and First Minister in the new Northern Ireland Assembly, began as Craig's political adviser before becoming Vanguard's deputy leader. 'David was typical of many young professional men that made themselves available,' Craig told me. 'It was really the new blood from that element that transformed the situation and gave Vanguard its appeal.' I asked him about the fears that Vanguard , with the motor-cycle outriders and all the paramilitary paraphernalia, aroused in the nationalist community. 'It was an act of deliberation to indicate that we meant business. That was its significance,' he said. 'We had people in military formations even though there was no question of arming them. It was more than the speeches that brought the response from the loyalist people.' But there is no doubt that Craig's speeches, which he always wrote himself, played their part and in the case of many young loyalists to calamitous effect. Every word a politician uttered, be it from the lips of Ian Paisley or William Craig, could be taken literally by young minds bent on seeking revenge for IRA atrocities and political justification for it. The words Craig spoke on 18 March 1972 at a vast rally of up to 100,000 in Belfast's Ormeau Park were the message thousands wanted to hear. 'We must build up a dossier of the men and the women who are a menace to this country,' he warned, 'because if and when the politicians fail us, it may be our job to liquidate the enemy.' The words 'liquidate the enemy' were met with loud loyalist cheers and sent shivers down nationalist spines. I asked Craig about his notorious speech.

Why did you use those words?

Because I did mean to liquidate the enemy.

Literally?

Well, not in terms of personalities but in terms of organization, yes.

Did you realize what you were saying?

Yes.

Did you think how those words might be misinterpreted?

No. I didn't expect them to be interpreted in any other way than the normal meaning.

Wasn't it a dangerous use of language in the circumstances of the time?

It was a dangerous situation. One had to stop talking in grey and white terms. This is black and white.

It was certainly black and white to many of those I spoke to who subsequently became senior figures in both the UDA and UVF. In the atmosphere of 1972, there was no room for subtlety. The UDA's Andy Tyrie, who had great admiration for Craig and became one of his close paramilitary allies, had no doubt what his political hero meant.

I thought that he was being honest in the sense that he felt that that was the only way to deal with the enemy. He didn't mean democratic nationalists, he meant *violent* nationalists. He meant the people who were involved in the bombing and the shooting and the petrol bombing. He meant to liquidate those people. That would have prevented the trouble carrying on the length of time it did carry on.

Did you agree with that sentiment, liquidating the enemy?

I never saw it any different. I always felt the only way to beat terrorism was to terrorize the terrorist – and be better at it.

UVF men like Bobby Morton, who was later sentenced for conspiracy to murder, felt the same about politicians' stirring words. 'We all have to take on responsibility for this [conflict] and not least the politicians,' he told me. 'They were only too happy to lead us by the nose at one stage, "Get into them boys!", "Protestant Ulster!", "We will fight and we will die!" Well, they never fought and they never died. It was left to people like me to go out and act on their behalf.' Ian Paisley categorically denies that he ever exercised such influence.

Oh yes, they do blame me. They say I got them put into prison and I've heard them all and I read their magazines. Their slanders are outrageous, and all I can say is they're not worthy of comment because if they had been worthy of comment, the vast majority of the electorate of Northern Ireland wouldn't have voted for me the way they do. There's no one that's stood more abuse from the paramilitary elements that I have stood, and you can go back and look at their magazines and I was bad man number one.

Two days after Vanguard's Ormeau Park rally and Craig's threatening words, the IRA planted what is thought to have been its first car bomb with devastating effect. A hundred pounds of explosives packed within a vehicle were detonated, killing four Protestant civilians, two policemen and one off-duty UDR man. Nineteen people were seriously injured. The policemen were shepherding the crowd away from the area where a suspect device was thought to be when the bomb exploded in Donegal Street, the place to which they were heading for safety. The Provisional IRA admitted responsibility and said they had given adequate warning. Craig's words were not forgotten.

Four days later, loyalists received the most bitter blow of all when the British Prime Minister, Edward Heath, announced that the Stormont parliament that had governed Northern Ireland for fifty years was being suspended and Direct Rule from London was being introduced. The particular point at issue was that Faulkner and his unionist Cabinet had refused to hand over control of security to Westminster as Heath had insisted, leaving the British Government no alternative other than to assume direct responsibility for the running of the province. But no doubt the underlying reason was Westminster's recognition that the province could not carry on being run in the way that it had been for the previous half-century, and which had resulted in the escalating violence. Heath announced the Government's decision to the House of Commons.

> The United Kingdom Government remain of the view that the transfer of this responsibility [law and order] to Westminster is an indispensable condition for progress in finding a political solution in Northern Ireland. The Northern Ireland Government's decision therefore leaves us with no alternative to assuming full and direct responsibility for the administration of Northern Ireland until a political solution to the problems of the province can be worked out.[2]

In a subsequent broadcast to the nation, Heath announced that the Government's decision to introduce Direct Rule from Westminster afforded the opportunity for 'a fresh start' and he appealed to Catholics to make a new beginning. 'Now is your chance,' he said. 'A chance for fairness, a chance for prosperity, a chance for peace, a chance at last to bring the bombings and killings to an end.'[3] Similar words and sentiments were to echo down the next two decades as successive British governments wrestled to find a solution to the same problem. Heath's words served only to antagonize Protestants even further as he appeared to be dancing to the IRA's tune in abolishing what had traditionally been seen as a Protestant parliament for a Protestant people. Direct Rule meant that the old Stormont government departments were abolished and a new Northern Ireland Office (NIO) was created, run by largely English civil servants under the direction of the Secretary of State for Northern Ireland. It was in effect colonial rule. Although the decisions were implemented by Northern Ireland civil servants, the decisions themselves were made by London. To Protestants Direct Rule was an affront and a sign of continuing Government weakness in the face of IRA violence. Although Stormont was only supposed to be suspended for a year, it remained in limbo, apart from one brief intermission in 1974, until almost the end of the century.

I was seldom away from Belfast during this momentous period and remember standing on the vast sweep of lawn in front of the now empty Stormont parliament trying to estimate the size of the flag-waving crowd that stretched as far as the eye could see. I had never witnessed anything like it before. People felt angry, bemused and betrayed as they looked for guidance from their now powerless political leaders who stood far away on the Stormont balcony like toy figures. I made out Brian Faulkner, William Craig and John Taylor and remember Faulkner's voice amplified over loudspeakers saying something about 'the power of our people being the power of our numbers'. There was no doubt about the numbers but the power was no longer there. I was surprised to see John Taylor standing there as the Official IRA had pumped ten bullets into him almost exactly one month before. Symbolically he was the most important person on that balcony, living proof that however great the IRA onslaught, the Protestant people and Ulster would survive. John Taylor still has vivid recollections of the moment.

Brian Faulkner decided to address the masses from the balcony of parliament buildings and he thought it would do me good if I got out of hospital for a couple of hours to experience this historic moment. The doctors thought about it and I was allowed out for two hours as long as I went straight back into hospital again. So I stood there, very feeble, very weak, as once you've been shot ten times it takes a while to get your strength back.

And you stood next to Brian Faulkner.

Oh yes, he gave me pride of place because I was like a resurrection from the dead. One of the newspapers was sure I was going to die and wrote my obituary that night in advance of my death.

What was the scene like as you stood on the balcony?

It was a scene of people who were increasingly alarmed and felt that with one thing after another they were losing power in their own country. They had lost control in matters of housing and in local government [as a result of reforms] and they had lost their 'B' Specials. Now they were losing their parliament and they just felt that they were on the slippery road towards eventual unity in Ireland.

Did you share that feeling?

Oh yes, I felt we were losing ground, certainly, yes, absolutely.

It was around this time in early 1972 that I first encountered the UDA, in the gloomy back streets off the Shankill Road. I was aware of their existence but knew very little about them apart from the fact that they were some form of vigilante organization. I remember running into one of their patrols when I was driving around a loyalist area one dark night trying to find out where someone lived. Some, I think, wore bush hats and some had scarves across their faces; a good many were carrying clubs. I showed them my press card and was allowed to go on my way. I subsequently made more enquiries about the UDA and was directed to the Woodvale area at the top end of the Shankill Road which was the fiefdom of the Woodvale Defence Association (WDA), the largest of all the defence associations that had come together in 1971 to form the umbrella UDA. The WDA was run by a man called Charles Harding Smith who went on to become the UDA's first Chairman. With the abolition of Stormont, loyalists now became more conscious of the need to get their message across and the UDA in its various forms gradually began to emerge from the shadows. I was taken to an upstairs room of a club where I was introduced to two men, neither wearing masks. The room was small and dingy and smelled of stale beer. There was only one window, heavily reinforced with wire net to prevent the glass from shattering into the room should the premises come under attack. To my surprise one of the two men was an Englishman called Dave Fogel, known locally as 'Big Dave', who was number two to Charles Harding Smith. Fogel sounded as if he came from Essex and cut an incongruous figure in a Shankill drinking club. He had first arrived in Northern Ireland in 1965 as a private in the British army and had served as a soldier in the province until 1968. His job was to look after the stores where he first learned all about guns and how to use them. When he left the army, he married a Protestant girl he had met in Belfast and settled down in the Woodvale area, which is how he came to be involved in the WDA. He had first become involved in the original Woodvale vigilante group following the IRA's shooting of three Protestants on the nearby Crumlin Road in the rioting that followed the Orange parades of 27 June

1970. Fogel's military experience and his knowledge of guns more than made up for the fact that he was not an Ulster Protestant and he was recruited by Harding Smith following a meeting at a pigeon fanciers' club off the Crumlin Road where the WDA was first formed. Harding Smith loved pigeons. He asked Fogel to 'put some order' into his men and give them some military training. 'The first thing I did was to tell each likely man to find one more reliable man. Then I did the same with them. That way we got a decent number – about forty. I began to train the men as a military unit. We marched and drilled and used a field out in Antrim for some training – crawling over the grass, up rope ladders, hand-to-hand combat, target practice. I showed them how to make fire-bombs. We also carved wooden guns for our training . . . But it would be dishonest to pretend that real guns didn't exist.'[4]

Some time after our first meeting, I filmed the WDA training in those fields outside Belfast and it was exactly as Fogel had described, although rather more comic as a series of overweight loyalists panted for breath as they 'monkey-climbed' a rope suspended above the ground and went through the motions of less-than-agile hand-to-hand combat. Fogel clearly enjoyed his position of power. Today, leading a quiet life in semi-retirement somewhere in England, he feels slightly embarrassed at the kind of person he was. 'I was walking around the streets with the power of life and death over people,' he told me. 'I must at times have been drunk with it. It wasn't the power that people have given you by votes but the power given you by violence.' There was no doubt that Fogel's colleague, Ernie 'Duke' Elliott, whom I met with him on that first occasion, was even harder. 'If somebody needed thumping,' Fogel remembered, 'Ernie would take care of it and that bloke would never come back for a second helping.' But despite his obvious physical attributes, somehow I felt Ernie Elliott did not fit the Shankill stereotype. He was small, thickset, with a shock of dark hair, highly articulate and politically sophisticated. He talked of how Protestants and Catholics were both victims of their history and maintained that what the working classes of both communities had in common was greater than the differences that appeared to set them apart. Elliott talked like a socialist whose political ideas would not have been out of place in the ranks of the Official IRA. I later discovered that Fogel and Elliott had met the Officials in Dublin to explore the possibility of finding common ground and subsequently had also met one of their representatives in Belfast. 'Ernie and I were political people,' Fogel told me. 'We were trying to see if we could come to a working-class accommodation with our Catholic neighbours.' Nevertheless, I always found Elliott's political ideas puzzling – for a loyalist. I was less surprised when, later that year, he ended up dead. On 7 December 1972, his body was found in the boot of Dave

Fogel's car, the result of an internal UDA feud. Fogel thought he was being framed. The feud was not the last. I was told Elliott had gone to a club in the loyalist Sandy Row to demand the return of some weapons. He never came back. He was the first non-security-force Protestant to be killed by a Protestant and I was shocked when I heard of his death. He was also the first person I had met in Northern Ireland who later ended up dead. As the years went by, there were more.

It was as a result of meeting Fogel and Elliott in that small, dark room that I watched my first weapons lesson. A couple of dozen loyalists of all ages were gathered in a room where one of their senior colleagues produced a Sterling submachine-gun and proceeded to demonstrate how to strip it down and clean it. Presumably they already knew how to use it. Suddenly I realized the conflict I found myself in the middle of was for real. At the time, the UDA was seriously short of the weaponry it knew it would need if it was to present a real challenge to the IRA. As Fogel told me, 'Of the weapons held by Protestants, two-thirds were legal [shotguns etc.] and a third were antiques.' Harding Smith decided it was time to update the UDA's fire-power. In the spring of 1972, he contacted a Belfast arms dealer, John Campbell, who set about arranging meetings in London where the deal could be done. Campbell sent out word that £50,000 was available to spend on arms.[5] Harding Smith chose one of his young colleagues, John White, to travel to London with him. White's family had been burned out of their house in New Barnsley 'by Catholics' and had moved to the Shankill where their home, on the borderline with the Falls, had again been attacked during the riots of August 1969. 'I felt compelled to do something to protect the community in which I lived so I became a vigilante,' White told me. 'Eventually, with atrocity after atrocity being committed in the area in which I lived and with people being murdered and blown to pieces, I felt that the security forces weren't able to deal with it. Something had to be done and that's why I joined the UDA.' Memories of the Four Step Inn and the Balmoral Furnishing Company were still fresh in John White's mind. Now he was preparing to get the guns to hit back. The Belfast dealer, John Campbell, apparently found that guns were in short supply and, according to White, was finally contacted by a dealer in London who said that he could acquire 'quite a large number'. With that assurance, one of White's colleagues was dispatched to London to examine the merchandise for himself. He was impressed by the weapons he saw, which included AK 47 assault rifles, and put in an order for a quarter of a million pounds' worth, considerably more than the UDA had told Campbell was originally on offer. When I expressed surprise at the amount of money at the organization's disposal, White explained that as, by the spring of 1972, the UDA had 'in excess of 30,000 members', raising

£250,000 would be no great problem. It would be less than a tenner a head, a small price to pay to defend Ulster. Fogel believes that both the amount of money available and the estimate of the size of the UDA at this time are grossly exaggerated.

White and Harding Smith went to London to conclude the deal in the Hilton Hotel. 'We were going to look at final shipment and work out the logistics of taking control of the arms and passing on the money.' On 29 April 1972, as they were standing in the foyer, the UDA delegation was arrested. The London 'arms dealer' turned out to be a member of the Security Service, MI5. 'We had seen the weapons and had lengthy discussions with the so-called "gun dealer" who was supplying them, said White, 'so we had no reason to be suspicious at the outset. We felt very silly and realized that we had been conned right from the very start. I suppose we were very naive in the way we tried to acquire these arms. But that was to change as we later became more professional as we went along.' White and Harding Smith were tried in December 1972 and acquitted on grounds of entrapment.

While Harding Smith was under lock and key in London awaiting trial, a temporary leadership took over the UDA, fully expecting that 'temporary' would be a considerable time since it would be many years before they expected Harding Smith and John White to return to Belfast after both had been caught red-handed in London. The new acting Chairman was a glazier from the Crumlin Road called Jim Anderson. During Harding Smith's absence, the UDA grew enormously and was structured even more formally along military lines. West Belfast became a 'battalion' with three companies under its command. The loyalist estates to the north of the Shankill – Springfield, Highfield and Glencairn – became A company, Woodvale became B company and the Shankill Road became C company.[6] The organization was now able to summon thousands of men on to the streets at a single command.

With such numbers at its disposal, the UDA leadership decided to confront the Government and the army on the issue that was a permanent affront to Protestants – the so-called 'no-go' areas that the IRA had established in West Belfast and Derry following the riots of 1969. These areas were barricaded off and were 'no-go' to the police and army, which meant that the IRA could train and operate behind them with impunity. Protestants and their politicians were furious when IRA men with masks and guns openly paraded their control of parts of the United Kingdom before the television cameras. In the sprawling Catholic estates of West Belfast – Andersonstown, Turf Lodge, Ballymurphy and the Falls – and the Bogside and Creggan in Derry, the Queen's writ did not run. The British Government was reluctant to order the army in for fear of another 'Bloody

Sunday' and of alienating the Catholic population still further. Loyalists saw this as another example of appeasement of the IRA and were determined to force the Government to act. Through the late spring and early summer months of 1972, the UDA erected its own 'no-go' areas and said it would not remove them until the IRA were forced to remove theirs. The potential for serious conflict was enormous and the last thing the army wished to face was a 'war' on two fronts. I remember watching the WDA prepare a complex operation to erect 'no-go' areas in the Willowfield area of East Belfast as part of a wider UDA operation. Men in masks stood before blackboards and maps holding pointers, giving local commanders their instructions with military precision. I was never sure it was really going to happen until, the following Saturday, 27 May 1972, it did.

The operation started when darkness fell with masked men hijacking a bread van on the Shankill Road and driving it over to Willowfield to add to the UDA's barricades. When I arrived, there were hundreds of men marching up and down in military formation while the police and army looked on with a mixture of bewilderment, apprehension and frustration on the other side of the barricades. One army officer tried to persuade the UDA not to be silly and go home. He met with little success. 'This is what makes a nonsense of being a soldier in Belfast,' I overheard him say, as he withdrew with mission unaccomplished. Next it was the turn of the RUC. A kindly, understanding, softly spoken police inspector tried the more gentle approach, appealing to the UDA's sweet reason. That was in short supply, and he too finally withdrew from the barricade. I knew it was only a matter of time before there was a confrontation and it was bound to be unpleasant. I went up to one Protestant woman who was watching the proceedings from her garden gate – it was now about two o'clock in the morning – and asked her what she made of all this. 'I'm glad to see them,' she said. 'It's time "ours" did something.' I suspected she spoke for tens of thousands of loyalists. As dawn began to break, the army had had enough. The Paras were sent in to smash the barricades and send the loyalists home. With a loud roar, the army Saracens revved up and drove straight into the barricades, smashing the Shankill bread van and scattering Ulster's defenders. Surprisingly, shooting broke out which threatened to lift the confrontation to a new and potentially terrifying level. I crouched at a corner and watched the bullets fly down the street. These were Paras and memories of 'Bloody Sunday' were still fresh in my mind. 'Bloody Sunday' had been my introduction to Ireland. The army's removal of the UDA's 'no-go' areas was, in an incongruous Ulster way, a victory for the UDA. Because, if the army was even-handed, having smashed the UDA's barricades, why could it not go on to do the same to the IRA's in Belfast and Derry? But there were to be more confrontations between the army and the UDA before that finally happened.

By now the loyalist killings were well under way. They began slowly and spasmodically at first and became chillingly more frequent as day by day loyalists saw the security and political situation apparently getting worse. Most of the killings were purely sectarian and at this stage seldom claimed directly by the organizations responsible. The exception was the first loyalist victim of 1972, a member of the Catholic ex-Servicemen's Association (CESA) called Bernard Rice (49), who was shot from a passing car on 8 February while walking by Ardoyne shops at the top end of the Crumlin Road. The killing was claimed by the Red Hand Commando. A month later, loyalists claimed their second victim with the shooting of a young Catholic, Patrick McCrory (19), at his home in Belfast on 13 March, less than a fortnight after the Abercorn bomb. Whether these killings were linked to any particular event or an instinctive reaction to the deteriorating situation it is impossible to say, especially as at this stage they appeared to have been carried out at random without any central direction. The following month, on 15 April, loyalists killed their third Catholic, seven-teen-year-old Sean McConville, who was shot from a passing car while walking along the Crumlin Road. But it was in the build-up to the Protestant marching season in May, June and July that the sectarian killings really increased. In May, nine Catholics were killed, one of them a thirteen-year-old girl, Martha Campbell, who was shot while walking along Springhill Avenue in the nationalist Ballymurphy estate. In June, loyalists killed five more Catholics and in July, a further nineteen. To put the grim statistics into perspective, in the first seven months of 1972, the loyalist paramilitaries killed thirty-six Catholics while the IRA killed eighty-one members of the security forces and fifty-five civilians. Most of them were victims of the Provisional IRA, as the Official IRA had declared a ceasefire on 29 May 1972 – to which it adheres to this day.[7]

There was also a political reason for the dramatic escalation in loyalist killings during these summer months. On 27 June the Provisional IRA had announced a ceasefire following secret talks orchestrated by the MI6 officer in Northern Ireland, Frank Steele, who had discussed the preliminaries with Gerry Adams and David O'Connell [a member of the IRA's Army Council] at a meeting outside Derry. As a result, an IRA delegation was secretly flown to London for talks with the Northern Ireland Secretary, William Whitelaw. The delegation consisted of the IRA's Chief of Staff, Seán MacStiofáin, Seamus Twomey, Gerry Adams and Ivor Bell from Belfast; Martin McGuinness from Derry; and David O'Connell from Dublin.[8] The talks got nowhere since the IRA delegation was uncom-promising in its demand that Britain should withdraw from Northern

Ireland by 1 January 1975. Frank Steele told me he was 'appalled at their naivety and lack of understanding of political realities'. On the return flight to Belfast, he confronted the IRA delegation and gave them a basic political lesson. 'I said if they really wanted a united Ireland, they were wasting their time shooting at British soldiers and bombing Northern Ireland into an industrial and social slum. They should be trying to persuade the Protestants and the unionists that they would have some sort of satisfactory life – jobs, housing and so on – in some sort of linkage with the South.' Given the evolution of the Provisionals' thinking over the next two decades that culminated in the Good Friday Agreement of 1998, the lesson was not lost on Adams and McGuinness, who were to become the effective leaders of the Republican Movement through the late seventies, eighties and nineties.

Loyalists viewed the 1972 IRA ceasefire with great suspicion, fearing that, following the suspension of Stormont, it was the next step on the road to a united Ireland with the British Government doing a secret deal with the IRA. In the week following the IRA's announcement, the loyalist paramilitaries gave their response by killing four Catholics and an English visitor, Paul Jobling (19), who was shot by mistake and his body dumped on waste ground. When the IRA ceasefire ended twelve days later following a confrontation between the IRA and the army in Belfast's Lenadoon Avenue, loyalists shot dead three more Catholics in retaliation for the IRA's return to violence. But the most intense spate of loyalist killings–nine dead Catholics in seven days – came in the aftermath of 21 July 1972 when the Belfast Brigade of the Provisional IRA planted twenty-six car bombs in Belfast, slaughtering eleven people and injuring 130. That day became known as 'Bloody Friday' and was a watershed in the loyalists' response to IRA violence. Any inhibitions there may have been about targeting innocent Catholics were literally blown away.

Chapter Nine

Killing Fields

It was a busy Friday lunchtime in Belfast on 21 July 1972. Office workers were on their lunch break and women were getting in the shopping for the weekend. Memories of the short-lived IRA ceasefire were fading fast in the welter of bloodletting that both sides had unleashed in the wake of its breakdown. The day before, loyalist paramilitaries had carried out yet another sectarian killing when they shot dead Anthony Davidson (25), a Catholic, at his home off the Springfield Road. One of the lunchtime drinkers near the city centre was Bobby Norris, who was now living in a Protestant area having been intimidated out of the home in which he had been brought up in the once mixed Lower Ormeau Road, in the pattern of population shifts that had become so depressingly familiar in Belfast. It was only a week since Bobby had lost one of his good friends, David Poots. Bobby, who was working in a bar at the time, saw David just before he disappeared. He chatted with him and warned him to take care when he left as it was 12 July, always a tense time but even more dangerous in the current atmosphere. David assured his friend he would be fine as he knew everyone in the area. His body was later found dumped on waste ground, and it was clear to Bobby that David had met a horrific death. 'He had been taken away and tortured. He'd been badly beaten and had his private parts cut off, removed and hidden in his mouth. He was an inoffensive lovely chap who had been brought up and raised amongst Catholic people. For this to happen to someone who was so thoroughly decent, angered me so much.' No particular republican group ever claimed responsibility, no doubt because of the savagery of the killing. It was probably republican retaliation as loyalists had shot dead two Catholics that same day, Jack McCabe (48) and David McClenaghan (15).

That Friday lunchtime nine days later, with David's death still fresh in his mind, Bobby Norris was playing darts in the pub with another friend (who was subsequently also killed by the IRA). Suddenly there was a huge explosion. 'The windows just came down round us and we thought the bomb was actually right beside us, beside the door. It transpired it was a few hundred yards away, and everyone rushed outside to see where it was. We couldn't see anything except smoke coming up over the roof-tops. And as we went out, there were more explosions. It just seemed to be one after another. We were just getting back off the ground and another one went off.' The IRA had launched its biggest ever bomb offensive – and against exclusively civilian targets. Warnings had been given but not far enough in advance for the areas to be cleared. The carnage was horrendous: eleven people killed and 130 injured. The IRA claimed they had never intended to kill civilians, which is what they always said, but the excuse sounded hollow amid almost unbearable television pictures of the slaughter. The worst scenes were at Oxford Street bus station where six people died, two of them soldiers. Bobby Norris has never forgotten it. 'The overwhelming memory I have, like everyone else's, is of bodies being shovelled into bin bags in Oxford Street which was only 100 or 200 yards away. It's something you live with every minute. It's imprinted in everyone's mind.' One police officer who was nearby at the time told me he had tried to put 'Bloody Friday' at the back of his mind for twenty-five years.

> The first thing that caught my eye was a torso of a human being lying in the middle of the street. It was recognizable as a torso because the clothes had been blown off and you could actually see parts of the human anatomy. One of the victims was a soldier I knew personally. He'd had his arms and legs blown off and some of his body had been blown through the railings. One of the most horrendous memories for me was seeing a head stuck to a wall. A couple of days later, we found vertebrae and a rib cage on the roof of a nearby building. The reason we found it was because the seagulls were diving on to it. I've tried to put it at the back of my mind for twenty-five years.[1]

Not long afterwards, Bobby Norris became involved. He was not alone. 'Bloody Friday' brought the loyalist paramilitaries as many, if not more, recruits as 'Bloody Sunday' did for the IRA.

That lunchtime, David Ervine was also in a pub, upstairs in a lounge with a reasonable view of Belfast. Up to that point he had avoided involvement with any loyalist paramilitary organization, but 'Bloody Friday' was the turning point.

> I watched as the puffs of smoke went up and it was only later that you realized that each of the puffs of smoke was somebody's life. One of the guys killed was called Ervine and he just lived a couple of streets away from me. He was the same age as me and a lot of people thought it was me. And then I thought it might have been me – or mine. I got off the fence and probably naively felt that the best means of defence

was attack. I joined the Ulster Volunteer Force and quickly began to do what I believed was right and challenged the threat to my society.

What were your emotions that day?

I don't think they were rational. I would be telling lies [if I said anything else] and I'm somewhat shamed by saying that they weren't rational. I think I could have countenanced anything and probably did.

What did you want to do?

Hit back. Hit back. But the problem of hitting back at faceless, unknown people is difficult. It leads to frustration and what many loyalists have then done is take it out on the community that they perceive as harbouring those who are inflicting the damage.

On innocent Catholics?

That's what's happened.

The UVF that David Ervine and his contemporaries joined was very different from the one that Gusty Spence had left behind when he went to gaol in 1966 for the murder of Peter Ward. For almost six years, Spence had watched the bloody conflict unfold through the bars of his prison cell in Crumlin Road gaol. He had seen his community on the Shankill devastated by the bombing of the Four Step Inn and the Balmoral Furnishing Company and been repelled by the UVF's murderous response when it targeted innocent Catholics in McGurk's Bar. According to Spence, when the McGurk's bomb went off, IRA prisoners in the gaol cheered thinking it was a police station or army base that had been hit. When they discovered that it was a UVF bomb that had killed fifteen Catholics, there was shock and horror. 'I can still taste the electricity on the tip of my tongue,' remembers Spence, 'and it was only through firm discipline that there weren't deaths in Crumlin Road gaol that morning.' Spence himself was appalled at what his colleagues had done and let the UVF leadership outside the gaol know in no uncertain terms how he felt. He saw himself as a soldier, and soldiers did not massacre innocent civilians. Spence, whatever his enemies thought of him, lived by a code and respected IRA men who lived by it too. Two days after Joe McCann, a legendary Official IRA figure, was shot dead by the British army on 15 April 1972, Spence wrote an extraordinary letter to his widow. A bond already existed since McCann had once done Spence a favour by releasing two UVF men who had been captured by the Official IRA.

My dear Mrs McCann,
I would like to tender to you my deepest and profoundest sympathy on the tragic death of your beloved husband, Joe.
   There are those who would find it strange to hear from someone such as myself but I can assure you that whilst your husband and I may

have been opposed to each other in politics, we shared that common
bond that is known only to those who fight their own respective
corners to the best of their ability. He was a soldier of the Republic
and I a Volunteer of Ulster and we made no apology for being what
we are or were.

Joe once did me a good turn indirectly and I never forgot him for
his humanity and even though I never got the chance to thank him
personally, I am almost sure that he knew how I felt and that I was
grateful to him . . .

I, too, am a family man with a wife and four lovely children and this
aspect is the most heart-rending of all because the women suffer in our
coming and in our going and it is they who have the most courage . . .

I salute your husband as an honourable and brave soldier.

Very sincerely and truly,

Gusty Spence.[2]

No doubt during this momentous time, Spence was growing restless in
gaol, feeling that if ever the UVF needed his organizational and leadership
skills, it was now. He could give advice to his family and comrades on visits,
but that was not the same as doing it face to face in the harsh world of the
conflict outside. Spence was a hands-on person, and in Crumlin Road gaol
there was a limit to what the hands could do. But there were some outside
who decided that Spence should have a taste of freedom.

In April 1972, a young Shankill man called Winston Churchill Rea – or
'Winkie' as he was universally known – had finally plucked up the courage
to ask Gusty Spence for the hand of his daughter, Elizabeth, in marriage.
'Winkie' had never met the legendary Spence before and was under-
standably nervous about doing so for the first time, especially under such
circumstances. Spence only had one half-hour visit a week and the Saturday
that 'Winkie' went up to the gaol, he was expecting to have the full thirty
minutes so he would have plenty of time to ask for Elizabeth's hand in the
manner that Gusty would expect. When he arrived, he found the Spence
family already there and the visit divided in two. 'I had the privilege of the
last fifteen minutes,' 'Winkie' told me. 'I was very nervous because Gusty,
even in those days, was a folk hero. For the seven days before the visit, it was
on my mind and as I entered the gaol that day I was actually shaking. But
once I got in and sat down and we started talking, the shakes left me. I told
him I was in love with his daughter and I would like to marry her.' Spence
told his prospective son-in-law that he had been doing some checking up
and one of his fellow prisoners had said, 'Don't let your daughter marry that
head case.' Nevertheless, Spence said he disagreed with the advice and was
happy to give 'Winkie' his daughter's hand in marriage.

As the wedding day approached – Saturday 1 July 1972 – Gusty was given forty-eight hours' leave to attend. He was met outside the prison on that morning by 'Plum' Smith and another colleague from the Red Hand Commando, who had also, with Smith, been one of its founder members. Spence said he was 'escorted to certain places' where he had conversations with those who were the UVF leadership at the time. They told him there was a need to restructure the organization in the light of the IRA's onslaught and presumably said they needed his help. Spence, being a 'soldier' and man of honour, said he was duty-bound to go back to gaol as he had given his bond. He then went on to the wedding. 'We had a good day,' he said. 'I was teetotal then. I had no alcoholic beverages whatsoever.' Early on Sunday morning, Spence was approached by senior UVF officers who said they did not want him to go back to gaol as his services were needed outside. He repeated what he had said the previous day, that he could not do it but 'what *they* did – and I'm saying this tongue in cheek – was their business'. Several nods and winks were exchanged. Spence's nephew, Frank Curry, was given the responsibility of driving Gusty back to gaol. As they were driving up the Springmartin Road, two cars pulled in, one in front of them and one behind. Spence was sandwiched.

I can't put my hand on my heart and say that my heart didn't skip a beat. At first I wasn't sure exactly who it was but I was reasonably sure. My nephew, who was driving the car, hadn't a clue, so he struggled and got a broken nose. These hooded gentlemen lifted me, put me in the back of the car and drove off.
   Were you surprised?
Not really.

Spence had been 'kidnapped'. It was like Robin Hood escaping from Nottingham Castle. His new son-in-law, now on honeymoon in Liverpool, was not surprised. 'The wedding happened to coincide with the time when law and order had practically broken down in Northern Ireland and there was a lack of leadership on the outside. There was leadership there but *the* leader was missing and that was Gusty.' The RUC said he might have been captured by the IRA and they feared for his life. When a body was found on waste ground on the Shankill the following day, a police spokesman said it was 'almost certainly' Spence. In fact it was a Catholic, John Hanlon (38), another victim of loyalist sectarian killing. Spence remained at liberty for four months and became known as the 'Orange Pimpernel', embellishing still further the legend that already surrounded him. While evading his captors, he gave a famous interview to David Boulton of Granada Television's *World in Action* in which he said the UVF

would use its guns 'against anyone who would defy the constitution of
Ulster' and expressed his desire that the organization should 'play a much
more active role than it has been taking'. Asked about the escalating loyalist
sectarian killings, Spence was unequivocal in his reply. 'Random killing is
to be deplored at any time,' he said, 'and I would say to anyone engaged in
sectarian murder, "Cease it." He also protested his innocence regarding the
murder of Peter Ward.

Spence used his unexpected liberty to reorganize and re-equip the UVF,
which was in danger of being eclipsed by the thousands of rival UDA men
who poured on to the streets. For much of the conflict, there was little love
lost between the two main groups of loyalist paramilitaries and, from time to
time, their rivalry erupted into murderous feuds. Spence, who had an
encyclopaedic knowledge of the old Ulster Volunteer Force, restructured
the organization along identical lines with sections, platoons, companies,
battalions and brigades. He also instituted a uniform whose most distin-
guishing feature was a black leather jacket, which he wore during his
television interview. But the priority for the UVF, as it was for the UDA, was
to get its hands on sophisticated weaponry to match the IRA's Armalites
now coming in from America. But the UVF, because of its contacts with the
security forces, and in particular the Ulster Defence Regiment (UDR), did
not have to look so far afield, nor entrust itself to dodgy intermediaries that,
earlier that year, had led the UDA into the embarrassing MI5 'sting'. I asked
Spence how the UVF went about getting guns. 'We stole them. From
everywhere. From the army, the police, anywhere we could get them. I
prefer not to use the word "stole". We procured them.' The most successful
UVF procurement took place on 23 October 1972 when an armed unit
raided the Territorial Army depot at Lurgan and made off with 104 guns and
an assortment of ammunition. 'Unfortunately, the van broke down or we
would have got a lot more. Many more were left behind,' Spence lamented
without complaining at the arms they had got. 'They were top-class
weapons. Self-loading rifles (SLRs), Browning pistols and Sterlings [sub-
machine-guns].' Nor was the UVF short of explosives after twenty tons of
ammonium nitrate, the essential ingredient for home-made fertilizer bombs,
were subsequently spirited away from Belfast docks. Spence left the UVF in
good health.

The 'Orange Pimpernel's' luck finally ran out when he was re-arrested
by soldiers of the Parachute Regiment on 4 November 1972. He was
identified by their commanding officer, Colonel Derek Wilford (who had
led the battalion on 'Bloody Sunday'), who noticed that Spence had dyed
his hair but had not been able to conceal the tattoo marks on his hands.[3]
When he returned to Crumlin Road gaol, no doubt to a hero's welcome
from his loyalist comrades, he found himself sharing prison life with 'Plum'

Smith of the Red Hand Commando, who had been arrested shortly after
he had escorted Gusty to his daughter's wedding, and had been sentenced
to ten years a few months later for the attempted murder of a Catholic
called Joseph Hall. Smith admits he did not know who the person was,
other than that he was a Catholic. He just picked him out and shot him. By
now such killings were almost routine.

> He was just walking along the street. That would have been the
> standard shooting of that time, from a passing car – 'travelling
> gunmen' as they were known. People didn't know who the IRA
> leaders were, who the commanders were or who was in the IRA.
> People just took the attitude that if people were in the nationalist
> community, they supported the IRA and gave them solace and
> people looked upon them as targets.
> **So a Catholic from a nationalist area was fair game?**
> In those days, that's how people looked upon it. When I look back,
> I think it was pure sectarianism and bigotry but we were all kids then
> and that's the way the world looked to us at that particular time. If I
> were born in any other part of the world where there was no trouble
> like this, I would never have killed or shot anybody and I would
> never have joined a paramilitary organization. That goes for Protes-
> tant kids and Catholic kids as well.

'Winkie' Rea also became associated with the Red Hand Commando and
ended up in gaol the following year with his newly recaptured father-in-
law. By this time, loyalist and republican prisoners had been moved to the
compounds of an old RAF camp known as 'Long Kesh', which to the
satisfaction of the inmates and the frustration of the authorities looked like
and was run like a German prisoner-of-war camp in the Second World
War. Rea was sentenced to eight years for possession of a Sterling
submachine-gun and for driving cars to and from Divis Street where
two Catholic postmen, Anthony Coleman (30) and David McAleese (38),
were shot dead from a passing car on 18 February 1973. Rea protested his
innocence. It was only the second case to come before the newly
constituted Diplock Courts (so called after Lord Diplock's report), where
a single judge sat and dispensed justice without a jury. The dubious honour
of being the first belongs to Billy Sloan of the UDA, who apparently sat
through the entire proceedings reading a book and was sentenced to life.

By the end of 1972, there had been 121 killings that were classified as
'assassinations'. Two-thirds were victims of what republicans were to refer to
as the 'loyalist death squads'. There was worse to come. As the year drew to a
close there was a power struggle within the UDA as Charles Harding Smith

returned from his trip to London via the Hilton Hotel and Her Majesty's pleasure. 'Until Smith came back, there was no such thing as a power struggle,' Dave Fogel told me. 'When we came together, we were the "Godfathers" and we agreed the overall direction. When he returned, he wanted to be "top dog". He was aware that I didn't agree with his strategy as I wanted a more political angle.' Harding Smith soon took control of the UDA in West Belfast, ousting Dave Fogel, and became joint Chairman of the organization with Jim Anderson who had been acting as caretaker while Harding Smith was away. By this time, a third candidate for the succession had emerged in the person of Tommy Herron, the UDA brigadier from East Belfast where he had powerful support. Fogel, who had been running West Belfast in Harding Smith's absence and even 'negotiated' with William Whitelaw – he remembers his 'puffy red face and bulging eyes' – was squeezed out and decided that, for the good of his health, it was time to go. He believed his life was under threat. Ernie Elliott had gone and Fogel feared he might be next. In January 1973, he left Belfast and disappeared into anonymity in England. Fogel survived, as did Harding Smith – but only just. Harding Smith was targeted on two occasions, it is thought, by the same gunman from a rival UDA faction in West Belfast and was lucky to escape with his life. On the first occasion, the gunman, a close associate of Andy Tyrie, put two .300 bullets into Harding Smith's chest from his sniping position above an opticians' shop opposite UDA headquarters on the Shankill Road. The second assassination attempt came after the lucky brigadier had been discharged from hospital. A masked man walked into his office and shot him again.[4] Harding Smith was not prepared to push his luck any further and, taking the hint, sought refuge in England like Dave Fogel, where he later died of natural causes, taking his secrets to the grave with him. Tommy Herron was not so lucky. He was reported missing from East Belfast on 14 September 1973 and his body was found by a roadside in the south of the city two days later. He had one carefully aimed bullet in his head. His legally held weapon was still in its shoulder holster. Thirty thousand loyalists attended his military-style funeral.

By the spring of 1973, the UDA power struggle that was to lead to the exile of two of its protagonists and the murder of the third, had been resolved at a meeting at the Park Avenue Hotel in Belfast, called to decide the succession between Harding Smith and Tommy Herron after the acting Chairman, Jim Anderson, had decided to stand down. Andy Tyrie, the commander of West Belfast's A company, a supreme conciliator and politician, was in the chair and emerged as the compromise candidate since the election of either of the other two would probably have resulted in defections or far worse. No one was more astonished than Tyrie.

That was a surprise to me. When I went to that meeting it was to put forward ideas on how to consolidate the organization and bring it forward. I felt at that time we'd become an organization that was controlled by so many other people. I had put suggestions forward of how the organization should develop and how we should look at different facets other than purely defence. I felt we should look at a political future, a historical future, and social issues. We should look at every possible aspect if it was to remain as a defence organization.

But you were supposed to be there for six months and you ended up staying fifteen years.

What had happened was that other people had been fighting with each other and they couldn't agree. So they put me in charge on a temporary basis to convince people of the things that I felt were wrong. The job just grew.

Tyrie survived for so long because he was not only a consummate political operator within the UDA, but also, behind an affable exterior, extremely tough. Had he not been so, he would probably have gone the way of Harding Smith, Dave Fogel or even Tommy Herron. Tyrie always managed to stay one step ahead of his enemies.

Soon there were those within the UDA who had another view of its role which had nothing to do with politics and social issues and the kind of thing Tyrie was talking about. It was about killing. They decided that in order to protect the parent body, the UDA – which, unlike the UVF and the Red Hand Commando, was legal – a separate unit should be formed within the organization. It was to consist of what its members called the 'élite' and became known as the Ulster Freedom Fighters (UFF). It was nothing more than a flag of convenience for the more militant members of the UDA. Although Andy Tyrie went on to become the UDA's 'Supreme Commander', he has always denied responsibility for the UFF. John White, who had recently been acquitted of attempting to buy arms in London with Charles Harding Smith, was one of the UFF's founder members.

The decision to set up the UFF came about because of the hard-core activists within the UDA. It was felt that a more efficient, streamlined organization needed to come into being because, you must remember, at that particular time the UDA was a very, very large organization, comprising of almost 30,000 and more members. It was felt, because of the activities that were being carried out, that it had to be a more streamlined, more efficient, and more effective organization. So a group got together and decided that they would set up this other organization to put together the main activists who were willing to take the war to the IRA.

Take the war to the IRA?

Yes, take the war to the IRA. They felt enough wasn't being done and that we had to embark on a campaign that would directly affect the IRA and would put pressure on the IRA in order for them to desist from what they were doing in our communities.

But most of the killings that the UFF carried out were not against the IRA, they were against innocent Catholics.

I think at the start of the campaign the vision was that the IRA had full support within their communities and therefore it was felt that in order to put pressure on the IRA, the same effect would be achieved by conducting a campaign against the communities where the IRA found its support.

So the nationalist Roman Catholic community was re-garded as a legitimate target by the UFF, was it?

Well, in the end, it was felt that the IRA gained very popular support within their communities and it was seen as a strategy that if pressure could be put on the IRA by their communities, then that would have an effect and that they would consider desisting from the attacks on loyalist communities. So there was a clear strategy and methodology behind the UFF activities.

It was as simple and brutal as that, was it?

Well, it was simple and it was brutal, you know, but it was a tactic of retaliatory action against a community who was inflicting great pain in our community.

The UFF's strategy was to show the IRA that loyalists could be even more brutal. The IRA might claim, when civilians were killed as a result of its operations, that it was a regrettable 'mistake'. The UFF made no such apology. Its killing of Catholic civilians was deliberate and could vary from a general reaction to IRA violence to a response to a particular IRA atrocity. On 12 June 1973, the IRA telephoned a warning about a car bomb it had planted in Coleraine, County Derry, but the wrong location was given. The bomb exploded, killing six pensioners on an outing. All of them were Protestants and most of them were over seventy years old. As with 'Bloody Friday', their deaths were yet another 'mistake'. The new leadership of the UFF met and ordered its units to retaliate. 'Jim', who had been brought up on a fiercely loyalist estate in South Belfast, was one of those instructed to carry out the order. He had become one of the UFF's earliest recruits, tired of seeing Protestants being killed on an almost daily basis and angered that the IRA was 'getting the upper hand'. He offered his services and was duly sworn in.

Basically it was the same criteria as being sworn into the UDA, but it was more of a solemn oath – that you would defend your country with your life. Whereas in the UDA you were sworn in to defend your country but whether you decided to do that or not was a matter of your own conscience. But with the UFF, you actually were swearing to lay down you life if need be for your country.

And were you prepared to do that?

I was, yes. Coming from the background I came from, which was a very strict Protestant upbringing, I felt that if I could do anything for my country I would do it regardless of the consequences, even if it meant laying down my particular life for it.

And laying down somebody else's life for it, killing someone – were you prepared to do that?

I was, yes, at that particular time.

I said he did not look like the kind of person who would go out and kill somebody as he was mild-mannered, neatly groomed and softly spoken. 'Jim' said that looks could be deceptive. Killing, he thought, would 'bring a speedy conclusion to the conflict'.

Four days after the death of the six pensioners in Coleraine, 'Jim' was ordered to exact revenge. The killings had made him feel sick. 'They'd probably spent all their lives doing their day's work and were on an outing enjoying themselves. They were coming home and were blown to bits.' With some other UFF members, he went to Andersonstown, a 100 per cent Catholic area, and picked out a victim, a seventeen-year-old Catholic student. He told me what he did.

I went out with a group of other Volunteers from the UFF and we picked up a Catholic and we took him away and we executed him.

Murdered him.

Yes.

Shot him dead.

Yes.

A Catholic?

Yes.

Any Catholic?

Yes.

Why was he selected?

He was selected for no other reason than he was a Catholic.

No reason to believe he was involved in the Republican Movement?

No.

'Jim' and his men took the student into a field. One of them had been chosen to pull the trigger but at the last minute he declined. 'I couldn't honestly say whether he had a clash of conscience or something. Obviously he didn't proceed with what he was supposed to do.' 'Jim' took the gun and without hesitation shot his victim through the head without saying a word. He served fourteen years of a life sentence for murder and now, with hindsight, regrets what he did. 'It's easy to say that, but unless you were sitting in my shoes, you couldn't understand what I was feeling. At that particular time, I thought it was right. I've now learned to be a bit more tolerant of people's views and aspirations.'

Ten days after the killing of the young student, John White himself carried out one of the UFF's most brutal killings. Senator Paddy Wilson, a leading member of Belfast City Council and election agent for Gerry Fitt MP (then also leader of the SDLP), was one of Belfast's best-known and most popular politicians. A former senator in the Upper House of the recently suspended Stormont parliament, he had always refused to carry a gun for his personal protection on the grounds that he could never live with the thought that he had shot 'somebody's son, or husband or father'.[5] On the evening of 26 June 1973, he had been having a drink in McGlade's Bar in Belfast city centre with Irene Andrews, a friend who was a Protestant and one of Belfast's best-known ballroom dancers. They left the bar at around 11.30 p.m. and drove away in Wilson's red mini. The car was found five hours later in a quarry just outside Belfast, near the spot where the three Scottish soldiers had been shot dead by the IRA over two years earlier. The bodies of Paddy Wilson and Irene Andrews lay horribly mutilated in pools of blood on either side of the car. Senator Wilson had been stabbed thirty times and his throat had been cut from ear to ear; Irene Andrews had been stabbed twenty times. There had been no killing like it in Northern Ireland before. The bodies were found after a call to a local paper from a 'Captain Black' of the UFF. 'Tonight we have got Senator Paddy Wilson and a lady friend,' the voice said. 'Their bodies are lying in the Hightown Road. After the IRA have murdered a retarded boy, we are not going to stand any longer for what those animals have done to us in the past four years. There will be more deaths in reprisal.' The 'retarded boy' was a reference to Alan 'Rocky' Meehan (18), who was shot on 9 July 1972 – the day the IRA ceasefire ended. His death subsequently drove others to join the UFF – including 'Jim', who lived close by. John White was later given two life sentences for murder.

Twenty-three years on, John White walked into Downing Street as a member of a loyalist delegation that had come to talk peace. Inside Number Ten, he shook John Major's hand. But that was only after over 2,000 more deaths.

Billy Giles with his parents, Sam and Lily, at his graduation inside the Maze prison.

Billy Giles inside the Maze prison, 1990.

The Relief of Derry. The famous painting that shows, in the foreground, Elizabeth Ash, her son Captain Thomas Ash, and her daughter Mrs Michael Browning, whose husband Captain Michael Browning stands aboard the *Mountjoy.*

Sir Edward Carson with Ulster Volunteers, 1912.

Sir Edward Carson signing the Ulster Covenant, 1912.

Ulster's
Solemn League and Covenant.

Being convinced in our consciences that Home Rule would be disastrous to the material well-being of Ulster as well as of the whole of Ireland. subversive of our civil and religious freedom. destructive of our citizenship and perilous to the unity of the Empire. we. whose names are underwritten. men of Ulster. loyal subjects of His Gracious Majesty King George V.. humbly relying on the God whom our fathers in days of stress and trial confidently trusted. do hereby pledge ourselves in solemn Covenant throughout this our time of threatened calamity to stand by one another in defending for ourselves and our children our cherished position of equal citizenship in the United Kingdom and in using all means which may be found necessary to defeat the present conspiracy to set up a Home Rule Parliament in Ireland. ¶ And in the event of such a Parliament being forced upon us we further solemnly and mutually pledge ourselves to refuse to recognise its authority. ¶ In sure confidence that God will defend the right we hereto subscribe our names. ¶ And further. we individually declare that we have not already signed this Covenant.

The above was signed by me at   Belfast.
"Ulster Day." Saturday. 28th September. 1912.

Edward Carson

God Save the King.

Lord Moyola, formerly Major James Chichester Clark, Prime Minister for Northern Ireland 1969-71.

James Murdock (second from right) and the Reverend Ian Paisley look on to a coffin covered with flowers, at a protest against the disbanding of the 'B' Specials.

James Murdock's farmhouse, where Ian Paisley took Noel Docherty and Billy Mitchell for their UPV meeting in 1966.

Noel Docherty, 1998.

The bombing at McGurk's Bar, 1971.

William Craig at a
Vanguard rally, 1972.

Gunmen of the UFF. UVF gunmen.

UDA marching in Belfast, circa.1972.

John White, co-founder of the UFF in 1973. Currently prisons spokesman of the UDA's political wing, the UDP.

John White's victims: Irene Andrews (left) and Senator Paddy Wilson (right).

David Ervine in the UVF compound in Long Kesh prison.

Billy Hutchinson (left) and Eddie Kinner (right) in Long Kesh.

Eddie Kinner (right) and Martin Snodden (left) in Long Kesh. Both served several life sentences for bombing Conway's bar in 1975.

Augustus 'Gusty' Spence following his re-arrest, after his 'kidnapping' by the UVF in 1972.

Gusty Spence in the UVF compound.

The UVF communications system in Long Kesh.

Gusty Spence.

Gusty at home in 1998.

The Reverend Ian Paisley, 1986.

Robert 'Basher' Bates, one of the 'Shankill Butchers', who was shot dead by a relative of one of his victims in 1997.

Lenny Murphy, leader of the 'Shankill Butchers', who was shot dead in 1982. The IRA were thought to be responsible.

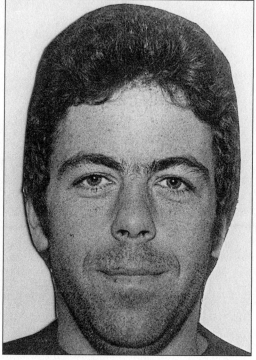

Winston Churchill 'Winkie' Rea's house in the early 1980s. Outside stands the 12th of July protest placard.

Michael Stone attacking mourners in Milltown Cemetery, 1988. The Browning pistol was part of the loyalist consignment smuggled in from Lebanon in 1987.

The Shankill Road fish shop, devastated by an IRA bomb in 1993.

Funerals of those murdered by UFF at Greysteel, one week after the
Shankill bomb attack.

Gusty Spence announcing the loyalist ceasefires at Fernhill House, 1994.

Loyalist UDP and PUP delegates at Downing St, 1996. Left to right: Hugh Smyth, Gary McMichael, John White and David Ervine.

Chapter Ten

Returning the Serve

For more than a year, the Stormont parliament building was silent, with only the cleaners entering the debating chamber to dust the leather seats and polish the furniture. No politicians' feet clattered along its marble corridors and halls as they had done since it was first opened by the Prince of Wales in 1932 when the parliament moved from Belfast City Hall to Sir Arnold Hornley's magnificent, neo-classical edifice on the outskirts of East Belfast.[1] Symbolically, the new Northern Ireland Office administration had set itself up in Stormont Castle, a contrasting neo-gothic building half a mile away that looked a bit like Count Dracula's castle. This became the home-away-from-home for the Northern Ireland Secretary, who had a flat above the office, and his team of civil servants, who had to wrestle with the problem of how to end the mayhem and bring politics back to the province. It was only ever the intention to suspend Stormont for a year until such time as structures could be agreed that would return democratic politics to Northern Ireland, although not on the basis on which they had been exercised for the previous fifty years. How to do it was the question. While the MI6 officer, Frank Steele, and his successor, Michael Oatley, made it their business to disappear into the woodwork of the two communities to make assessments and establish contacts, William Whitelaw and his civil servants pored over scenarios that might produce peace. The result was a White Paper called 'Northern Ireland Constitutional Proposals', published on 20 March 1972, almost a year to the day since Stormont was suspended. What it outlined, to the consternation of loyalists, was a new devolved government, called an 'Executive', in which nationalists and unionists would share power within a wider political framework involving the Irish Republic. The Government made it clear that 'any new arrangement for Northern Ireland should . . . be so far as possible acceptable to and accepted by the Republic of Ireland'.[2] This notion, referred to as the 'Irish Dimension', represented a totally new departure in British Government policy and triggered the first split in the hitherto monolithic Unionist Party. Many more were to come. The fact that William Craig jumped ship ten days later to form his own Vanguard Unionist Progressive

Party was an indicator of the great unease among many of those left on board. The UDA announced that it would give Craig and his new party 100 per cent support. (The political arrangements outlined in the White Paper bore an uncanny similarity to those of the Good Friday Agreement reached exactly a quarter of a century later.)

Whitelaw moved with lightning speed to fill the dangerous political vacuum and by the end of June 1973, elections had been held for the new Northern Ireland Assembly with pro-White Paper candidates in a clear majority. Nevertheless, the loyalist opposition, led by Paisley and Craig, was significant if not yet serious, with more than 20 per cent of the vote. Brian Faulkner who had undergone a remarkable transformation from Unionist hard-lines to liberal, declared that the result showed that voters 'have rejected violence, either from the IRA or from paramilitary organizations on the other side'.[3] It was earlier that month that the IRA had slaughtered the six pensioners in Coleraine and the UFF had shot dead the young student and savagely mutilated Paddy Wilson and Irene Andrews. Paisley described the result as 'the voice of free-born Ulstermen saying to Messrs Heath and Wilson [then leader of the Labour opposition] "You will not push us into a united Ireland." '[4]

One of the Vanguard members elected to the Assembly was a young trade unionist from Derry called Glen Barr, who was invariably referred to by the media and other politicians as a senior member of the UDA. Barr denies he ever was – at least in the military sense. 'I never joined the UDA,' he told me. 'I certainly was very much associated with the UDA as the senior political spokesman for the organization but, as such, I was never in the military side which most people would have thought was the real UDA. I was never asked to take the oath and never forced to take the oath. I think that people just accepted me for what I was.' Barr, sworn in or not, and the UDA's recently elected new Chairman, Andy Tyrie, were to become key figures as political events unfolded. Vanguard, the UDA and their trade union allies had already flexed their industrial muscle at the beginning of 1973 when they called for a one-day strike on 7 February following the detention of two Protestants in the Long Kesh prison 'camp', making them the first loyalist internees. In Belfast and other parts of the province, there was an electricity blackout which showed the potential of what loyalist workers could do, but far from gaining widespread support, the strike alienated most Protestants, who were appalled by the catalogue of violence the one-day strike produced. Four people were shot dead: two UDA (one killed by the IRA, the other by the army), one UVF (shot by the army) and a Protestant fireman shot dead by loyalists while fighting a blaze. In addition, there were twenty-seven injuries, eight bomb blasts and sixty-eight arrests. Billy Hull, the Harland and Wolff shop stewards' convenor who led the Loyalist Association of Workers (LAW) which was allied to Vanguard and the UDA in the strike, declared that the 'power of the [loyalist] grass roots' could no longer be ignored.[5]

With the Assembly elected, the Government now had to put in place the two vital components of its political initiative: a power-sharing executive and the 'Irish Dimension'. The two were interdependent and, to loyalists, equally contentious. After ten hours of discussion on 21 November 1973, members of the Unionist Party under Brian Faulkner, the SDLP under its leader, Gerry Fitt, and the Alliance Party (moderately inclined Catholics and Protestants who wanted to end the old sectarian divisions) finally agreed to share power in the devolved government. Faulkner was to be Chief Executive and Fitt his Deputy. The Reverend William Beattie of Paisley's DUP (its founder being away in America) described the decision in words of which his leader would have been proud as 'the greatest betrayal since Lundy'; William Craig warned it was unacceptable to most of the loyalist majority and they were 'going to make this Executive unworkable'; and Prime Minister Edward Heath said it offered 'a real prospect of lasting peace'.[6] The inevitable happened and a fortnight later the Unionist Party split again when five of the Ulster Unionist MPs at Westminster declared that they could not support their leader. Faulkner was becoming increasingly isolated and perhaps blinded to political realities at home by mainland approbation for his courage in leading unionists out of the past.

The tightrope he walked became even more unsteady when, that same day, he attended the first Anglo-Irish Conference since partition, held at the Civil Service Staff College at Sunningdale in Berkshire. There, in what became known as the 'Sunningdale Agreement', Faulkner finally agreed to accept a Council of Ireland that was to consist of a Council of Ministers drawn from the two jurisdictions and a consultative Assembly made up of members of the new Northern Ireland Assembly and the Dublin parliament, Dail Eireann. The Council of Ireland was the SDLP's *quid pro quo* for agreeing to go along with power sharing and the British Government's hoped-for guarantee that the Irish Republic would crack down on the IRA and extradite terrorist suspects. The unionist opposition closed ranks against Faulkner and the political structures he had agreed to. Under the banner of the United Ulster Unionist Council (UUUC) the dissidents pledged to bring power sharing and Sunningdale down as they claimed they were unacceptable to the vast majority of the loyalist people of Ulster. A united Ireland, they believed, was just around the corner. On 4 January 1974, the Ulster Unionist Council voted by 427 votes to 374 to reject Sunningdale, 'the proposed all-Ireland Council settlement'.[7] Faulkner resigned and went out on his own followed by the minority of unionists who agreed with him. However, events over which they had no control suddenly played into the hands of Faulkner's opponents. At Westminster Edward Heath faced his political Waterloo over the miners' strike and summoned his faithful lieutenant, William Whitelaw, back to London to become Home Secretary, in the hope that he would be able to use his emollient powers of persuasion to make the miners' leader, Arthur Scargill, see sense. Heath called an election on the basis of 'Who runs Britain?' and the UUUC ran candidates on the basis of 'Who runs Ulster?' The outcome was disastrous for both Heath and Faulkner. Heath lost and Harold Wilson once again became Prime Minister. The UUUC swept the board, winning eleven of the twelve Westminster seats – the exception being the unwinnable constituency of West Belfast with its huge nationalist majority, which was held by Gerry Fitt. To Paisley, the February 1974 election result was a turning point. 'It was a magnificent victory,' he told me. 'We swept the board. What did the British Government do? Ignored the ballot box. The people of Northern Ireland said we have had enough.'

Surprisingly against a background of what for most loyalists was a traumatic series of political events, the UVF declared a ceasefire. On 17 November 1973, it issued a statement saying the cessation would last for forty-three days until the New Year. Before the ceasefire, the UVF was responsible for detonating more than 200 bombs in comparison with the IRA's 300.[8] The statement said 'without fear of contradiction' that the UVF was responsible for 97 per cent of loyalist violence 'with the exception of sectarian murders' and declared the organization would be working with loyalists who opposed power sharing and Sunningdale for 'a restoration of a democratic system of government'. If that did not happen, the statement threatened, the UVF would carry on with its military campaign. By this time, Billy Mitchell had risen to become a senior member of the UVF and was one of the prime advocates of the ceasefire. Looking back, he described the mood of the time.

> During the conflict there were times when you did take time out to sit down and think. We always expected the conflict to blow over in about eighteen months or so. Nobody expected it to go on. By the end of 1973 it had been going on about four years and a lot of us were saying, 'When is this going to end? Are we going to fight for ever?' There was a feeling that there had to be some sort of resolution. We knew nothing about conflict resolution. We didn't even know the term. But we knew there had to be a different way, that we couldn't go on sending people out to blow up pubs or to go out and shoot people – and at the same time to see our pubs and our shops being blown up and our people shot. It didn't look as if the politicians were going to resolve it politically so we needed space. We felt if we called a ceasefire and stopped the hostilities, perhaps we could engage politically and maybe even ourselves come up with

some political thoughts. We just felt that continued acts of violence weren't taking us anywhere.

At the beginning of 1974 when I was making a film about the impact of Sunningdale, I was taken to the basement of a club in the Shankill Road where three masked UVF men were sitting at a table surrounded by several others holding SLR rifles. There was clearly one spokesman for the group who sat there, with black mask, black sweater and revolver on the green-baized table in front of him. He outlined the UVF's position.

> Whilst we were fighting the IRA, we were leaving the constitutional and the political crisis to the politicians. We woke up and realized that we'd been fighting a war for four years yet our country's been sold down the river by the politicians. We'd been leaving the political war to the politicians whereas in actual fact the politicians had been losing that war. So we called a ceasefire and went to the politicians and told them we weren't going to fight the Provos for ever. We want to see peace but we want to see a real, lasting peace not peace at any price; a peace that will satisfy both the Ulster Protestants and the Irish nationalists. Some solution will have to be worked out between what the press call 'the men of violence'. The politicians can never give us peace. The men who pull the triggers are the only men who can take their fingers off the triggers. The Provisionals will have to accept the fact that the Protestant people of Northern Ireland will not give up their Protestant liberties. Our objection is to the Provisional IRA and their supporters who are trying to take away our liberties and our traditional way of life at the point of a gun.[9]

It was only when I came to research Loyalists nearly twenty-five years later that I realized that the hooded spokesman was Billy Mitchell. Given what had finally happened by 1998, his words of 1974 were prophetic. He remembered the interview and the political climate in which it was done. 'Unfortunately in 1974 we didn't have a strategy and we didn't have a political philosophy,' he said. 'We had a gut feeling that the politicians weren't going to resolve it, that only the paramilitaries could stop the violence and that there had to be some form of compromise where we could accommodate each other's aspirations. We didn't have a strategy for doing it then. Perhaps we had to go to gaol to find one.'

What was unknown at the time was that Mitchell, with the blessing of the UVF leadership, had not only talked with the Official IRA in Dublin, which was also on ceasefire, but had met the Provisional IRA at a secret location in the middle of Ireland to explore the possibility of peace. At the beginning of 1974, Mitchell told me he had sat down with David

O'Connell of the IRA's Army Council and Brian Keenan, a leading Provisional from Belfast, at a fishing lodge by Lough Sheelin just outside Mount Nugent, County Cavan. Although few would have thought it, there was potentially some common political ground. For the loyalists, Desmond Boal, a former Stormont MP for the Shankill, Paisley's political mentor and the sharpest advocate at the Belfast bar, had advocated a form of federal or 'amalgamated Ireland' as the answer to the age-old conflict. For the Provisionals, David O'Connell, along with Sinn Fein's President, Ruairi Ó'Brádaigh, had written the Republican Movement's policy document, Eire Nua (New Ireland), which was based on a federal Ireland too. On 8 January 1974, Ó'Brádaigh had publicly welcomed Boal's proposals as a real alternative to Sunningdale, saying that it was 'approximately' what Sinn Fein had been saying for the past two and a half years. A week later, O'Connell echoed the sentiment.[10]

Mitchell remembered the encounter in the fishing lodge. 'Again there was nothing structured. We weren't going to go in for recriminations. It was to find out, you know, "What do you want? What are you after? What will you settle for?" And we were trying to say, "Well, this is what we want." It was more of an exploration to find out what people wanted. We didn't go there to say, "You've done this, that and the other." What we were saying was, "How can we reach an accommodation, how can we do something about this?" Although there was some agreement on social and economic issues, which were never the problem anyway, there was no meeting of minds on the central political issue. 'They had the one-track mind with the thirty-two-county [united] Ireland and even within unionism, Boal's "amalgamated Ireland" wasn't acceptable. [Neither Paisley nor Craig showed any enthusiasm for it.] Obviously, as history has shown, nothing was resolved. Probably we were a few small voices on the loyalist side. What we did wasn't particularly liked or welcomed but we felt we had to do it. And unfortunately nothing came of it. At least we tried.'

Although the talks with both wings of the IRA proved fruitless, the UVF did get its reward for trying when on 4 April 1974, Merlyn Rees, the Secretary of State for Northern Ireland in Harold Wilson's new Labour Government, told the House of Commons that the ban on the UVF and Sinn Fein was to be lifted, allowing both organizations to participate in the political process. Brian Faulkner, now Chief Executive of the new power-sharing Government, disagreed strongly with Rees' decision to lift the ban. The following month, he referred to 'the whole rotten gamut of paramilitary organizations'.[11] Nevertheless, while welcoming the decision and recognizing that there was a need to develop a political party of its own, the UVF maintained that it had to remain an armed force.[12] A few days later, it dipped its toe in the political water by announcing that it would cause widespread disturbance unless bus fares in Belfast were reduced.[13] On 26 April 1974, some members of the organization had also gone into up-market fundraising with 'criminal' elements by lifting £8 million of paintings, including a Goya, a Rubens, and two Gainsboroughs, from a stately home in County Wicklow, south of Dublin. The gang cut the paintings from their frames, made off in a car, and apparently sold them on the black market abroad. Some of the UVF members who had taken part in this 'unauthorised' operation were subsequently 'court-martialled'. But by the spring of 1974 the UVF was not just agitating about bus fares in Belfast but had gone back to killing Catholics. Clearly the UVF had realized that 'a democratic system of government' was not going to be returned and was now carrying out its threat to return to 'military' action. By this time, the IRA was not only killing members of the security forces with chilling regularity but had extended its campaign to England. On 4 February 1974, it had planted a bomb in the boot of an army coach on its way from Manchester to Catterick military camp in Yorkshire. It exploded on the M62 motorway, killing nine soldiers and three civilians. The UVF decided it was time to return to the bombing campaign that had previously caused such bloody mayhem – no doubt using in its bombs some of the twenty tons of ammonium nitrate fertilizer it had stolen from Belfast docks. On 29 March it attacked Conway's Bar in Greencastle, killing two Catholics, and on 2 May it bombed the Rose and Crown Bar on the now largely nationalist Ormeau Road, killing six Catholic civilians. Between the two explosions, the UVF lost one of its men, Joseph Neill (25), who was apparently blown up by his own bomb in a house in Portadown. But these killings were as nothing compared with the slaughter to come.

On 17 May 1974, two UVF units, one from Belfast and one from mid-Ulster, hijacked four cars and drove them across the border. The cars were packed with explosives and one left in Monaghan town and the other three in Dublin. At 5.30 p.m. the cars that had been parked in the centre of Dublin exploded almost simultaneously without warning as office workers were on their way home for the weekend. Twenty-six civilians died in the blasts, of whom twenty were female, two of them baby girls. Half an hour later, the car bomb left in Monaghan exploded, killing a further seven civilians. The combined death toll of thirty-two was the biggest loss of life in a single day in the whole of the current conflict – even greater than the 'Real IRA's' Omagh bomb on 15 August 1998 that claimed the lives of twenty-eight people. One of the young women who died in the Dublin explosions was twenty-one-year-old Anna Massey who was due to be married six weeks later. Anna had spent the previous night writing 120 wedding invitation cards with the help of her father, Frank. The wedding cake had been ordered and the wedding dress was being made. By mid-evening on Friday, Frank was getting worried that Anna had not arrived home from work and was growing increasingly concerned, having seen news of the horrific bombings on the television. He jumped into the car and tried to drive into the centre of Dublin to see if he could find his daughter, but was turned back. The family tried to ring the hospital but all the lines were jammed. Between ten-thirty and eleven o'clock, the police arrived at their door and asked if Frank and his wife could come to the hospital. There the matron showed them a ring and a watch with Anna's name on it. They identified her body in the morgue at one-thirty the following morning. The family was devastated. 'There's not a day goes by when we don't think of that child,' Frank told me with tears in his eyes.

No person has ever been brought to justice for the bombings and Frank and many of the relatives of those who died that day are now convinced that there has been a cover-up because elements of British Intelligence were involved. 'All I'm looking for is justice,' he told me. 'I want to know who did it and why. If [only] someone would come along and say, "Yes, I made those bombs." I don't want them to be put in prison or executed or anything like that. Why were twenty-six people murdered in Dublin and seven in Monaghan, within a hour of one another, and hundreds injured and still carrying their injuries today? So there's two questions in my mind to be answered. Who did it and why?' I told him the UVF did it to make Catholics across the border suffer like Protestants in the North had suffered at the hands of the IRA. I said that although it was possible that elements of the UDR may have assisted in the making of the bombs given the close association – and even dual membership – of some of its members with the UVF, especially in the Portadown/Lurgan area of mid-Ulster, I did not believe it was a British Intelligence plot. I knew he was disappointed to hear me say it.

I asked David Ervine, who was a senior member of the UVF in Belfast at the time, about these bombings although he himself had nothing to do with them. He said they were 'returning the serve'. I knew what he meant but was surprised he had used the expression. I sensed too that he regretted doing so the moment the phrase left his lips. In fact he was only being brutally honest, as that was how the bombings would have been seen at the time by many loyalists who had witnessed the IRA wreak havoc in their own areas and kill dozens of their civilians. 'I think certainly there were many within the unionist community who felt, and I may have felt it too, "Now you know how we feel." We're not there and we don't see the blood and brains and the destroyed, dismembered people. You don't see that. You're remote from it. It's a bit like watching Bosnia on television.'

'Returning the serve?' I repeated. 'Slaughtering dozens of innocent people?' 'You asked me a question,' he said, 'and I gave you an answer in determining why people do things.' I knew David Ervine wished he had put it another way.

Chapter Eleven

Strike

Ironically, on 14 May 1974, three days before the Dublin and Monaghan bombs, the House of Commons passed an amendment to the Northern Ireland Emergency Provisions Act legalizing the UVF and Sinn Fein in accordance with Merlyn Rees' announcement of the previous month. That same day, a momentous series of events were set in train that sent a clear message to Harold Wilson's Labour Government, and every one of its successors, that there could be no political settlement in Northern Ireland that did not command the broad support of the province's Protestant majority. The February general election was tantamount to a referendum on power sharing and Sunningdale, and the answer from loyalists was a resounding No, which, as Paisley rightly said, the Government at Westminster ignored. The problem was that what British Governments thought was best for Northern Ireland was seldom viewed in that light by most of its citizens. As the new Secretary of State, Merlyn Rees, observed, it was only when he went to Belfast that he realized that the new political structures were hated by loyalists. 'They'd fought their election campaign on the slogan, "Dublin is but a Sunningdale away",' he told me. 'They saw it as the supreme sell-out, the supreme betrayal. Within a day or two of my arrival in the province, Brian Faulkner came to see me and told me in so many words that he couldn't carry the Unionist Party with him on Sunningdale. He said, "I cannot carry it. I have lost my reason to be. I'm beaten, overwhelmed by the vote against my sort of unionism or the unionism I'm trying to carry out."' Rees recognized that one of the weaknesses of Sunningdale was that it had been negotiated and signed in the midst of the golf courses of stockbroker Berkshire. 'They ought to have met in Belfast and learned the realities of life,' he said. But even if Sunningdale had been signed on the moon, it would have made little difference to the loyalist response.

The day Westminster was legalizing the UVF, the new Assembly in Belfast was rejecting a motion from the loyalist opposition condemning power sharing and the Council of Ireland. The motion was defeated by forty-four votes to twenty-eight. Faulkner's supporters left the Assembly with smiles on their faces while Paisley's supporters looked glum. Then, to everyone's surprise, at 6.08 that evening, a virtually unknown shipyard shop steward called Harry Murray informed a handful of journalists at Stormont who were prepared to listen that a group known as the Ulster Workers' Council (UWC) was calling a strike. Few had ever heard of the UWC. He went on to announce that the electricity supply would be reduced from 725 megawatts to 400.[1] His audience could be forgiven at the time for thinking it was a joke. A joke it was not. What few of them knew was that careful planning had gone into the proposed strike to create the impact the strike the previous year had not had and to apply the lessons learned from it. The Ulster Workers' Council was the umbrella title the organizers had deliberately chosen so people would associate the strike with industrial action taken by workers. But its purpose was nothing to do with pay and conditions or trade union recognition: it was to use the power of the workers in the province's key industries and the paramilitary strength of the UDA and UVF to bring down power sharing and Sunningdale. Loyalist politicians opposed to both, led by William Craig and Ian Paisley, gave the strike the cloak of political respectability. Craig told me he had no problem in working alongside the loyalist paramilitaries. 'I had no hesitation in working with the UDA. I had some reservations about the UVF but since it was made clear no violence was involved, it became easier to have an agreed programme.' The main thing was to ensure the absence of the violence that had so alienated law-abiding Protestant support in the strike a year earlier when five people had been killed during one violent day. It was clearly not going to be easy with literally thousands of loyalist paramilitaries taking to the streets and the prospect of confrontation with the police and the army. The last thing the organizers wanted were scenes of clashes between loyalists and the RUC. Discipline was essential.

Every Wednesday night during the previous month, meetings of up to thirty men representing all the loyalist paramilitary organizations had been held to discuss strategy, not just among themselves but with loyalist workers from key industries.[2] These regular meetings had been called by Vanguard's economic spokesman and the Assembly member from Derry, Glen Barr, who went on to become the chairman of the strike coordinating committee. Bar was bright, personable, good-looking and media-friendly – the perfect person to get the strikers' message across. He had also been the trade union convenor at the giant electricity-generating station at Coolkeeragh, which was a useful credential given the important role that the power stations were to play in the strike. Andy Tyrie, the UDA's Chairman, gave his full support to what Barr was trying to do. 'Tyrie and myself had decided to set up a political think tank amongst the

ordinary working class and the paramilitary people to try and break the
mould of our political thinking and the workers came in with the idea of a
strike,' Barr told me. 'Andy and I debated it at great length and after a long
time a decision was made to go ahead. Originally, the strike was to be for a
whole variety of reasons but I felt it had to have a focus and I suggested we
should look at the possibility of focusing on the Assembly debate on the
Sunningdale Agreement and that's what we did. Andy agreed and he
instructed the workers an the rest of the paramilitaries that that would be
the date for the strike. And that's what happened.' By this time the loyalist
paramilitaries had come together under the banner of the Ulster Army
Council, the organization in whose name a dramatic statement was issued
following Harry Murray's surprise announcement of the strike. 'If Westminster is not prepared to restore democracy, i.e. the will of the people
made clear in an election, then the only other way it can be restored is by a
coup d'état.' I asked Glen Barr if a coup d'état was always the intention.

I think we used to bandy about dramatic words and use dramatic
phrases in those days. I think we didn't fully understand what we were
getting ourselves into. Here we were, a bunch of working-class
fellows, and all of a sudden we were handed all of this power, and this
responsibility in our communities. We hadn't been trained so we used
all these romantic phrases and emotional things that we read in comics
and books and stuff like that. The coup d'état basically was that we
were going to take over the country ourselves rather than have it
handed over to a united Ireland. We were saying, 'If you're not going
to run it, then we'll run it and if we can't run it, there'll be a scorched
earth policy. We'll burn the country rather than hand it over to a
united Ireland.' So all of these romantic things were said. The strike
seemed to be the best way to try and bring the British to their senses.

When you began, did you really think you would succeed?
People talk about this 'brilliant planning'. The 'brilliant planning'
went on from hour to hour and we were responding on many
occasions to what other people were doing. We just went along day
to day, and that's how the whole thing ran.

From the beginning, Tyrie believed the strike would be successful. 'If I'd
gone in with any other attitude,' he told me, 'I'd be wasting my time even
attempting to do it.' But his biggest concern was whether the workers
could deliver what they promised.

I had a meeting with the workers in my back garden when I lived in
Glencairn and we discussed the possibilities of a strike. I had to say to

them, 'Look, every time we have a stoppage it finishes up in violence.' And we talked about it and they said, 'We think we can deliver the goods. We can cut the power, we can bring the workers out.' I said, 'That's great.' I told them if we could do it from a non-violent point of view, it means we will win because up till then we had been so predictable: there was going to be a strike, there'd be violence and the security people knew exactly how to deal with it. I said, 'If we can do it like that, we won't have a problem.'

But it was easier said than done. When the strike began on Wednesday 15 May, there was clearly little evidence of mass support, although many did heed the UWC's call for a general work stoppage. Even some of the strike leaders' families did not know what was going on. Harry Murray's wife quite seriously asked him that morning why he was not going to work. The wife of another did not believe her husband when he said there was a strike until she went into the kitchen to make breakfast and found that there was no electricity. She thought a fuse had gone.[3] The power workers fulfilled the promise they had made in Andy Tyrie's garden by cutting off 75 per cent of the power in Glen Barr's home town of Derry and 60 per cent throughout the province. As anticipated there was a total stoppage in the shipyard, total because any of those having second thoughts about laying down tools had their doubts removed by being told that unless they joined the strike, they would find their cars burned out in the car park. Workers who arrived at Mackie's engineering plant were turned back at gun point and others who tried to get to work were prevented from doing so by UDA barricades manned by masked men with cudgels. Shops in East Belfast that showed any reluctance to close immediately put up the shutters before petrol bombs came through their doors. The port of Larne was totally sealed off. Without such widespread intimidation the strike would never have got under way. At the time, the strike leaders were reluctant to admit that there had been intimidation but now they are more honest. 'There was intimidation,' Andy Tyrie admits today, 'but it was very subtle – like taking photographs of people going to work with no film in the camera.' I pointed out it was not that subtle if you were on the receiving end. 'I suppose it's not, but it's better than people getting killed,' he admitted. 'When we woke up on Wednesday morning, there was no strike so what we had to do in the best possible way – you call it "intimidation" – was to get the members of the Ulster Defence Association to advise people to support the strike. You can call it intimidation. You can call it what you want – and it worked. It didn't work the first day and it took a few days before it got going. Once it had gripped, there was no violence. I still maintain that was the most important thing about the strike.' Glen Barr was more straightforward.

We felt that if we called the strike, it was going to have to be for whatever length of time it took to bring about our demands. A lot of people were saying, 'We don't want another one of these two-day wonder strikes that Vanguard called last year. We all lost two days' wages and it achieved absolutely nothing.' People were still in this mindset and so we decided we were going to have to put up barricades. We couldn't be seen to be provoking the security forces but at the same time we had to get the message through to our own people. Yes, there was intimidation. Andy called it 'discouragement', which was much more diplomatic. That's precisely what we did. Everybody zooms in on that, and our critics throughout the years have always said, 'but you threatened your own people'. We didn't have to after the third day.

You didn't have to because you'd threatened them for the first two days and if you hadn't done that, the strike would never have got off the ground.

Probably, yes.

By the fourth day of the strike there were power blackouts of six hours but these were overshadowed by the horror of the Dublin and Monaghan bombs which had exploded the evening before.

The army did move in to remove the barricades but, as soon as they arrived, the UDA melted away as Tyrie had ordered them to do to avoid any confrontation. The moment the soldiers went away, the UDA came back and so did the barricades. Tyrie's strategy was sophisticated. 'They [the authorities] would have to use violence to break the strike up and they would be seen as the bad guys. The real plan was that if there was any violence, it would have to come from the establishment. They would have to make the mistakes and we knew what to expect. They expected violence so we didn't give them any.' The tactic worked not just because it made sense given the experience of the strike the year before but because the army were also of like mind. The last thing the General Officer Commanding (GOC) Northern Ireland, Sir Frank King, wanted was for his men to be involved in a shooting war with the loyalist paramilitaries as well as the IRA. Soldiers, too, had been ordered to avoid confrontation wherever possible. When I interviewed Sir Frank in 1974 shortly after the strike was over, he told me in soldier's language why he had taken the course that he did. 'Certainly if you get a very large section of the population which is bent on a particular course, then it is a difficult thing to stop them. You can't go round shooting people because they want to do a certain thing.'[4]

As Tyrie and Barr both said, after the third day of the strike intimidation or 'discouragement' was no longer necessary as the action gained support by the day. Protestants gradually realized that this time the strike was for real and, as no blood was being spilled, felt they could give it their support as most of them agreed with the reason why it had been called. The argument made by the UWC and the loyalist politicians who supported it – Craig, Paisley and John Taylor, who had thrown in his lot with the strikers – that the Government had ignored the clearly expressed wish of the people in the February election, struck a powerful chord in even the most law-abiding Protestant's heart. Most could live for a while with no electricity but not with the prospect of a united Ireland. As John Taylor told me, 'The London Government refused to acknowledge that the Sunningdale Agreement did not have consent in Northern Ireland, and any democracy to be successful must have the consent of the population, not necessarily the support, but certainly the consent. But they'd lost consent here and they refused to recognize this reality. So the people took to the streets. The workers' strike was the final way of dealing with the problem that they were challenged with.' I asked Merlyn Rees why he had not confronted the strike and ordered the army to break it instead of giving in to the UWC.

> I didn't let them win. They were going to win anyway. It wasn't like a coal miners' strike in Sheffield. It could not be done, that's the short answer. We couldn't do a Prague. You can't put down a popular rising by killing people. We're not Russia. The police were on the brink of not carrying out their duties and the middle classes were on the strikers' side. This wasn't just an industrial dispute. This was the Protestant people of Northern Ireland rising up against Sunningdale and it could not be shot down.

Merlyn Rees' view was identical to Sir Frank King's. Nevertheless, it would be wrong to think that the army stood around and did nothing. An extra 2,000 troops were flown in, many of them with special skills to help run the power stations, but there was a limit to what they could do. For example, they could not run the giant Ballylumford power station between Belfast and Larne without the help of senior staff who were not inclined, nor in any position, to help. Soldiers also helped man the sewage works and keep the water supply running but they were only putting fingers in the dyke. Moreover, as Glen Barr remembers with some amusement, every move the army made was countered by the UWC.

> I think that the security forces felt that if they escalated the war, they were going to be sitting ducks in the power stations. They didn't want

that. At one stage the army announced that they were going to take over the distribution of bread and I quickly said, 'If you do that, you're going to have to bake it first, so I'm going to call out the bakers.' So they very quickly lost that idea. They then took over the distribution of oil, so we didn't give them any oil. Everything they did, we responded to negatively.

And they couldn't run the power stations.

They couldn't run the power stations, they couldn't run the petrol stations, they couldn't run the bakery, they couldn't run the sewage works. So every time there was a move by the army or by the Northern Ireland Office, we stepped it up again.

Had there been any sign of a popular loyalist backlash against the UWC for depriving them of their creature comforts, things might have been different. But there was not. For the first time since the outbreak of the Troubles, the majority community felt it was hitting back, not at the IRA, but at the British Government at whose door it laid many of its ills.

It was a bizarre situation. I went to Belfast and met Glen Barr and Andy Tyrie at the Vanguard offices at Hawthornden House, which the UWC was using as its strike headquarters. The scene was chaotic with queues of people waiting for passes and permits to provide essential supplies like bread and milk. It seemed incongruous that those who said yes or no to the requests were not the elected politicians, sitting powerless in the Executive half a mile away up the road at Stormont, but a mixture of paramilitaries and workers, most of whom had probably never even run a raffle. And the British Government was letting this happen. Shortly after the strike was over, Merlyn Rees told me he was 'lancing the boil'. The 'boil' was Sunningdale. But it was hardly a policy.

In loyalist areas, there was little outward sign of hardship as neighbours swapped bread, milk and stories in an atmosphere reminiscent of the Second World War, when Belfast as well as London was blitzed. Andy Tyrie says that, during the strike, Protestant and Catholic communities in some areas actually exchanged bread and milk since nationalists baked one and loyalists delivered the other. On the fiercely loyalist Taughmonagh estate to the south of Belfast, Jackie McDonald, who was a UDA commander at the time, reminisced as if he had been running the social services.

Each UDA brigade, or battalion or whatever, ran their own areas. They provided people with whatever medication they needed, whatever food they needed, whatever transport they needed. When I talked to people on the street they were saying to me, 'My husband

can't go to work and we have a family to keep.' I said, 'Well, I can't
go to work and I have a family to keep too. But if you want to keep
yourself part of the British Isles, we're going to have to sacrifice
something. It's better sacrificing little things now than what you'll
have to sacrifice eventually if this doesn't work out.'

Could the strike have been successful without the UDA?

No. Although we've had our differences with some of the
politicians since, I think at the time even they would admit you
have to have the bodies on the streets to literally force your will upon
the people – sometimes against their wishes maybe, but for a better
end and that's what happened.

Feelings of the loyalist paramilitaries towards the politicians who were their
partners in the strike were mixed. There is no doubt they greatly admired
William Craig. Tyrie said he was a politician who was prepared to put his
money where his mouth was, and Glen Barr believed he was the one
politician who came through the strike 'in shining armour'. 'At the very
start of the strike, Craig told us that he didn't think it would succeed,' Barr
remembers. 'He felt that probably we were wrong but that he would sink
or swim with us. He was totally dedicated and committed to it.' They were
not sure about John Taylor, whom most regarded as an opportunist; and
they had decidedly mixed feelings about Ian Paisley. Shortly after the strike
began, Paisley went off to Canada to attend a funeral. There were those
among the paramilitaries – and the British Government too – who thought
he was getting offside for a while to see how things worked out. If the
strike turned out to be a fiasco, then Paisley would not be tainted by it. If it
was successful, he would make sure he was on hand to take the credit.

By the time Paisley returned towards the end of the first week of the
strike, the increasingly unwieldy UWC Co-Ordinating Committee had
been streamlined into a much tighter body with Glen Barr in the chair.
On the morning of Monday 20 May with the strike into its sixth day,
Barr was chairing a meeting of the new committee at Hawthornden
House (Vanguard headquarters) to discuss the business of the day. It was
scheduled to start at nine o'clock and last for an hour, and Barr gave
instructions that no late arrivals were to be admitted. The men around the
table were, after all, effectively running the country. He placed two UDA
men on the door outside with strict instructions not to let anyone in,
regardless of who they were. As he did so, Barr looked through the big bay
window and saw Ian Paisley arriving outside. 'He believed that he was
going to walk in and take the strike over,' Barr recalls, 'and he got a very
rude awakening.' Sammy Duddy, who was one of the guards on the door,
knew what he had to do.

Paisley arrived seven minutes late and tried to brush me aside. I was only a wee lad of ten stone. I said, 'You're not going anywhere,' and he said, 'Do you know who I am?' I said, 'Why, have you lost your memory? Of course I know who you are, but I've been told you're not to be admitted here. The meeting's already started and these people can't be disturbed.' So Paisley went outside and came back with a hastily written note and said, 'Can I put that under the door then?' I thought about it and said, 'OK.' So Paisley bent down and put it under the door. A few seconds later Andy Tyrie came out and said to Paisley, 'What kept you?' and he said, 'This man wouldn't let me in,' and I remember Andy saying, 'This man's under orders here, nobody gets in. The meeting started at ten and you were in full knowledge of that.'

Paisley was finally admitted after the meeting had adjourned for a cup of tea. When the committee returned to the room, Barr found Paisley sitting in his chair.

I asked him to move and he started to complain that two ruffians had stopped him outside. I suggested that he wasn't as big a man in the room as he might be outside and would he please move. He made an excuse and said he had a bad back and the chair that he was sitting in, which was my chair, was the most comfortable in the room. So we physically lifted him, chair and all, and moved him down the table. He then got the message that he wasn't in charge of the strike and nor was he going to be allowed to be in charge of the strike. He was instructed very forcibly to fall into line or get out. He wasn't too happy.

The following day, the General Secretary of the Trades Union Congress (TUC), Len Murray, and some of his colleagues from Transport House in London flew into Belfast, not to show solidarity with the strikers but to lead a 'back to work' march to the shipyard. What they planned to do illustrated the gap between the perception of the strike in London and the political reality on the round. When Len Murray arrived in the province, he announced on the radio that the strike was not a strike. 'It is a stoppage of work imposed by an unrepresentative group of people on the vast mass of people in Northern Ireland who want to go to work today and tomorrow and next week and all the time.'[5]

Fifteen minutes before the march was due to leave its assembly point and heroically march to Harland and Wolff's shipyard, only a handful of people were there and few of them were workers. As the march left, the numbers

amounted to only around 200. Len Murray and his colleagues got a warm
reception, but not the kind they had anticipated. Glen Barr has vivid
recollections of that day.

> There were always women's groups within the UDA and there was
> one very, very active one in the Shankill. We used to call the hair
> styles in those days 'beehives' and when you got one of these women
> of about six foot with a beehive on top of her head, they were like
> Amazons. They really were quite frightening. We had one of these
> ladies in the Shankill and she got all these women down [for the
> march] and they pelted Len Murray with eggs and flour and every
> damned thing. I've faced those women myself at times and it was
> frightening. I don't know how Len Murray felt, but he never came
> back to Northern Ireland after that. That was the end of the 'back to
> work' march.

A second march later in the day attracted barely twenty supporters.
Intimidation no doubt played its part in the embarrassing turnout but
the absence of any significant support was more likely the result of an
English misreading of the situation than the work of the UDA's 'bully
boys'. Len Murray left the province, shaken and chastened.

Given the TUC's painful experience, people might have thought that
the Prime Minister, Harold Wilson, would have adopted a more subtle
approach, but as the days went by and the province bordered on total
collapse with talk of sewage overflows and dreadful epidemics, Wilson
threw discretion to the winds. On Saturday 25 May, the eleventh day of
the strike, Harold Wilson made a broadcast to the nation in which he did
not pull his punches despite Merlyn Rees' advice. Looking straight into the
camera with a mixture of defiance and scorn, he declared the strike was
being run by 'thugs and bullies' and that people in the rest of the United
Kingdom had had enough.

> British parents, British taxpayers have seen their sons vilified and spat
> upon and murdered. They have seen the taxes they poured out almost
> without regard to cost – over £300 million this year – going into
> Northern Ireland. They see property destroyed by evil violence and
> are asked to pick up the bill for rebuilding it. Yet people who benefit
> from this now viciously defy Westminster, purporting to act as
> though they were an elected government, spending their lives
> sponging on Westminster and British democracy and then system-
> atically assault democratic methods. Who do these people think they
> are?[6]

Wilson's taunts would have gone down a storm in millions of living rooms across the nation as he articulated what most English people felt, but that was not the message received by Protestants in Northern Ireland. The beleaguered Brian Faulkner was horrified and anticipated the reaction that Wilson's infelicitous broadcast would have. It was not loyalists who were killing British soldiers but the IRA. In fact only two of the 214 soldiers killed to date were the victims of loyalist violence.[7] Protestants were insulted, incensed and deeply offended, not least when they heard their community referred to as 'spongers' since they still took great pride in the traditional work ethic. Glen Barr could hardly believe his ears. 'I thought great stuff. This is fantastic. We'll make him an honorary member of the UDA after this. I think that was the best thing that happened to us yet. Anything after that we couldn't go wrong.'

Three days later, as ruddy-faced Ulster farmers laid siege to Stormont with their tractors and trailers, Brian Faulkner and the Executive resigned. Bonfires were lit in loyalist areas all over the province. The strikers and their community had won. Sunningdale and power sharing were almost a quarter of a century ahead of their time.

Chapter Twelve

Inside and Out

One of the people who had been instrumental in persuading Billy Mitchell and the UVF leadership to call its ceasefire at the end of 1973 and engage in dialogue with both the Official and the Provisional IRA was Gusty Spence. Although he had been in prison since 1966, his influence extended far beyond the compound wire of Long Kesh. In 1974 he had become a convert to non-violence and believed his decision was vindicated when Merlyn Rees legalized the UVF just before the UWC strike, thereby freeing the organization to become involved in politics. In the dangerous vacuum left by the collapse of the Executive and Sunningdale, the UVF, again encouraged by Spence, formed its own political wing, called the Volunteer Political Party (VPP), under the leadership of Ken Gibson, who had been one of the UVF's strike leaders. But Spence's conversion from violence to politics did not happen overnight. 'There are no roads to Damascus in my opinion, only in biblical times,' he told me. 'I can only speak personally. It was a process that I went through, that I rationalized in my own particular case. I had attempted to persuade and use whatever influence I had with the UVF hierarchy on the outside to call a ceasefire, at least for a limited period but hopefully for a longer period in order to get some political dialogue going. They did do that. People had become disenchanted with the political leadership that they had been getting which was leading us nowhere, just up a blind alley.'

Whatever the sceptics may say, there is no doubt that Spence's conversion was genuine as evidenced by a tape-recording he made around Easter 1974. By this time he had been joined in Long Kesh by his son-in-law, 'Winkie' Rea, who had been sentenced to eight years for possession of a Sterling submachine-gun. Although Rea was associated with the Red Hand Commando, he joined Spence in the UVF compounds of the prison as the two organizations were closely linked. Shortly after he had married Gusty's daughter, 'Winkie's' parents had emigrated to Australia to get away from the Troubles and, incarcerated in Long Kesh, the only way he could communicate with them was by the restricted number of letters prisoners were allowed every week. His father-in-law came to his rescue. Gusty was taken ill and sent from gaol to Musgrave Park hospital to undergo major surgery. At some stage, the enterprising patient managed to get hold of a tape recorder and he smuggled it back into the prison to the admiration and delight of his men. 'Winkie' saw his opportunity. 'When I knew this tape recorder had arrived in the camp I went and asked if I could borrow it to make a tape to my mother,' he told me. 'I felt it would be a lot better than letter writing.' Gusty obliged and supervised the making of the recording, not just of 'Winkie' but of himself and some other prisoners. The tape, which I listened to and annotated, is proof that Spence's conversion to non-violence was genuine. Gusty delivered the epilogue, explaining that, although this was a tape from a son to his mother, he wanted to say how proud he was of 'Winkie'.

Most of the men in Long Kesh are young men from sixteen to twenty-one. I am very proud of them. They're a credit to the men who suffered and died in many foreign fields in defence of the British cause. This is the stage after fighting all my life that I want to see peace in Northern Ireland. We need to sit down and hammer it out. We've been called 'fascists' and 'communists' but we have a singular title, 'loyalists'. We're loyal to a cause, a shining beacon. We're not afraid to be called 'fools' for freedom's sake. We don't promise revenge or retribution. We need to politicize people. For too long in Northern Ireland have hatred and bigotry been the overriding factors. I have an awesome duty in this camp to give hope and inspiration and at present there is a ceasefire.

But shortly after Gusty made the tape, the ceasefire effectively ended, although its end was not formally declared. The UVF's bombs in Dublin and Monaghan were enough. Spence was mortified at the return to violence. 'My reaction was one of shock and horror. In my opinion, it was futile. Force begets force. Violence begets violence. Whatever influence I had, had been dispensed with. I ran the prison. They [the UVF] leadership ran the outside. I wouldn't let them interfere in the running of the prison and obviously they wouldn't let me interfere on the outside. There was nothing I could do about it. Unfortunately, a harder element took over with the collapse of the ceasefire.' The fact that Ken Gibson ran as the candidate for the newly formed Volunteer Political Party in Westminster's general election of 10 October 1974 and was almost humiliated, confirmed the ascendancy of the 'hard men' inside the UVF leadership. Gibson stood in the West Belfast constituency, a gold-plated nationalist seat, to measure the degree of support for the new party against the Shankill's legend, the veteran Johnny McQuade. Gibson polled 2,690 votes while McQuade polled

16,265. It was hardly an auspicious beginning for the UVF's first foray into politics as its subsequent statement acknowledged. 'The low poll for the VPP candidate indicates that the general public does not support the political involvement of the UVF. It would therefore be fruitless to promote the Volunteer Party as a party political machine.'[1] The UVF went back full-time to what it did best. Killing.

Less than a fortnight after the election, two Catholic half-brothers, Michael Loughran (19) and Edward Morgan (27), were walking to work along the Falls Road at 7.30 in the morning. As they reached the junction with Northumberland Street, a car drew up and a gunman shot them both dead. The men in the car were two nineteen-year-old teenagers, Billy Hutchinson and Thomas Winstone, both members of the UVF's junior wing, the Young Citizens Volunteers (YCV), which Hutchinson himself had founded. Hutchinson was the driver of the car and Winstone the gunman. Both pleaded guilty and were sentenced to life. The judge said they had set out that day to tour Belfast looking for victims and when they found them, shot them down in cold blood. As Winstone left the court, he made a clenched fist salute and shouted, 'No Surrender! Up the UVF!'[2] Hutchinson does not deny what he did but is reluctant to be specific.

I always have difficulty in talking about it. I was involved in the murders of these two people. I played a role and I don't like to get involved in talking about what I did or what my colleagues who were with me did. As far as I was concerned, we were members of an active service unit and all involved in the murder of those two people, irrespective of our roles. I think that if we start to say that we only played this part or played that part that we're denying responsibility. The responsibility is on the person who plans it to the person who pulls the trigger and that includes the people who all play their roles in that. I see the role as part of that active service and part of that murder.
   Do you regret your part in the murder of those two young men?
   No, I don't have any regrets. I believe that I was part of the war and that war had to be fought. I certainly don't regret anything that I've done in the past.

Billy Hutchinson served sixteen years in gaol, and initially encouraged by Gusty Spence, whom he described as his 'mentor', went on to take a degree in Social Science and a diploma in Town Planning. 'I suppose I came out of prison better than most,' he said.

Spence ran the UVF compounds like a military camp. With their round-roofed Nissen huts, high wire and watchtowers they looked like prisoner-of-war camps and as their inmates, both loyalist and republican, felt that that was what they were, they lived out the role as Spence described.

> The compounds were run on British army lines with made-up beds, highly polished boots, pressed uniforms etcetera. There was a daily regime. Reveille was at eight o'clock in the morning, followed by showers, breakfast, and then a parade. Then the day was laid out. Initially we relied happily on military matters, field craft and all those things. There weren't that many fields in the compound, you know, but we practised all those things that made a person a more proficient soldier.

Gusty's military regime suited many of his men. It gave purpose to their incarceration and confirmed them in their belief that they really were soldiers who had become prisoners of war for defending their country. It also made the long days seem shorter. Bobby Morton, who later came under Gusty's compound command, loved every minute. 'When I first met him, I marched into his makeshift office and he was dressed totally in black with a Sam Brown belt and a cap comforter. He was a figure of authority and a person with charisma. I felt a little humble.' Morton stood to attention and saluted. 'I remember when he came into our hut one day, we were all there sitting playing cards. I stood up to attention and everybody else just looked at me as if to say, "Why are you standing up?" I thought that was the right thing to do. You know, treat the man with respect. He is the commanding officer.'

Spence more than any other single person sowed in the hard soil of Long Kesh the political ideas that were to flourish many years later in the form of the UVF's new political party, the Progressive Unionist Party (PUP). Many of its leading figures – David Ervine, Billy Hutchinson, William 'Plum' Smith and Gusty Spence himself – were to play vital roles in the peace process that led to the Good Friday Agreement of 1998. Without their experience in Long Kesh, it is unlikely that such a political cadre would have emerged. Spence encouraged them to question everything and accept nothing. Contrary to popular opinion, republicans were not the only ones who received their political education courtesy of the Northern Ireland Prison Service.

Three days after Billy Hutchinson was arrested and charged with double murder, David Ervine was arrested too. He was caught red-handed on 2 November 1974 with a gelignite bomb in a stolen car. 'It was a made-up bomb in East Belfast,' he told me. 'I was alone and stopped by a police patrol. The army technical officers were summoned and they very quickly tied a rope around my waist and around the army technical officer's ankle and I was sent off into the night with a pistol trained on me to defuse the bomb. They described what I had to do in a sequence of orders. Open the boot, open the back door, open the front door, open the bonnet, open the front

door, open the back door, then lift the bomb out on to the pavement.'
Ervine was later sentenced to eleven years. Like all other UVF prisoners,
when he entered the compounds he was interviewed by Gusty Spence who
asked him the question he asked all new inmates, 'Why are you here?'
Ervine was affronted. 'I said, "Possession of explosives," and he says, "No,
no, no, no, no. *Why* are you here?" I thought, "Arrogant bastard – for
defending my people!" But it was a question that caused me some concern
because I don't know that I'd thought very long about why I was doing
what I was doing and why I subsequently ended up in gaol. I would say that
question was a beginning for me on a road that was about analysis and about
trying to understand not only what was happening to me as a person but
what's happening to our society, generation after generation after generation. Gusty unlocked the door, pushed it slightly ajar and gave me the offer
to walk through it or not as was my choice. I think that was as good for me as
anything that's ever happened to me in my life. I don't advocate prison for
reflection but it's certainly the place to do it.' That was how David Ervine's
political education began, as it did for so many other UVF gunmen and
bombers over the next two decades. The UDA did undergo a similar process
but, as we will see, more outside the prison than in, as most of its key political
strategists managed to remain at liberty.

As 1975 approached, both the UDA and the UVF were more interested in
killing than talking politics. The IRA had kept up its campaign with
murderous effect, especially in England, where its active service units had
carried out two horrendous bomb attacks: the first was on the Horse and
Groom pub in Guildford on 5 October 1974 and killed four off-duty soldiers,
two of them women, and a civilian; the second on 21 November, on two pubs
in Birmingham, the Mulberry Bush and the Tavern in the Town, resulted in
the deaths of twenty-one civilians. In its wake, the Home Secretary, Roy
Jenkins, introduced the Prevention of Terrorism Act that gave the state powers
unprecedented in peacetime over the liberty of the individual. When the IRA
finally declared a ceasefire at Christmas 1974, which, theoretically at least,
lasted through most of 1975, loyalists were even more apprehensive, fearing
that a secret deal was being cooked up between the British Government and
the IRA. 'There were suspicions that secret negotiations were going on,'
remembers Eddie Kinner. 'The feeling within the loyalist community was that
the British Government was going to sell them out.' These suspicions were
well founded and although loyalists did not know it at the time, the MI6
officer, Michael Oatley, was involved in talks with a member of Provisional
IRA's Army Council and others, during which 'structures of disengagement'
from Ireland were indeed discussed. Precisely what those 'structures' were was
deliberately left vague by the British, who were happy to let the IRA think
they meant political withdrawal from Northern Ireland when in reality, at this

stage, they were only about withdrawing troops.[3] The fact that the Government admitted talking to Sinn Fein (but never the IRA) and the fact that the IRA was on ceasefire were enough to suggest to the loyalist paramilitaries that their community was about to be sold out. They reacted as they had always done before but now with a savagery that, with the retaliation it provoked from the IRA, made 1975 one of the bloodiest years of the conflict, in which loyalists killed 121 people and republicans 120. The UDA and UVF out-killed their enemy by one.

Although, as ever, the vast majority of their victims were civilians, the loyalist paramilitaries did begin the year by killing a leading IRA man from Lurgan, John Francis Green (27), who had escaped from Long Kesh disguised as a priest – in his brother's clothes who was a priest – and was hiding out in a farmhouse across the border in Monaghan. To the UVF in mid-Ulster, Green was a high-profile target. Because of the IRA Christmas ceasefire, he had been home to Lurgan to see his family, during which time soldiers had come to his house as part of a routine check-up on a well-known republican family. Green had decided it was too risky to hang around, despite the ceasefire, and made off back to Monaghan, but even there his movements were well known to the Irish police, the Garda Siochana. The farmhouse he had made his hide-out was not enough to protect him. Gunmen broke in and shot him through the head. No group ever claimed responsibility although the killing is thought to have been the work of the UVF's border unit, possibly with some inside help from the security forces who would have known about Green's movements. Apparently two bullets were left in the shape of a cross. When I interviewed his brother, Leo Green, for *Provos* – he had been a prominent figure in the IRA's prison protest and hunger strike of 1981 – he told me he believed his brother's killers were either 'loyalists or the British army or a combination of both'. He said seeing his dead brother with 'the body and the face mutilated by gunshot wounds' had been a traumatic experience. He had his suspicions, too, about the motive for the killing, apart from the fact that his brother was an active IRA man. 'I would suggest that it would have annoyed the loyalists that there was a truce with the British Government and there may well have been fear that some sort of negotiated settlement was going on behind their backs. Probably my brother's killing would have been designed to anger and provoke the IRA into breaking the truce.' But the IRA was not provoked and the ceasefire held, at least for the moment. The IRA said Green had been 'murdered by British forces', which is how the Provisionals often referred to the loyalist paramilitaries, who they were convinced were working hand-in-glove with the security forces. Evidence to substantiate at least some of the Provisionals' claim was to emerge later. There were rumours and allegations that Captain Robert Nairac, a legendary army intelligence and liaison officer who was later kidnapped and killed by the IRA, was involved in Green's death, but the allegations were never confirmed. It was, as with the Dublin and Monaghan bombs, a conspiracy theory that was never proved.

Since those cross-border bombs, the UVF had almost exclusively relied on guns and not explosives to kill those it regarded as its enemies, but by March 1975, two months into the IRA ceasefire, bombs were being made up again. Eddie Kinner and Martin Snodden both volunteered for a mission. Kinner was eighteen and Snodden twenty at the time. The target for the bomb attack was Peter Conway's bar on the Shore Road that runs parallel to the M2 motorway to the Belfast suburb of Greencastle. The bar, along with the Europa Hotel, was probably close to holding the record for the most bombed premises in Belfast. It had already been attacked four times, most recently almost exactly a year earlier when two Catholics, thought to have been security men on the door, were killed while trying to carry out the bomb that the UVF had planted. Not surprisingly, Conway's was now surrounded by a thirteen-foot-high wire mesh fence. On 13 March 1975, Kinner, Snodden and a third UVF man called George Brown (22) set out to bomb the bar for what would be the fifth attack in five years. They had been told that an IRA meeting was taking place inside and never thought to question the intelligence. 'As far as I was concerned,' Kinner told me, 'the UVF had come back with that information and they had selected the target so I was prepared to go and attack it.' I asked him if he was really concerned about the precise nature of the target.

Did you care if it wasn't a meeting of republicans and it was just a Catholic bar?
I didn't particularly care.
If it was a Catholic target.
Yes.
A sectarian target.
Yes.
That's the way you were thinking at that time?
My attitude was that they are inflicting that on my community. They [Catholics] harbour IRA men that were carrying that out in my community. They didn't expel IRA men from their community that attacked my community.
But it really wasn't like that. The vast majority of Catholics didn't support the IRA. People in that bar didn't necessarily support the IRA. They were just innocent Catholics having a drink.
I think, in terms of how I felt then, it didn't matter.

Kinner collected the bomb, a gas cylinder containing fifty pounds of explosives, enough, as Kinner said, to turn Conway's into a car park. 'We were told that there was a forty-second fuse on the bomb and if we wanted, we could cut it in half to reduce it to twenty seconds. We were told to plant it in the hallway and not to enter the bar, then to light the fuse, walk away and leave it.' At 8.30 that evening, twenty to thirty people, most of them regulars, were sitting around drinking and chatting when they saw a gun come round the door and open fire. Half a dozen shots were fired into the bar as people dived for cover. Then, six seconds later, the time taken to empty the revolver, there was a huge explosion. The UVF men had placed the bomb in the hallway as instructed but as they did so, someone opened the door and knocked the cylinder over. Kinner remembers being hurled away by the blast and bouncing off the security fence. 'As I was flying through the air I knew this thing had gone off. I was in complete shock at that stage. I didn't feel any pain although I had been seriously burned. I got up and looked round and saw "Geordie" Brown lying there. I saw that his foot had been blown off and he had chest and head wounds. He was groaning and I just called his name. I just hadn't a clue what I could do. I felt totally helpless. I felt that there wasn't anything that could be done for him and I knew that he was going to die. I think he lasted six weeks.' Martin Snodden came round in the debris of the bar, crawled out of the rubble and tried to make his escape, flames leaping from his back. He made his way towards the M2 motorway, pursued by an angry crowd who had realized that he was one of the bombers, and tried to hide under the motorway bridge. But he was spotted by the crowd. 'I heard them shouting, "There's the bastard, there!"' They caught up with him, beat him and then dragged him back to the motorway bridge from which they were going to hang him. 'That's when the military police came on the scene and took me off the crowd and proceeded to beat me. Shortly afterwards the RUC came on the scene and they took me off the military police and proceeded to beat me. The crowd was gathering then at that stage and the RUC then took me to Greencastle police station and beat me there as well. At that point the medical officer came in and told the RUC they needed to take me to the hospital.'

When Snodden came round in the Royal Victoria hospital the following morning, he heard that a thirty-eight-year-old Catholic woman, Marie Doyle, had been killed in the explosion. 'I was devastated, to be honest,' Snodden said. 'As far as I was concerned, I was going out to attack and kill the IRA. It wasn't my intention to kill any woman or any other civilian.' Eddie Kinner was more sanguine. 'The fact that it was a woman made it difficult. At that stage I would have felt that had it been a man I would have felt somehow better about it. I would have been able to justify it more as an IRA man than a woman.' Among the death notices for Marie Doyle in the *Irish News* were several from the IRA and its women's wing, Cumann na hBan. One was from 'The Republican Political Prisoners' in Armagh gaol where Mrs Doyle's daughter, Mary, 'our comrade', was serving a sentence for IRA activity.[4] No doubt had the bombers known it, Marie Doyle would have been seen as a 'legitimate' target as the mother of an IRA prisoner. (When her daughter was finally released from gaol, she became the partner of Terence 'Cleaky' Clark, Gerry Adams' chief bodyguard.) Kinner and Snodden both received life sentences for murder. The following month, on 5 April 1975, the IRA retaliated, killing five Protestants in the Mountainview Tavern on the Shankill Road. One of them was a member of the UDA. The attack made nonsense of the IRA ceasefire. The very same day the UVF had also bombed McLaughlin's bar, killing two Catholic civilians. A week later, on 12 April, loyalists struck again, killing six Catholics, four of them women, in a gun and bomb attack on the Strand Bar in the nationalist enclave of Shot Strand in East Belfast. The dreadful cycle of tit-for-tat bombings reminiscent of 1971 had started up again.

Through the months of late spring and early summer, violence set the agenda, despite the culmination of the Government's latest political initiative following the collapse of the Executive and Sunningdale the previous year. Merlyn Rees had organized elections for a Convention at which all of the province's politicians were to chart their own way forward. The elections were held on 1 May 1975 and the United Ulster Unionist Council (UUUC) that had swept the board at the Westminster election in February 1974 did so once again. As the UUUC had gone to the polls on a promise of no power sharing and no Irish Dimension, there was no chance whatsoever of any agreement. The Convention died and was subsequently wound up, marginalizing the province's politicians yet again and leaving the field wide open for the republican and loyalist killers.

By the time of the Convention election, loyalists were already killing their own in a bitter internal feud between the UDA and the UVF. On 7 April two UDA men, Hugh McVeigh (36) and David Douglas (20), had been abducted while delivering furniture and 'executed' by the UVF.

Their bodies were not found until nearly five months later when they were uncovered in a shallow grave near Islandmagee along the beautiful County Antrim coast. They were identified by their tattoos. A hole had already been dug before the two UDA men were taken with hands tied behind their backs to the remote spot. They were made to stand by the grave and shot at close range: Douglas was grabbed by the back of the neck and shot through the top of the head; McVeigh, the more senior of the two, was shot in the side of the head.[5] One of the senior UVF officers who took them to their place of 'execution' was Billy Mitchell, though it was not he who pulled the trigger. One of the UVF men was then given money to buy grass seed to scatter over the top of the grave. As a result of a seventy-seven-day trial costing £2 million, Billy Mitchell and three other UVF men were given life sentences for the murder of Douglas and McVeigh.

Billy Mitchell, the former Baptist Sunday-school teacher, served fourteen years of his sentence and while in gaol in 1979 became a born-again Christian and resigned from the UVF. He did not wish to talk about his role in the killings as clearly it is something that he still finds painful and of which he is ashamed. 'I'd accept the responsibility for what I have done,' he said. 'Everyone has got moral responsibility. But there were circumstances where morals went out the window.' Beyond that he would not go.

Of all the atrocities committed by both sides during 1975, however, one in particular stands out. The Miami Showband was one of Ireland's most popular groups, attracting Beatle-like devotion from its fans, both Catholic and Protestant, on both sides of the border. On 30 July they had just played a highly successful gig in Banbridge. One of the band, Stephen Travers, remembers it well because after their performance they had been served with Irish stew instead of the usual sandwiches. It was after two in the morning before they had finally packed up and hit the road for Dublin, a good couple of hours' drive away. Half an hour later, as they approached the border town of Newry, they were stopped at a checkpoint. Men in army uniform approached the Volkswagen van in which the members of the band were travelling and proceeded to ask them the usual questions. The 'soldiers' were in fact members of the UVF's Mid-Ulster Brigade with what is suspected to have been a carefully laid plan. Stephen Travers painfully recalls that horrific night.

They came up to us and said the usual, 'Goodnight, fellas. How are things? Can you step out of the van for a few minutes and we'll just do a check.' We stepped out and they told us to put our hands on our heads and we were lined up with our backs to the van facing the field. And they started joking with us, asking us how the gig went and saying, 'I bet you'd rather be at home in bed than be here.' So we were obviously joking with them and Brian McCoy who was the trumpet player and singer in the band nudged me and said, 'Don't worry, Steve,' he said, 'this is an army checkpoint.' Round about that time I heard somebody at the back of our van where I always kept my guitar, it's very precious. When I realized that somebody was at the back, I very naively and very stupidly took my hands off my head and walked back to ask them to be careful and, rather indignantly, to ask them what they were doing there. They turned me round, pushed me on the shoulder and punched me in the back, back into the line-up. I realized then that these people weren't fooling around. What they were actually doing in the back of the van was putting a bomb inside and about to say to us, 'Well, that's great, fellas, thanks for your cooperation, jump in and off you go!' They intended the bomb to go off while we were travelling maybe through Newry or towards Dublin. If it had gone off then, nobody would have known about this bogus checkpoint and the van would have blown up and the whole world would have said, 'Well, who can you trust? The Miami Showband are carrying bombs.' It was a great plan if you think about it. But, unfortunately for them, the bomb went off when they closed the back of the van and instantly killed the two guys that were standing there, one of them the one who had just pushed me. I later saw a picture of one of them some months later. He didn't have any head, just a black torso, no head, legs or arms, which reminded me very vividly of what could have happened to me but for the grace of God.

As the bomb went off, killing two of the UVF men, Harris Boyle (22) and Wesley Somerville (34), the surviving gunmen opened fire. Stephen Travers was hit with an explosive 'dum dum' bullet but miraculously lived to tell the tale.

It entered my right hip, went through me and exploded inside into about thirteen pieces. The rest of it went through my lung and exited into my left arm. I was blown up into the air [by the bomb] and as I came down into the field I could have counted every thorn and leaf. My awareness was heightened and there was a vivid red colour that I could see. It was very, very red. The next thing I remember was hearing Fran O'Toole and, I think, Tony Geraghty, who was my best friend in the band, crying, 'Please don't shoot me, don't kill me.' Then I heard the gunfire as they killed them. I was told later that Fran, the good-looking lead singer, was shot twenty-two times in the face.

Another member of the band, Brian McCoy, was also killed, and one more, Des McAlea, survived with Stephen Travers.

Three UVF men, Thomas Crozier, James McDowell and James Somerville (whose brother, Wesley, was blown up by the bomb), were subsequently arrested and sentenced to life imprisonment for what became known as the Miami Showband massacre. McDowell was a sergeant and Crozier a lance corporal in the Ulster Defence Regiment (UDR), which confirmed, at least in this instance, the nationalist assertion that there was collusion between the security forces and the loyalist paramilitaries.[6]

The UVF leadership tried to cloak its embarrassment and deflect the universal condemnation that fell on its head by issuing the following statement under the heading 'Ulster Central Intelligence Agency – Miami Showband Incident Report'.

> It would appear that the UVF patrol surprised members of a terrorist organization transferring weapons to the Miami Showband minibus and that an explosive device of some description was being carried by the Showband for an unlawful purpose. It is obvious, therefore, that the UVF patrol was justified in taking the action it did and that the killing of the three Showband members should be regarded as justifiable homicide. The Officers and Agents of the Ulster Central Intelligence Agency commend the UVF on their actions and tender their deepest sympathy to the relatives of the two Officers who died while attempting to remove the bomb from the minibus.[7]

Combat, the UVF journal in which the statement appeared, also carried a sympathy note from 'A' Company of the Ninth Battalion of the Ulster Defence Regiment.

A fortnight later, on 13 August 1975, the IRA retaliated with a bomb and gun attack on the Bayardo Bar on the Shankill Road. Four Protestant civilians and one UVF man were killed. One of those convicted and sentenced to life for the murders was a leading member of the IRA, Brendan 'Bik' McFarlane. McFarlane was to play a key role in the IRA's 1981 hunger strike, and subsequently led the 'Great Escape' from the Maze prison (as Long Kesh was later called) on 25 September 1983, when thirty-eight IRA prisoners staged a mass break-out. McFarlane has never spoken about the attack on the Bayardo Bar and has not been encouraged to do so by the IRA leadership because the attack was seen as purely sectarian. The IRA always maintained that its campaign was never directed against Protestants as such.

But if ever there had been doubts about the IRA's assertion, they were shown to be manifestly well-founded when an IRA unit from South Armagh operating under the flag of convenience, the 'Republican Action Force', stopped a minibus at Kingsmills in South Armagh that was carrying Protestant workers home. The gang asked if any Catholics were on board. The driver stepped forward, and the gang gunned the rest of the passengers, ten Protestants, to death. The attack was in itself retaliation for six killings the day before by the Mid-Ulster UVF: they had attacked two families, the O'Dowds near Gilford, County Down, and the Reaveys of Whitecross, County Armagh. The UVF shot dead three members of each family. I remember covering some of the funerals and wondering where it would end.

Chapter Thirteen

Heroes and Villains

Every year on 12 July tens of thousands of Orangemen march through the centre of Belfast to a field in the south of the city where they gather to celebrate King William's famous victory at the Battle of the Boyne in 1690, and join together in prayers of thanksgiving. Most then adjourn to the pub. The scene is a colourful and noisy spectacle as the giant Lodge banners sway through streets that thunder to the sound of flute bands and drums. Pavements are lined with thousands of flag-waving loyalists, many of them women dressed from head to toe in Union Jack colours, singing and dancing to the sounds of the 'Sash'.[1]

One of the Lodges in the parade is Lodge 633, known as the Old Boyne Island Heroes, the biggest and one of the oldest on the Shankill Road with a history that goes back to 1823. Its old banner was adorned with the giant gantries of the shipyard from which the Lodge takes its name and where hundreds of its members have worked down the years. Today its banner depicts Sir Edward Carson signing the Ulster Covenant on one side and King William on the other. The 'Island' in the title refers to Queens Island, on which the Harland and Wolff shipyard has long stood. In its heyday, the company employed 20,000 men and just about every man from the Shankill worked there. Today the workforce is barely 2,000. The Old Boyne Island Heroes is in the blood of most of its members, or 'brethren', many of whom joined as junior Orangemen at the age of eight or nine and, if they were lucky, had the honour of carrying one of the four 'strings' that balance the swaying Lodge banner in the great parade of the Twelfth. They would have been paid a few shillings for it too. Eddie Kinner, whose family has long been closely associated with Lodge 633, remembers first being allowed to hold one of the strings in 1966. 'I can remember carrying it and waving at people and at family relatives and friends. You were proud of it and you thought that you were taking part in a tradition that was part of your cultural heritage.' Eddie McAdam, who was born and reared on the Shankill, and whose father and grandfather also marched with the Lodge, also carried a string at the age of eight and still sees the Twelfth as the greatest day of the year. 'When you're walking down the Shankill Road early on the Twelfth morning with the sound of the drums echoing off the walls and you're with your brethren and all your friends, you know you're going to have a fantastic day. We are not just a Lodge. We are mates. It's a very proud moment. No Twelfth ever changes and every one will be the same.' On 1 January 1999, Eddie McAdam became Master of the Lodge. David Warren, a past Master and still its Secretary after fifteen years, has been a member of the Old Boyne Island Heroes for over three decades, following, too, in the steps of his father and grandfather. 'It's part of my heritage, part of my culture, part of my religion,' he told me with pride. The Lodge commands a loyalty from its members that is as fierce as their loyalty to the Crown. When one of its best-loved members, Albert 'Buttons' Graham, died at the age of nearly eighty, he requested that the Lodge's old banner depicting the shipyard and its gantries be buried alongside him. His brethren did as he wished.

But the Old Boyne Island Heroes is no ordinary Orange Lodge. I asked whether the Lodge number – 633 – referred to the RAF's famous 'Dam Busters' Squadron 633, which destroyed the great German dams of the Ruhr in 1943. I thought it might have been a patriotic reference but was politely corrected. The only bomber on Lodge 633's banner, under the words 'In fond memory of our fallen brethren', is one of the names of five UVF Lodge members killed during the current conflict listed on the Lodge's smaller bannerette. Aubrey Reid was one of four UVF men blown up in 1975 when the bomb they were carrying in their car exploded prematurely; Noel 'Nogi' Shaw was 'executed' as a result of an internal UVF feud, also in 1975; John Bingham was a UVF commander shot dead at his home by the IRA in 1986; Brian Robinson was killed on 'active service' by undercover soldiers in 1989;[2] and Robert 'Basher' Bates was shot dead in a revenge attack in 1997. A sixth name, that of Colin Craig, gunned down by the INLA in 1994,[3] was once listed on the bannerette but removed when it was thought he had been an informer. Few of them were 'defending Ulster' when they died, although, in the eyes of their comrades, they had played their part in doing so before.

There is good reason for the Old Boyne Island Heroes being known locally as the 'UVF Lodge' and, although its officers do not welcome the reference and point out that the majority of its members have no connections with the UVF, they do not deny the association and are proud of their members who have died, as they see it, in defence of their shared heritage and tradition. Whereas most Orange Lodges expel members who have served prison sentences for terrorist offences, the Old Boyne Island Heroes do not. 'We don't throw them out because they're brethren,' Eddie McAdam explained. 'We could throw out house burglars or sex offenders and the like, but to us these guys are not criminals, they're victims of circumstances. If they hadn't lived in Northern Ireland at the present time, they wouldn't be in gaol. These men feel they fought for their country and we're not to judge them. In the Lodge room they weren't terrorists. They were our brethren.' David Warren echoed the sentiment. As one senior member of the Lodge told me, 'If you hadn't done gaol, you weren't a real member.' Given its catchment area, if ex-prisoners were excluded, the Lodge would have a good deal fewer members.

The most notorious of the five UVF men whose names adorn their bannerette is Robert 'Basher' Bates, who was one of the leaders of the infamous 'Shankill Butchers', the UVF gang who terrorized the nationalist community from the end of 1975 onwards by abducting their victims and then literally carving them up with butchers' knives. All of them were innocent Catholics. When Bates' brethren found out about his horrendous activities they were shocked but did not disown him. Bates was a good friend of David Warren. 'I knew him very well and he'd been a personal friend for twenty or thirty years and to me he was a gentleman.' I expressed some surprise at the description, knowing what 'Basher' Bates had done, but David stood by his portrayal of his friend. 'He was an easy-going, decent fellow and as far as the Lodge is concerned, a man of good standing.' Bates was eventually arrested and sentenced to life. When he was finally released from prison, the Old Boyne Island Heroes welcomed him back. When he was shot dead on 11 June 1997 in a revenge attack by a relative of one of the 'Butchers'' victims, the brethren turned out in force to pay their respects.

In October 1975, as that dreadful year of killings continued with all the savagery with which it had begun, the UVF leadership called for a 'big push'. Aubrey Reid and his three UVF comrades, who were blown up by their own bomb on 2 October (an 'own goal' in security force language), may well have been intended to be part of it. Whether or not the 'Shankill Butchers' were part of it too remains unclear.

Although the UVF leadership, element of which remain in position today, never publicly disapproved of the 'Butchers'' methods, they were not unhappy with their effect. The only difference between gunning down innocent Catholics on street corners and carving them up in dark alleys was the means not the end. The end, from the very outset, was to terrorize the nationalist community into putting pressure on the IRA to stop, and the 'Butchers' made their contribution to that in a way that no others did. This may be one of the reasons why they were never stopped. Another reason is that the UVF leadership was frightened or incapable of doing so. Although the organization had its own command structure, individual units could, without too much difficulty, become laws unto themselves should the individuals be strong and ruthless enough and capable of striking as much fear into their colleagues as they did into their 'enemies'.

The 'Shankill Butchers' gang, for a gang is what it was, was led by a psychopath called Lenny 'the Butcher' Murphy, who had a passionate hatred of Catholics and who clearly took pleasure in the act of killing, be it pulling a trigger or wielding a knife. Over the years, eleven members of his gang murdered nineteen people, most of them Catholics. Three of the 'Butchers' were never prosecuted. Murphy had come out of gaol in May 1975 where he had been on remand facing a murder charge. The case had fallen apart after he had murdered his accomplice, the prosecution's chief witness, by throttling him in his cell and pouring cyanide down his throat.[4] When Murphy returned to the Shankill, he already had a fearsome reputation behind him and was intent on setting up his own 'cell' within the UVF's platoon made up of those of like mind prepared to do his bidding. 'Like mind' invariably meant being prepared to 'kill Taigs'. Murphy set up 'headquarters' in the Brown Bear pub on the Shankill Road. One of his recruits was William 'Billy' Moore, whom he met by chance in the pub. Moore was a particular asset because he owned a black taxi which plied the Shankill Road – paying, of course, his dues to the UVF – and also owned some butchers' knives and a meat cleaver which he had taken with him when he left his job as a meat packer in Woodvale Meats on the Shankill Road.[5] When I spoke to a long-standing member of the UVF about the 'Shankill Butchers', he told me that the reason the gang had driven around in a taxi with knives was because, if they were caught, the sentence would have been much shorter than had they been apprehended with guns. The UVF leadership did not authorize their killings, he said, but did not do an awful lot to stop them.

Lenny Murphy's initial contribution to the 'big push' was what he told his gang was to be a robbery of Casey's Wholesale Wine and Spirits warehouse, a Catholic-owned business between the bottom of the Shankill and the Falls Roads. It resulted not in a robbery but in the slaughter of its four Catholic employees, two sisters and two eighteen-year-old young men. Murphy shot three of them in cold blood through the head and the neck and another member of the gang shot the fourth. The following day, Merlyn Rees banned the UVF once more. Many were astonished he had not done so before. But Belfast had not yet seen the butchery that was to become the hallmark of Murphy's gang.

On 22 November 1975, the IRA killed three young soldiers, two of them nineteen and one twenty, in a gun attack on their observation post outside the IRA stronghold of Crossmaglen in South Armagh. The day before they had also killed another soldier in nearby Forkhill by booby-trapping what appeared to be an abandoned rifle. Four dead soldiers in half as many days in the notorious area known as 'bandit country' gave Murphy an excuse, if he needed one, to retaliate. He instructed Moore to get his taxi and they headed off with two other members of the gang to look for a 'Taig' in the nationalist section of the Antrim Road, only a few minutes' drive away. Just after midnight on 25 November, they intercepted a lone Catholic, Francis Crossan (34), who had been having a drink with friends and was now walking towards Belfast city centre. He was hit over the head with a wheel brace, dragged into Moore's taxi and driven to a dark alley off the Shankill. Murphy then slashed their victim's throat until the head was almost severed from the trunk – a feature that was to become Murphy's personal calling card in future atrocities. When morning came, Francis Crossan's body was found by a horrified elderly neighbour, who saw a bloodied corpse with its head almost at right angles to the body. No group claimed responsibility.[6]

The following day, an RUC murder squad led by Detective Inspector Jimmy Nesbitt from 'C' Division, which covered the Shankill area from its headquarters in Tennent Street, started to investigate the killing and began a remarkable piece of detective work that, many murders later, finally brought Lenny Murphy and most of the 'Shankill Butchers' to justice. Murphy was arrested on 13 March 1976 and charged with attempted murder but, after plea-bargaining with the Crown, pleaded guilty to possession of firearms and ammunition and was sentenced to twelve years, of which he was to serve six. Remarkably, Murphy, the 'Master Butcher', continued to direct his gang from inside Long Kesh, which had now become known as the Maze prison. Robert 'Basher' Bates, Billy Moore and other 'Butchers' were finally arrested in 1977 and after a long period on remand were sentenced on 20 February 1979. Bates pleaded guilty to ten murders and Moore to eleven. Both received life. Passing sentence, the judge, Mr Justice O'Donnell, declared, 'I see no reason whatever, apart from terminal illness, why either of you should ever be released.'[7] But they were. Moore lived but Bates did not. Lenny Murphy was released in 1982 and, shortly afterwards, was shot dead by, it is thought, the IRA.[8]

The question of knowledge of the 'Butchers'' activities, not just on the part of the UVF leadership but by the organization's rank and file, has never been satisfactorily answered. I asked Gusty Spence why the 'Shankill Butchers' had not been stopped, given that it was a fair assumption that, even if the UVF leadership were not controlling Murphy and his gang, they must have had their suspicions about who was responsible for the serial killings. 'I wasn't surprised,' he said. 'I don't think they had the "bottle" or the guts to stop them.' It appears – astonishing, if true – that other men of the UVF platoon to which Murphy and the others officially belonged were unaware of their comrades' activities. Gorman McMullan was a member of the same platoon. His view of Lenny Murphy and his killers was not unlike the Old Boyne Island Heroes' opinion of one of their brethren, Robert 'Basher' Bates.

> I regarded them as a decent bunch of lads. Like everything else in life, there were maybe one or two out of that group who would have found their way into prison anyway. But I would say that 70 to 80 per cent of those charged with the 'Shankill Butchers' would probably have gone through life without ever being in prison themselves.
> **But how can you call them a decent bunch of lads when they committed the horrendous crimes that they did?**
> I still found them a decent bunch of lads. I knew them not as people who were monsters. I knew them as human beings.
> **They carved people up, tortured them, slaughtered them. A decent bunch of lads?**
> Well, in every bunch of lads you have ones who are the leaders and ones who are led. Quite a few of them were led and they remain to this day decent fellows.

Jimmy Nesbitt, who was later awarded the MBE in recognition of his services fighting terrorism and who knows more about the 'Shankill Butchers' than anyone else, gave a simple answer to the question of how much those in charge of the UVF knew. He said their actions were not sanctioned by the leadership because the leadership was afraid of them.

By the end of 1976, a new leadership had taken over at the top of the UVF with the approval of Gusty Spence who, with many of his comrades both inside the gaol and out, had had enough of the 'Shankill Butchers' and the cycle of tit-for-tat sectarian killings. Spence sent out a statement expressing his support for the new men in charge.[9]

> For some time, the name of the UVF has been abused. Rumours have been allowed to circulate to the effect that funds have been mis-appropriated and that gangsterism is rife in our ranks. All this has served to damage our relationship with the people and we hope that the new Brigade Staff will soon set about the painstaking task of renewing our lost confidence . . . it is not our wish to wage war on anyone except armed republicans determined to overthrow Ulster in order to force us into an Irish Republic.

A senior member of the new leadership told me that the change was the result of great dissatisfaction among the UVF rank and file over both political and military issues. On the political level, there were suspicions that there had been more meetings with republicans (the previous contacts having been broken off in 1974), while on the military front there were concerns that some of the UVF's operations were not in the best interests of Ulster. That may have been putting it mildly. The professed aim of the new leadership was to move away from what were seen as sectarian tribal killings and concentrate on attacking members of the Republican Movement and the INLA. After an interval of well over two years, the UVF leadership both inside the gaol and out were once again thinking and speaking as one.

But although the UVF launched bomb attacks on a republican Easter parade and an IRA funeral in April 1977, the organization's ability to act was severely hampered by the increasing number of its Volunteers who were going to gaol.

Chapter Fourteen

Bad Years

In the five years from 1972 to 1976 the average number of killings in Northern Ireland was running at just over 300 a year. Over the next five years, from 1977 to 1981, they declined to an average of just under 100 – a dramatic fall of two-thirds. For the first time the Government and the security forces felt they were getting on top of the terrorists on both sides. In that period the UVF prison population roughly doubled, a growth that was reflected in the sentencing of other loyalist and republican parami-litaries. The decline in violence and the corresponding increase in the number of prisoners were no accident but the result of a deliberate change in government policy. The 'special category' status[1] that had allowed loyalist and republican prisoners to run their own lives in compounds like prisoners of war was abolished by Merlyn Rees, and all those sentenced for offences committed after 1 March 1976 were to be treated as common criminals like prisoners elsewhere in the United Kingdom and subjected to a structured and disciplined prison regime. New wings had been built alongside the compounds that became known as the 'H-Blocks' because of their shape with each block containing four wings, one along each leg of the 'H'. The main difference for the prisoners was not only that for the first time they were locked up in cells, but that they were also no longer allowed to wear their own clothes or enjoy the other privileges that special category status had given them. The Government said they were criminals and treated them as such.

Through the late seventies, the 'H-Blocks' filled up as hundreds of paramilitary prisoners travelled along what republicans called the 'conveyor belt', from arrest and interrogation under special emergency legislation, via trial by the special non-jury Diplock Courts to incarceration in the specially constructed 'H-Blocks'. At the end of this line, which had been 'special' at every stage to deal with the emergency, the prisoners no longer enjoyed 'special' category status or, as they saw it, 'political' status. Although Merlyn Rees was the architect of the change in policy, it was his Labour successor as Northern Ireland Secretary, Roy Mason, who put it into practice with devastating effect. Mason, a tough, no-nonsense former Barnsley miner, saw the conflict in simple black and white terms. To him, the problem was one of terrorism, and the terrorists on both sides had to be defeated. Mason had no time for political niceties and initiatives. They had all been tried and failed. To the delight of unionists who had been demanding tougher security for years, Roy Mason was the man they had been waiting for and who they thought would never come. Mason, who took over from Merlyn Rees as Secretary of State on 10 September 1976, did not disappoint them and raised loyalist spirits by declaring that he was going to squeeze the IRA like a tube of toothpaste. He was backed in his determination by the new Chief Constable of the RUC, Kenneth Newman, who has been appointed from the Metropolitan Police four months earlier. Together, Mason and Newman were a formidable pair who made no distinction between republican and loyalist terrorists.

The engine that drove the 'conveyor belt' was the RUC's interrogation centre at Castlereagh, or 'holding centre' as it was officially and euphemistically called, where suspects could be detained and questioned under the emergency legislation for up to seven days.[2] The purpose of Castlereagh and the RUC's other interrogation centre at Gough barracks in Armagh was to break the suspect under intense questioning with the result that he (or she) would eventually sign a statement admitting guilt. These statements were admissible as evidence in the Diplock Courts as long as the judge believed that they had not been obtained as a result of 'torture' or 'inhuman or degrading treatment'. The normal rules of evidence were that statements were only acceptable in court if they had been given voluntarily without inducement or pressure of any kind. Clearly few hardened republicans or loyalists were going to sit down and confess all under the existing rules so the rules were changed. This inevitably gave the interrogators far greater latitude, which seemed to be confirmed when, in a celebrated and to civil libertarians infamous judgment, Lord Justice McGonigal said that a 'blow' to the nose that 'left it swollen and caused it to bleed' did not necessarily rule the statement inadmissible.[3] This was taken to mean that a certain degree of physical violence was permissible as long as it fell short of what the court would deem 'torture' or 'inhuman or degrading treatment'. McGonigal's judgment became known to republicans as 'The Torturers' Charter'. The point was well noted by Mr Justice Bennett, the English judge whom the Labour Government later appointed to investigate the allegations of brutality. He concluded that 'the uncertainty . . . about what is permissible and what is not, short of the use of physical violence or ill-treatment, may tempt police officers to see how far they can go and what they can get away with'.[4]

The result of these much tougher interrogations was an endless stream of allegations from republicans and loyalists that they had been severely ill-treated at Castlereagh, Gough barracks and elsewhere. They peaked in the summer and autumn of 1977, the year in which over 1,300 terrorist suspects were charged. At first, the allegations were dismissed as terrorist propaganda, and I must admit that initially I did not give them great credence until in the early summer of 1977 I started to investigate the allegations and concluded that a good number of them were true. There was clearly a pattern, and police surgeons who were examining suspects after they had either been charged or released expressed grave concern about the state they found some of them in. Republicans made great propaganda out of the allegations – so much so that most people either ignored or were unaware of the fact that a number of loyalists too were being subjected to the same treatment. I remember interviewing a UVF suspect in the summer of 1977 shortly after he had been released from Castlereagh without charge. He was still clearly in considerable pain as he described being beaten and demonstrated how he had been made to squat for long periods with his back to the wall. Gorman McMullan, who had been a member of the same UVF platoon as Lenny Murphy and the 'Shankill Butchers', was interrogated at Castlereagh in September 1977. He told me that the police tried to get him to say that he had been part of Lenny Murphy's gang who had murdered four Catholics during the robbery of Casey's Wholesale Wine warehouse on 2 October 1975. McMullan assured me he was not involved but came close to making the admission.

> There was a time due to the pressure that the police were putting on me physically and mentally that I started to question myself. I started to wonder maybe I had been on this job. Because of the abuse that I was receiving at the hands of the RUC in the interrogation centre, I was almost ready to admit to being involved in it just to get out of their clutches for however short a space of time.

McMullan's description of the treatment he alleged he received mirrored perfectly that described by an IRA suspect, Tommy McKearney, whom I had interviewed for *Provos* and who had been interrogated at Castlereagh the following month.[5] This is how Gorman McMullan described what he alleges happened at Castlereagh.

> Physically they were doing things that wouldn't show up as bruises. An officer stood behind me with cupped hands, smashed them into my ears. The pain in your eardrums was tremendous after it was

repeated several times. They also bent my fingers and my wrist backwards and forwards whatever way they could do it so that it wouldn't leave a bruise. Sometimes the pain was unbelievable and you were at the end of your tether. But I seemed to grit my teeth against that. It was the psychological stuff that affected me more.

In the end, McMullan admitted being involved in other robberies – that he said he *did* carry out – and was sentenced to six years.

By this time, the RUC had taken over the lead role in combating terrorism as politically it fitted the Government's new policy of regarding the republican and loyalist paramilitaries as common criminals, not as individuals doing what they did for political reasons. The army was not happy and from time to time over the next decade there was friction between the army hierarchy and the police. The reason the RUC was given 'primacy' was because in a 'normal' situation it was the police who brought 'criminals' to justice through the courts and as Roy Mason wanted to create the illusion of 'normality' in the province, the police and not the army were the ones to stand in the front line. In human terms, the RUC paid the price for doing so.

But despite the growing success of the security forces in the year when Billy Mitchell and twenty-five members of the UVF were gaoled for more than 700 years[6] and another nine UVF members were gaoled for over 100, Ian Paisley still denounced the Government for its weakness in the face of the IRA and demanded even tougher security and a return to majority rule. Andy Tyrie and the UDA shared his feelings about security.

> The message was coming through that the security people were being restrained from doing their job. They couldn't deal with it. They were being restricted. They were badly organized and badly equipped. Intelligence was very bad coming in. When I was approached about the strike, it was back to the workers again. It wasn't necessarily Dr Paisley. They came along and said to us, 'Look, this is all getting out of hand. We are not beating the IRA, we are losing. They seem to be able to bomb and shoot at will. We will have to turn around and tell the British Government look, as in 1974, we want this sorted out.' In 1977, we felt that they felt that they could deliver the goods on the strike again. We said, 'Yes, we would go along with you and support you.' It was very important because there were a lot of people being killed and bombed and we thought by doing the same thing again, we might make the necessary progress.

Paisley, once again backed by the Ulster Workers' Council (UWC) and the UDA whose combined efforts had spelled the end of power sharing and Sunningdale in May 1974, gave Mason seven days to meet their demands. But Roy Mason was not one to be bullied. 'I didn't intend Paisley and his cohorts to be able to run over the Secretary of State and Direct Rule and Her Majesty's Government. That would have been the last straw for us, wouldn't it? So I was determined that wasn't going to happen. There was a lot of intimidation, a lot of villainy.'[7] Mason was true to his word. Paisley and the UWC called a strike and were backed once again by the UDA in an attempt to repeat the success of the strike three years earlier. But the strike failed. The situation was different because the workers had little appetite for it and Paisley's familiar cry for tougher security did not have the same impact as the fear of a united Ireland had in 1974. But the critical factor was that this time the Government and the police had made their preparations and were ready to move against 'intimidation and villainy' and in particular against Andy Tyrie and the UDA whose barricades they unceremoniously removed from East Belfast. Mason, who, as a former Barnsley miner, had impeccable trade union credentials himself, was also able to win over the power workers. 'They were bought, so they were,' Andy Tyrie told me. They were convinced by the charm of the British Government that this wasn't the right thing to do.'

Furthermore, unlike in 1974 when loyalist politicians had been united, there was dissension in their ranks and the Unionist Party disassociated itself from the strike. Paisley blamed them for the failure but, as ever, claimed victory from the jaws of defeat. 'The Official Unionist Party, who were very ambivalent, backed out and, of course, backed the Government and that led to a division in Unionist ranks,' he told me. 'But our best election result was after that strike, when we were returned with more councillors than ever before and indeed more councillors than the Official Unionists had. So I think that there was an element of very strong grass-roots support.' But, with the strike over and, at least in the Government's eyes, Paisley humiliated, Tyrie and many in the UDA began to question the wisdom of continuing their association with the 'Big Man' whom they increasingly thought was marching them to the top of the hill and then leaving them there. Jackie McDonald, a senior UDA commander from South Belfast, was now convinced that the organization had to start to think for itself instead of being used, dumped and then attacked by politicians. He had initially questioned the wisdom of the 1977 strike.

My argument was that there's some intelligent people in the British Government. They'd had three years to think about how a strike would work again and we should have advanced our thinking three years too, but we didn't and our politicians at the time didn't advance their thinking either. They just thought, 'It worked before, it'll work again.' I think then we realized we need to start thinking for ourselves here. We need to take ourselves on, take a step further.

The failure of the 1977 strike heralded the break between Paisley and the UDA whose members were no longer prepared, as they saw it, to be used by him. Andy Tyrie, aided by the emerging figure of a powerful and politically astute UDA commander from Lisburn called John McMichael, set up a political think tank – the New Ulster Political Research Group – to work out the organization's own policy as its members no longer had any faith in mainstream loyalist politicians. Glen Barr, who had risen to prominence in the 1974 UWC strike when the press headlined him 'The War Lord', was Chairman, John McMichael was Secretary and Andy Tyrie was a Committee member. By this time, William Craig, who had been greatly admired by all three, had entered the political wilderness, having chosen not to give his support to the 1977 strike and having advocated, controversially and presciently twenty years ahead of its time, a voluntary coalition between nationalists and unionists at Stormont. The outcome of Tyrie's and McMichael's deliberations was a discussion paper called 'Beyond the Religious Divide', which advocated negotiated independence with a constitutional Bill of Rights as 'the only hope of achieving a united Northern Ireland'. It said there had to be a constitutional settlement that was 'acceptable to both sections' [of the community] and stressed that the idea 'is not the creation of a Protestant dominated state, nor is it the stepping stone to a united Ireland. It is an opportunity for peace and stability. It is an opportunity for Ulster people to get back their dignity.'[8] The idea of an independent Ulster never caught on for both political and economic reasons but 'Beyond the Religious Divide' did mark the beginning of the UDA's political development that would flourish almost two decades later in its political wing, the Ulster Democratic Party (UDP), which was to play a vital role in the events that led up to the signing of the Good Friday Agreement.

Nevertheless, throughout this period, the UDA's 'active' wing, the UFF, carried on killing, and although most of its victims were innocent Catholics, known republicans were also successfully targeted and shot dead. The UFF's highest-profile victim was Maire Drumm, the Vice-President of Sinn Fein and wife of the IRA veteran Jimmy Drumm, who was gunned down on 28 October 1976 while in Belfast's Mater hospital recovering from an eye injury. Three loyalist gunmen walked in, two of them dressed in doctors' white coats, and shot her dead. The Shankill Road UDA sent a message of sympathy. There had been some form of dialogue between the Provisionals and the loyalist paramilitaries around this time, again seeking possible common ground on the basis of a federated Ireland with an autonomous Ulster within it – which potentially was not a million miles from the UDA's own thinking – but the exchanges had come to nothing. The dialogue was effectively terminated towards the end of 1976 when the UFF killed Maire Drumm, whose husband had been involved in the talks, and the UVF underwent the change in leadership that Gusty Spence had welcomed.[9]

Throughout this time, the IRA also carried on killing and, despite its protestations about its campaign being non-sectarian, many innocent civilians were among its victims. The IRA's most shocking attack came on 17 February 1978 when it planted an incendiary bomb at the La Mon House hotel outside Belfast when the restaurant was crowded with diners. Twelve Protestants were virtually burned alive as the giant fireball turned the restaurant into an inferno. There had been only a nine-minute warning and it appears the fire-bomb had gone off prematurely. The IRA apologized for its 'mistake'. Gerry Adams, who was alleged to have become the IRA's Chief of Staff at the end of 1977 – a fact he denies as he has always also denied IRA membership – was arrested the morning after the La Mon bombing and charged with IRA membership, but the case never came to court.[10]

The IRA was badly hit by Castlereagh as were the loyalist paramilitaries, thus reducing the capacity of both groups to prosecute the 'war' in their different and bloody ways. It was the period when the IRA came closest to defeat and when it appeared that Roy Mason was living up to his promises to hit the terrorists hard. But by the end of the decade, the balance was swinging the other way. With IRA prisoners demanding the restoration of 'political' status by refusing to wear prison uniform or to wash and slop out their cells, the IRA outside the gaol intensified its campaign with two 'spectaculars' on one day to prove that it was far from defeated and still a military force to be reckoned with. On the morning of 27 August 1979, the IRA planted a bomb on board the *Shadow V*, a boat used by the Queen's cousin, seventy-nine-year-old Lord Louis Mountbatten, who was on holiday with friends in Mullaghmore, County Sligo, where he had spent the summer, without a bodyguard, for the previous thirty years.[11] Lord Mountbatten, his fourteen-year-old grandson, Nicholas Brabourne, the Dowager Lady Brabourne and the teenage boatman, Paul Maxwell, were all killed. As the shock waves reverberated around the world, the IRA struck again that same afternoon, killing eighteen soldiers, most of them members of the Parachute Regiment, in a double bomb attack at Warrenpoint just outside Newry. It was the army's biggest single loss of life in the current conflict and the Parachute Regiment's worst since Arnhem.[12]

That night, John Dillon's unit of the UVF held a meeting in Belfast to make plans. 'I remember the day well,' he told me. 'We decided that we were going to retaliate and through our intelligence we had known targets, men we believed to be members of the Provisional IRA.' The target was a Catholic man and father of ten called John Patrick Hardy (43), who lived on the nationalist New Lodge estate near the city centre. That night, Dillon was driven round the area to check out 'the target house'. He never questioned the 'intelligence' about his potential victim but took it on trust. If he was told John Hardy was an IRA man, Dillon believed it regardless of whether it was true or not. The following day, he picked up a motor-cycle and a hand-gun from another UVF member, William 'Budgie' Allen, and then went to collect a third person, who was to ride pillion and carry out the killing. Dillon drove round to Hardy's home and the gunman got off the bike and knocked at the door. Mr Hardy's teenage daughter, Elaine, who was making tea in the kitchen, came to the door with her father, who had got up from watching television in the living room, close behind her. Dillon heard two shots as John Hardy was gunned down in front of his daughter.[13] Despite what John Dillon had been told, John Hardy was seen as the victim of a purely sectarian killing but Dillon had no regrets. He told me he felt quite normal after the shooting, felt no remorse and certainly did not celebrate. 'I'm a soldier,' he said. 'I don't need to celebrate over a death.' He also denied that he was personally in any way sectarian. 'If I had been a sectarian person, we would not have travelled into the New Lodge. All we had to do was drive on to the Falls Road, which is two minutes away from us, and shoot the first person walking up and down because he was bound to be a Roman Catholic. We believed John Patrick Hardy was the target, we were given the details, moved out and took the target out.'

John Dillon was arrested almost three years later in June 1983 on the evidence of William 'Budgie' Allen, a member of the junior wing of the UVF, the Young Citizens Volunteers, from whom Dillon had collected the motor-cycle and gun. Allen was one of several UVF members who, like several IRA men, had become 'supergrasses' or, in the words of the RUC, 'converted terrorists', prepared to give evidence against their former colleagues in return for immunity from prosecution or lesser sentences, depending on the offences they had committed. As a result of Allen's evidence, the RUC charged forty-seven people with a total of 226 offences. Dozens more loyalists were charged on the evidence of other UVF 'supergrasses', as were scores of republicans on the evidence of the IRA equivalents. It suddenly looked as if the security forces had hit the jackpot and found an astonishing way of finishing the terrorists on both sides for good. Following his arrest, John Dillon was confronted by his accuser, William 'Budgie' Allen, in the interview room at Castlereagh. The police read out Allen's statement and asked if Dillon was the man Allen had referred to in it as the person to whom he had given the gun. Allen said he was. Dillon, who had kept a low profile and had never been arrested before, told me he felt 'sick'. He also told me that, although Allen was correct about his own role in the murder, he had given the wrong name for the gunman. 'He named an innocent man who was not even involved in the murder,' he told me. 'He never got the trigger puller. He got it wrong.' Dillon confessed to the murder and was sentenced to life. He told me he was the only one, of the forty-seven people whom Allen had named, who went to gaol as a result. In the second month of the trial, the case against the others collapsed after the judge found Allen's evidence 'totally unreliable'. Nevertheless, a year later, William Allen was given a Royal Prerogative pardon and released by the Conservative Secretary of State, Tom King.[14] I asked John Dillon if he had any idea where 'Budgie' Allen now was. 'I don't know,' he said. 'People say he's in England. I don't think he's on the Shankill Road unless people have given him good plastic surgery.'

In the end all the other loyalist and republican 'supergrass' trials went the same way since the Northern Ireland judiciary decided that, in the vast majority of cases, the evidence given by the 'converted terrorists' would not withstand scrutiny. Only those who made confessions like John Dillon, or against whom there was compelling additional evidence, went to gaol. Nevertheless, since most of those charged were remanded in custody for up to two years and more, they were removed from the streets. Not surprisingly, both loyalists and republicans protested that the 'supergrass system' amounted to internment without trial. Significantly in 1983 and 1984, there was a notable reduction in the number of deaths, shootings and bombs planted. But the other result, the effect of which was to be seen later, was that the dozens of loyalist and republican names that came out of these trials provided each side with a 'hit list'. Bobby Norris, a loyalist who was charged on the evidence of Joe Bennett, another loyalist 'supergrass',[15] had no doubt how precisely the IRA used the names produced at the loyalist trials to hit their enemies. 'It gave people a profile where they became targets for republican murder squads. In the Bennett case, four of the people charged are now dead. Three were murdered by republicans and one was hassled so much by the police that in the end he took his own life.' Bobby Norris was never convicted and was eventually released.

On 16 March 1983, while Norris was halfway through his trial after almost a year on remand, he heard news of a shooting over the radio as he was getting ready to go to court. When he got to Crumlin Road courthouse, he noted a fair number of his regular supporters who came along every day were missing and immediately feared that the shooting might have involved some of his friends. It did. Three UVF men had gone out in a stolen car to kill members of the INLA in an operation that had been planned for several months. The driver of the car was one of the men who had been arrested with Bobby Norris when the police swooped and picked up those named by Joe Bennett. According to Norris on the basis of the information he later received, this individual, whom he did not name, had been released and then obviously 'been turned by the RUC' and had been 'actually working for Special Branch' during the year that he and the others were on remand. The other two UVF men in the car were Bobby Morton and Billy Miller. Morton described to me what happened. 'We had worked out the logistics of what was needed and we had everything including weapons at the ready. We knew exactly what we wanted to do and it was just a question of carrying it out. Unfortunately there was intelligence from within our organization which led the security forces to apprehend us. There was an informer in our ranks.'

The three UVF men were driving through the university area of Belfast heading towards their target, allegedly members of the INLA, when the driver suddenly stopped at Elmwood Avenue, pushed open the door and ran away at great speed. The next thing Morton, who had been sitting beside him, saw was a car pulling up in front and a police Land Rover driving up from behind. The police leapt out and, according to Morton, immediately opened fire. Morton was seriously wounded but miraculously survived. Billy Miller, who was in the back seat, was fatally hit. He died on the operating table in hospital later that night. Morton remembers the shooting as if it were yesterday.

> There was no warning and no chance to surrender. It's a very peculiar situation because I could actually see the bullets coming at me, by which stage there was not much I could do about it. Then I felt them hitting me down the left-hand side. I remember thinking to myself, 'Hell with this for a game of darts!' Then I was drifting and knew I was dying. Obviously I couldn't see Volunteer Billy Miller who was sitting in the back seat. I understand he was shot in the chin, neck and chest.

The ambush took place only a few months after the RUC's special anti-terrorist unit had shot dead three Provisional IRA men, two members of the INLA and one uninvolved young man in three highly controversial shooting incidents in County Armagh in November and December 1982. These killings gave rise to what became known as John Stalker's 'Shoot to Kill'. inquiry[16] and gave the Republican Movement and its supporters a propaganda field day. But Bobby Morton would have none of it.

> Now I'd like to make a point here. Even though the police did what they did, I think it's important to remember from my point of view

that I have never been one to complain. I think if you can't stand the heat, you shouldn't be in the kitchen. I think there's a unit of the British army [the SAS] that says, 'If you want to play with the big boys, it's big boys' rules.' I knew what I was getting into and I take the consequences. I'm not complaining about 'shoot to kill'.

Bobby Morton was given a fifteen-year gaol sentence: twelve years for possession of a weapon with intent and three years for membership of the UVF. I asked him what happened to the driver of the car who ran away, the person who had been arrested on the word of the 'supergrass', Joe Bennett.

The evidence against him is overwhelming as we understand it. When the security forces put him on a plane, one can only conclude that he was working in collusion with them. We believe he went to England where he spent several years. He did make a request to come back to Northern Ireland and I was approached because clearly I have an input into whether he is allowed to come back.
Whether he lives or dies?
Yes. In the final analysis, I decide whether he lives or dies.
So the person that you believe was the informer could return to Northern Ireland today?
On my terms. That is a full and frank admission of his crimes against the loyalist people and indeed the UVF.

But the targeted attacks on 'combatants' like Bobby Morton and Billy Miller during this period were not all one-sided. Loyalists were killing republicans too and the UFF was highly active, in particular around the time of the IRA 'no wash' protest and the hunger strikes of 1980 and 1981. On 4 June 1980, the UFF shot dead John Turnly (44), a Protestant businessman who had 'turned coat', joined the nationalist SDLP and then the tiny Irish Independence Party. Three weeks later, the killers penetrated deep into the IRA's heartland of Andersonstown in West Belfast to turn their guns on the Irish Republican Socialist Party (IRSP), the political wing of the INLA, killing one of its most prominent figures, Miriam Daly (45), in her own home. They shot her five times in the head through a cushion to deaden the sound. Shortly afterwards, her ten-year-old daughter returned from school to find her mother lying in the hall in a pool of blood.[17] The UFF kept up the pressure on the IRSP, whose members were prominent in the campaign that supported the 'H-Block' prisoners' demands. On 15 October 1980, a fortnight before the announcement of the first IRA hunger strike, the UFF shot dead two more leading IRSP members, both of them Protestants: Ronnie Bunting (32), the son of Paisley's former lieutenant from the late sixties, Major Ronald Bunting, and Noel Lyttle (44), who was staying in Bunting's house at the time. The UFF penetrated the Turf Lodge area, another republican stronghold in West Belfast, smashed in the door with a sledgehammer at around three o'clock in the morning and shot Bunting and Lyttle dead in their beds.[18] But the UFF had two even higher-profile targets in their sights.

Three months later, after the first hunger strike had ended and the second was about to begin, the UFF shot Bernadette McAliskey (the former Bernadette Devlin who had been such a prominent activist in the early days of the conflict), who was one of the leading republican figures in the 'H-Block' campaign. The attack was planned and carried out by UFF members drawn from the UDA's South Belfast brigade, which also covered the Lisburn area. Jackie McDonald, who was a senior South Belfast commander at the time, had no hesitation in justifying the attack. 'It seemed that she was a hundred per cent against the Protestant people and the loyalist people,' he told me. 'She wanted a united Ireland. That photograph of her smashing the kerbstones [during the "Battle of the Bogside" in August 1969] with that look on her face just summed it up as far as most loyalist people were concerned and not just the paramilitaries. She was seen as one of the main movers behind the Republican Movement and as such a genuine target.' At breakfast time on 16 January 1981, the UFF smashed down the door of the McAliskey home in Coalisland, County Tyrone, and shot Bernadette seven times as she was dressing her children. Her husband, Michael, was also shot four times as he tried to prevent the gunmen getting in.[19] Mrs McAliskey and her husband would probably both have died had not an undercover British army unit been staking out the house and, after the shooting, arrested the UFF unit and given first aid to its severely wounded victims. The question of why the assailants were not apprehended before the shooting has never been satisfactorily answered. Inevitably there were suspicions, never proven, that the army wanted the attack to go ahead and to apprehend the gunmen afterwards. One member of the UFF unit was Raymond Smallwoods (31), a UDA member from Lisburn, who was sentenced to fifteen years. When he was released from prison, he became one of the organization's chief political strategists before he was shot dead by the IRA on 11 July 1994, just before the IRA and loyalist ceasefires. John McMichael, the UDA's South Belfast brigadier, was in court for the trial since the operation was believed to have been planned by him and his men. McMichael was not only Andy Tyrie's confidant and one of the authors of 'Beyond the Religious Divide', but was also thought to be the commander-in-chief of the UFF and the mastermind behind its offensive against prominent republicans. McMichael was himself subsequently killed by an IRA booby-trap bomb placed under his car on 22 December 1987. I put the UFF allegation to his son, Gary, who was to carry on his father's political work as the leader of the UDA's political party, the Ulster Democratic Party (UDP), which was to emerge in later years. 'I think it was recognized that my father was no angel,' he told me. 'He was a leader in a paramilitary organization. Perhaps he'd been there and done that and bought the T-shirt. He was a well-respected person within the loyalist community and his credentials were extremely strong. People saw my father as someone who said that loyalism was at war with militant republicanism and he was unashamed about that. At that same time, he was also making a contribution to trying to push not just loyalism but everyone beyond conflict.' I knew John McMichael and remember interviewing him in the late seventies – it was his television debut – in the upstairs room of the pub he ran in Lisburn. He was both articulate and tough, a prototype of the new breed of loyalist paramilitary and political leaders who would emerge in the late eighties and nineties. I thought that Gary McMichael's assessment of his father was pretty accurate.

But the UFF's most spectacular attack was on 14 April 1984, when its gunmen came within an ace of killing their number one target, Gerry Adams. Earlier that year, he had said that he was fearful that he 'may be assassinated at any time'.[20] At lunchtime, as Adams was leaving the magistrates' court in the centre of Belfast on the second day of his trial for a minor public order offence, three UFF gunmen drew up alongside his car and opened fire twenty times. They had obviously been monitoring his movements. Adams was hit four times and was rushed to the nearby Royal Victoria hospital where he was immediately treated by a surgeon. If one of the bullets had gone slightly lower, Adams would have been shot straight through the heart and would have died.[21] Members of the UFF unit were arrested shortly afterwards by an off-duty UDR soldier and two military policemen, inevitably fuelling the suspicion, again unproven, that the security forces let the attack go ahead in the hope that it would be Adams' last day on earth. Later, while filming in the Maze prison in the summer of 1990, I met one of Adams' attackers, a muscular giant of a man, covered in loyalist tattoos, called John Gregg, who told me that his only regret in trying to kill Adams was not his gaol sentence but the fact that he had not succeeded. For trying, John Gregg had become a loyalist hero.

Killing republicans was something of which the UDA was proud, but there was another side to the organization that severely damaged its standing in the eyes of the community it claimed to be defending. The racketeering in which it became involved in the 1980s seemed to confirm what the Government and the security forces had always said: that the terrorists were gangsters and mafiosi and that their political pronouncements were only cover for a reign of intimidation and terror. The UDA's racketeer – or as the organization saw him, fund-raiser-in-chief – was a Shankill Road man called James Pratt Craig, who, while serving a 'non-political' sentence in the early days of the Troubles, had been asked by the UDA's Chairman, Charles Harding Smith, to take command of the UDA prisoners in Crumlin Road gaol. Craig had a justified reputation as a hard man. When asked how he kept discipline among his fellow loyalist inmates, he is reported to have said, 'I've got this big fucking hammer and I've told them if anybody gives me trouble, I'll break their fucking fingers.'[22] By 1985, Craig had 'persuaded' a number of building firms working in Belfast and elsewhere that they needed 'protection' and that, inevitably, protection cost money. The protection Craig and his henchmen were offering was protection from his heavies. Builders lived in fear and paid up rather than have their equipment smashed or their employees – and themselves – threatened and killed. Hundreds of thousands of pounds entered the UDA's coffers and Craig's own pockets – as 'commission' for his fund-raising efforts – as building firms coughed up the monthly payments, too terrified to name names and blow the whistle on the racket. Craig was finally brought to court in 1985 when certain businessmen agreed to testify against him provided their identities were concealed, but the case collapsed when the defence argued that such concealment was a violation of their client's rights. When Craig was released and went back on to the Shankill Road, the West Belfast UDA are said to have told him they did not want him and could no longer afford him. Craig then went to join John McMichael who, with Jackie McDonald, was running the South Belfast UDA. McDonald, too, was concerned about the size of Craig's 'commission'. 'His argument would have been that he was the one that took the chances so he was quite entitled to some of the money, but I think he decided what percentage should go back.' McDonald knew Craig well and was part of his racketeering operation as he admitted to me, although it is not something of which he is proud. 'Through not being able to get a job anywhere else and not being able to look after my own family and being part of the organization that needed the money, eventually I did [join Craig] yes.' McDonald told me he saw it as the most effective and reliable way of getting hold of the money the UDA needed not only to run itself but to pay for the weapons it required. 'Nobody else was going to come along and say, "There's X amount of pounds. I know you need a few AK 47s," or "I know you need weapons to defend your country." Nobody was going to say, "There you are. There's a few pounds for you." '

By the end of 1988, Andy Tyrie made Jackie McDonald the UDA's South Belfast brigadier, following McMichael's killing by the IRA. Almost a year later, Jim Craig was himself shot dead by the UFF in a bar in East Belfast for what they called 'treason'. There were suspicions, never substantiated, that in addition to other instances of collusion with the IRA, Craig had set up John McMichael because he feared that McMichael was about to expose his lucrative racketeering business and end his operations. Craig, it was alleged, had done deals with republicans, carving up the rackets in West Belfast. It was suggested that he would have been doing the IRA a favour in helping dispose of the alleged leader of the UFF. The idea that McMichael was killed because he was about to clean out Craig's stables is, to say the least, unlikely as McMichael was fully aware of Craig's rackets and the South Belfast UDA benefited directly from them. John McMichael was not a knight in shining armour.

Jackie McDonald and some of the surviving members of Craig's team were finally arrested after the RUC had set up an anti-racketeering unit and appealed for help from builders and the public. One advertisement said:

> These are not just offences committed by gangsters in firms! If you are in business in Northern Ireland, no matter what the size of that business, you could be a victim of blackmail and intimidation. Terrorists use these means to raise money to finance death and destruction. If you are a victim, the police can help you.

The police finally persuaded some builders to let their conversations with the extortioners be tape-recorded. The investigation and the recordings had started before Craig met his violent end. One builder who agreed to assist the police had paid the following amounts to Craig and his associates through the 1980s: 1983 – £3,000; 1984 – £4,000; 1985 – £4,400; 1986 – £5,400; and 1987 – £7,800. Inflation and the increased cost of 'security' had clearly taken their toll. The builders were warned not on any account to contemplate giving evidence in court. If they did, it was suggested, they would never get there. Senior members of the building companies received Christmas cards from the UFF saying, 'We wish you a Merry Christmas and pray this is not your last.' But, despite the threats, the builders did give evidence, and after a trial in January 1990, some of the surviving members of Craig's team went to gaol. Jackie McDonald was sentenced to ten years for blackmail, intimidation and threatening to kill. Part of the evidence against him was a tape-recording of a conversation he had had with a builder following a television interview in which the Chief Constable, Sir John Hermon, asked for builders to come forward and help the police. I asked McDonald for his account of what happened.

I saw the builder the next morning and he said to me, 'Did you see Jack Hermon on the TV last night asking people like me to give evidence about people like you?' And I said, 'He's asking you to put your life in danger.' I got ten years for that – a threat to kill.

What happened to the builder?

Well, he's retired gracefully as far as I know.

Do you have any regrets about what you were involved in?

I have certainly. I would say without a shadow of doubt the worst thing that ever happened to South Belfast, John McMichael and myself especially, was that Jim Craig ever had anything to do with our organization.

But you and John McMichael were running South Belfast. You could have said to Craig, 'This is bringing the UDA into disrepute. It's gangsterism and it will stop or you will go.'

Believe it or not, we tried to do that as far as possible. We tried to eliminate as much of it as possible, but at the end of the day we still needed the money to meet our commitments.

By the end of the 1980s, those commitments were extensive, not just in terms of running the UDA and UFF but in acquiring from abroad the quantity of arms thought necessary to fight back against what was seen as the ever increasing threat of a united Ireland as London and Dublin grew closer together. For loyalists, these were 'bad years' politically too.

Chapter Fifteen

Betrayal

After the IRA's devastating twin 'spectaculars' on 27 August 1979 killing Lord Mountbatten, members of his family and eighteen British soldiers at Warrenpoint, the Prime Minister, Margaret Thatcher, flew to Northern Ireland to knock heads together. She had been in Downing Street for barely five months. The horrendous losses of that one day had been due to a black hole in the intelligence picture that might have been avoided had the police and army worked more closely together and seen each other as allies instead of rivals. But Mrs Thatcher, who had never shown any particular interest in Ireland, knew that tougher security and better coordination of intelligence were not enough. She knew that politics were part of counter-terrorism too. She was greatly influenced on that front by the Whitehall mandarin Sir Kenneth Stowe, who had been her principal private secretary when she moved into Number Ten after the Conservatives' election victory on 3 May 1979. The following October, after her visit to Northern Ireland, she made Sir Kenneth her senior Northern Ireland official, the Permenant Secretary. It was his view that a political solution to the conflict could be reached only if a way could be found of circumventing the unionist veto that the Government believed stood in the way of all political progress: if loyalists, as seemed likely, were to keep on saying 'No' to every political initiative the British put forward, then a situation would have to be engineered in which their veto had no effect. They would be huffing and puffing but not, as in the strike of 1974, blowing the house down. Sir Kenneth Stowe and his colleagues calculated that this might be possible if the political axis were swung from London and Belfast to London and Dublin. The strategy became known as the 'Belfast Bypass'. Mrs Thatcher, no doubt with some reluctance, was persuaded of the merit of the new strategy, not because she relished the prospect of doing business with the Irish Prime Minister, Charles Haughey, who had been involved in the gun-running scandal and the arms trial of 1970, but because she thought that in the process she might persuade Haughey to be tougher on terrorism and extradite the many IRA men and women on the run in the Republic to stand trial in the North.

Remarkably, the two Prime Ministers hit it off, each launching a charm offensive designed to achieve different ends. Haughey made no secret of his republicanism – 'his father was an IRA man from Swatragh' was one of Paisley's favourite jibes – and had frequently gone on the record saying he wanted to see a British withdrawal from Northern Ireland, and he saw this 'new' relationship with the British Prime Minister as the first step on the road to the peaceful achievement of his goal. Mrs Thatcher, not one to have green wool pulled over her eyes or fall for the blarney, was prepared to be nice to Mr Haughey to get what *she* wanted – a commitment from Dublin to crack down on the IRA in what loyalists saw, with some justification, as their 'safe haven' in the South. To general astonishment on both sides of the Irish Sea, the relationship proved productive. In May 1980, Haughey visited Downing Street and presented his new-found friend with an eighteenth-century Irish silver teapot. The following December, in the ominous shadow of the first IRA hunger strike, Mrs Thatcher paid a return visit, no doubt bearing gifts of equal splendour, to meet the Taoisach (the Irish Prime Minister) at Dublin Castle, the former seat of British power in Ireland. With her, she brought the most high-powered delegation ever to visit the Irish Republic, including the Defence Secretary, Lord Carrington, the Home Secretary, Geoffrey Howe, and the new Northern Ireland Secretary, Humphrey Atkins. Mrs Thatcher, it seemed, was serious and the joint communiqué that came out of the summit bore that out. To the delight of Charles Haughey and the fury of Ian Paisley, it stated that there was 'a unique relationship between the two countries' and that the two Governments were going to set up special study groups to examine 'the totality of relationships within these islands'. But, despite the impression that Haughey tried to create, the constitutional position of Northern Ireland had not been discussed. Mrs Thatcher, a unionist from hat to handbag, would have been horrified at the thought. Nevertheless, in historical terms, this new relationship forged between London and Dublin in 1980 laid the ground for the Anglo-Irish Agreement of 1985 and the Good Friday Agreement of 1998. Few would have thought it then, except for loyalists and Ian Paisley.

Once Christmas and the first IRA hunger strike were over, Paisley marched into action, condemning the 'historic breakthrough' in Anglo-Irish relations as treachery, betrayal and every other synonym he could call on. On the night of 6 February 1981, selected members of the press were escorted to a lonely hillside in County Antrim where they found Paisley at the head of 500 men dressed in combat jackets and lined up in military formation.[1] At a command, they waved bits of paper in the air, certificates for legally held shotguns. If it was theatre, it was more comic than menacing. Paisley was determined to alert Protestant Ulster, yet again, to the crisis it faced as London and Dublin prepared to bed down together. 'I felt it was going to go down the very road that O'Neill wanted to take us down and didn't succeed,' Paisley told me. I suggested that shotgun certificates were pure theatrics. 'Well, it had a very salutary effect on the Government, a very salutary effect indeed.' 'Waving shotgun certificates?' I asked. 'Yes,' he said with a loud Paisley guffaw, 'the fact that those men produced those certificates got you worked up. You'd have thought that we had brought a big machine-gun!'

Three days after the outing to the lonely Antrim hillside, Paisley donned yet again the mantle of his hero, Sir Edward Carson, and with great flourish and with members of his Democratic Unionist Party (DUP) signed the Ulster Declaration at Belfast City Hall, announcing a series of rallies across the province, as Carson had done in 1912. The rallies saw Paisley whipping up the crowds to fever pitch as he denounced every enemy, real or imagined, in sight. I remember watching him at his knockabout best in a field outside Banbridge when he likened Haughey and Thatcher to the Spider and the Fly, with Haughey enticing Mrs Thatcher into his parlour. To rapturous applause he assured his cheering loyalist crowd that Ulster Protestants were not 'fly'. The audience loved every minute. But the 'Carson Trail' led nowhere, except to a huge rally at the foot of Carson's statue at Stormont. Yet Paisley assured me that its great achievement was that the expression 'all relationships between both parts of these islands' was for a while 'forgotten about'. The reality was that the expression was not forgotten but evolved into a form of words that loyalists were to find even more threatening.

By this time, Gusty Spence's son-in-law, Winston Churchill 'Winkie' Rea, had been released from gaol, where he had been since 1973, and was angered to see Paisley marching up and down yet again. In earlier days, 'Winkie' had thought Paisley was Ulster's saviour, but his own experience and his years in gaol had taught him that Paisley was not. 'I used to go to Paisley's rallies,' he told me. 'I listened to what he had to say, "Ulster will fight and Ulster will be right", and I read into that the way I thought he meant fighting. Now perhaps he did not mean it that way, but I surely put that meaning into it.' I pointed out that Paisley would always emphatically deny that any such interpretation should be put on his words. 'I would accept that,' 'Winkie' replied. 'But at the same time I would ask him to accept what I read into what he was saying and I genuinely believed it.'

'Winkie' lived close by Carlisle Circus at the bottom end of the Crumlin Road where thousands of Orangemen assembled every year for the start of the great Twelfth of July parade. For four consecutive years, he made what he called 'a dignified protest' by hanging a placard outside his house that said, 'Remember the loyalist prisoners for after all 50 per cent of them are ex-Orangemen'. Two years into his protest, 'Winkie' saw Paisley leading his supporters along the 'Carson Trail' and feared that many of its younger members might go the way that he had – to gaol. 'When I heard about Paisley starting it all up again, I thought, "Here we go again. We're just going to go round in another cycle."' 'Winkie' felt he had to do more about it than just hanging a placard outside his house, so he and another ex-prisoner approached David Dunseith of the *Counterpoint* weekly current affairs programme at Ulster Television with a practical suggestion.

> We said to him, 'Listen, we're not long out of gaol. We're hearing Paisley ranting and raving on his "Carson Trail" and we feel we would like you to do a programme and perhaps it would help young people from falling into the same traps as we did ourselves.' He agreed and we did it. Basically the programme was just advising young people of today not to fall into the traps which we had fallen into ourselves.
>
> **What did you see Paisley doing at that time?**
> What he did at other times. I saw him leading people up to the top of the hill and then marching them down again. He then went home and other people, like myself and others, didn't go home but felt we had to do something. I saw all this reoccurring again. I wanted to warn young people. Speaking through experience, I knew that if there had been teenagers there who had gone on that 'Carson Trail' and been marched up to the top of that hill, when they came down, they wouldn't have gone on home.

'Winkie' Rea was later arrested again and held on remand on the word of another loyalist 'supergrass', John Gibson. Gibson was brought in to confront Rea at Castlereagh to confirm face to face the allegation that he had made in his statement to the police that Rea was the leader of the Red Hand Commando. 'As he came through the door, his head was bowed and he was looking at the ground rather than me,' 'Winkie' remembers. Rea denied the allegation and was eventually released when the case collapsed.

By the end of 1981 – a year that had seen Bobby Sands and nine other IRA and INLA prisoners starve themselves to death in the Maze prison – Paisley appeared at the head of yet another organization that he now called the 'Third Force' (the police and the army being the first two). The year itself had already been violent enough, but now the atmosphere was even more tense after the IRA had shot dead the Ulster Unionist Westminster MP, the Reverend Robert Bradford, in his South Belfast constituency advice centre on 15 November 1981. Paisley was outraged that the IRA had murdered a Methodist minister and Member of Parliament. 'The blood of the murdered not only lies on the skirts of those who did this evil deed,' he told the House of Commons, 'but on the British Government who by political and security policies created the circumstances in which such a crime can be done with impunity.'[2] Resorting to a now familiar tactic, Paisley called for a 'day of action' – or at least half a day as it was from noon onwards – nine days after the MP's murder. Under the circumstances, the response was good. During the course of the day, Paisley had an altercation with the barrister Robert McCartney, then an Ulster Unionist, who was to become his political ally fifteen years later in his opposition to the Good Friday Agreement. McCartney accused Paisley of 'outrageous conduct and irresponsible language' and went on to call him a fascist who was 'more interested in an independent Ulster, a mini-Geneva run by a fifth-rate Calvin', than in the union with Britain.[3]

Significantly, the UDA would have nothing to do with Paisley's 'day of action' or with the display over which he presided that evening in Newtownards town when the 'Third Force' made its debut. Loyalist expectations were raised as they saw 6,000 men, with all manner of dress and demeanour, marching through the streets in the pouring rain, carrying cudgels and trying to look like a private army. From the platform outside the town's historic eighteenth-century courthouse, Paisley boomed that he wanted to see 100,000 men on the march for Ulster – the figure Carson had raised for the original UVF. 'We demand that the IRA be exterminated from Ulster,' he roared. 'The aim of the IRA is to destroy the last vestige of Protestantism in our island home. But there is one army the Republic fears and that every other enemy of Ulster fears and that is the army of armed and resolute Protestants.' With the men of the 'Third Force' drawn up in front of him, he threw cautious language to the wind and rain. 'Here are men willing to do the job of exterminating the IRA. Recruit them under the Crown and they will do it. If you refuse, we will have no other decision to make but to do it ourselves.' His words were reminiscent of William Craig's in 1972 when he talked of 'liquidating the enemy'; the other ominous part was the threat 'to do it ourselves'. In his peroration Paisley assured his audience, 'These men are pledged to me and I am pledged to them, and by God's grace, we shall devise a way, plan a strategy, and put it into operation that will smash the London/Dublin talks.'[4] For most people, that rainy night in Newtownards was the first and last sighting of the 'Third Force'. But to Paisley, it represented something more, an updated version of his old Ulster Protestant Volunteers, many of whom had been former or serving 'B' Specials who had offered their services to defend their country. He was thinking more of a Home Guard than a UDA or UVF.

The Third Force was a force that we felt should come into existence and should have had the backing of the Government whereby we would go back to the old ways of working. The 'B' Specials were part-time men but there was also a 'C' Special force in the old days whose purpose was to defend our homes and houses. And I believed that people had a right to defend them. There were a lot of murders going on, dastardly murders. People had a right to defend their own homes. If you rung up the police, the police said, 'We can't do anything for you. You just have to take your chance.' So I felt that it was right that there should be a 'Third Force' organized.

Weren't you the grand old Duke of York who marched your men to the top of the hill and marched them down again?

Ian Paisley never went to the top of the hill and marched down again. I have always gone over the top. Other people have been afraid to go over the top. I've never asked anybody to do anything that I haven't been prepared to do myself.

Such a remark would prompt gales of laughter from Paisley's army of detractors, especially the loyalist paramilitaries who make the accusation that Paisley was *never* prepared to go over the top – as events were to show, yet again, only a few years later, when loyalists saw an even bigger threat looming.

Far from halting the evolving relationship between London and Dublin, Paisley had to stand by and watch it happen. Words, however loud and threatening, were not going to stop it. Charles Haughey's romance with Mrs Thatcher was short-lived as, following the Irish general election of 11 June 1981 – held in the emotional heat of the hunger strike – he was voted out of office and succeeded by a coalition Government headed by the Fine Gael[5] leader, Dr Garret Fitzgerald, a civilized and erudite man with a feeling for the sensitivities of Protestants in the North that Charles Haughey had never displayed. He instinctively knew how the majority community felt as his mother had been an Ulster Presbyterian. Just over a fortnight before Paisley paraded his 'Third Force' in Newtownards, Fitzgerald and Thatcher had announced that they were to set up an Anglo-Irish inter-governmental conference that would hold regular meetings in London and Dublin to discuss matters of mutual concern. In effect, that meant Northern Ireland. But the relationship was to go much further, driven, as ever, by violent events.

On 12 October 1984, the IRA blew up the Grand Hotel, Brighton, during the Conservative Party's annual conference and almost wiped out Margaret Thatcher and her Cabinet. The Prime Minister narrowly escaped death when the bathroom she had been in two minutes earlier caved in.

Five people were killed, including Sir Anthony Berry MP and Roberta Wakeham, the wife of the Government chief whip.[6] A few months later, on 28 February 1985, the IRA mortared Newry RUC station, killing nine police officers, two of them women. The IRA said it was 'a major and well-planned operation indicating our ability to strike where and when we decide'.[7] Few would have questioned the boast as the IRA carried on killing. By the time the July 1985 marching season reached its climax, the IRA had killed a further nine policemen (including four by a 1,000-pound remote-control bomb), two soldiers and two Protestant civilians. Furthermore, there was also now a political threat from Sinn Fein as loyalists saw their candidates win fifty-nine seats in the district council elections in May 1985 which the party had contested for the first time. Yet again, loyalists and the Government felt that something had to be done to combat the Republican Movement and now on the political front too.

The loyalist reaction was to form an organization called the Ulster Clubs based on the clubs that Carson had founded at the time of the Home Rule crisis. As in Carson's day, they were a means of rallying loyalists in every town, village and hamlet throughout the province to oppose what they saw as the Government's betrayal in its embrace of Dublin and its lack of will to smash the IRA. The issue came to a head in Portadown at the beginning of July when the authorities attempted to ban the district's Orangemen from marching down the town's Obins Street, a nationalist area known as the 'Tunnel', which for years had been the traditional route on their return from their annual church service at Drumcree. Every year, the parade had been a sectarian flashpoint as nationalists showed their resentment at having what they saw as Orange triumphalism rammed down their throats, while the Orangemen insisted on their right to march along their traditional route. To prevent them doing so, they saw as yet another attack on their heritage. Inevitably, violence erupted as the police tried to stop the march. For Joel Patton, who went on to form the 'Spirit of Drumcree' movement, the Orangemen's right to march from the church at Drumcree and down Obins Street became the supreme test. 'Way back in 1985, we felt that one of the crucial elements was how the RUC were going to be used,' he told me. 'Were the police going to be used against their own people – we saw that as the unionist and Protestant people – and were they actually prepared to act against them? Portadown was going to be used as that test. The Government and the police were testing the Protestant population. That was a pretty decisive time because the police did actually go in fairly strongly against Protestants and stop them from parading their route. It was a fairly violent time in Portadown.' As a result of the violence, Orangemen finally agreed to change the route of their march and in future years return from Drumcree church down the parallel and equally nationalist Garvaghy Road. The scene was thus set for the great confrontations at Drumcree that erupted in the mid-1990s.

Shortly after the showdown in Obins Street, the Ulster Clubs were formed with their nucleus drawn initially from loyalists in the Portadown and mid-Ulster area. The Clubs represented both a reaction to events and a fear of what was to come. According to Joel Patton, they were also a recognition that the RUC was no longer on the Protestants' side. 'The Ulster Clubs realized that the Government was going to use the police as a force as much to keep Protestant resistance down as to oppose terrorism which they saw coming from the IRA.' An executive committee, a loose mixture of Orangemen, local politicians and loyalist paramilitaries, was set up with the general purpose of opposing 'betrayal'. Precisely how they were going to do so was at the beginning not clear. Certainly at this stage there was no discussion of military means, although with John McMichael, the UDA's South Belfast brigadier and alleged commander of the UFF, and a leading UVF commander from mid-Ulster on the committee, such possibilities could never be ruled out. The Ulster Clubs decided to settle for street protests in which they hoped to mobilize thousands of loyalists from mid-Ulster and further afield to demonstrate, yet again, the power of Protestant numbers and their opposition to the sell-out to Dublin. Gregory Campbell, a rising young politician in Ian Paisley's DUP, willingly gave his support to the Ulster Clubs as did thousands of others. 'I think in every time of crisis, the natural unionist reaction is to form themselves into some type of defensive unit,' he told me. 'This has happened historically and I think the Ulster Clubs was a 1980s-style reaction. People simply gelled together. I think they were looking ahead and saying, "Well, the logic of this may mean us having to take some steps that some of us might have reservations about." But so severe was the time that we were prepared to contemplate that.' The Ulster Clubs were similar to Paisley's Ulster Protestant Volunteers in the late sixties, a reservoir of manpower on which loyalist politicians could call as physical back-up whenever the need arose. There was certainly no shortage of willing hands and feet with eighty-eight Clubs and a membership list of approaching 20,000. The particular attraction of the organization to many Protestants who would never have contemplated joining the UDA or the UVF was its loyalist 'respectability'. The lawyer and rising unionist politician David Trimble, who thirteen years earlier had served with Vanguard and twelve years later was to become the First Minister of the new Northern Ireland Assembly, was associated with the Ulster Clubs and wrote a learned paper on the implications of 'Dominion status' for the province.

At their formation in the summer of 1985 following the clashes in Portadown, the Ulster Clubs' membership was largely parochial, but the numbers were about to increase dramatically in the months ahead as the British and Irish Governments responded to the growing military and political threat from the IRA and Sinn Fein. Their response came in the form of the Anglo-Irish Agreement, signed on 15 November 1984 at Hillsborough Castle in County Down by the British and Irish Prime Ministers, Margaret Thatcher and Garret Fitzgerald. Mrs Thatcher was never enamoured of the idea but was eventually persuaded by her Cabinet Secretary, Sir Robert Armstrong, of the wisdom of going ahead. Sir Robert once told me he regarded the Agreement as the greatest achievement of his political career. It gave Dublin a direct say in the affairs of Northern Ireland by the establishment of a permanent representative's office at Maryfield just outside Belfast and through regular meetings of British and Irish ministers in what became known as the Anglo-Irish Conference. The Conference's agenda was to be all-embracing, dealing with political, security, legal and all other matters relevant to Northern Ireland and the two sovereign Governments. To the Irish, the Agreement was a way of stabilizing the situation in the North and thus minimizing the risk of its violence infecting the South; to the British, it was a way of stemming the worrying rise of Sinn Fein by boosting John Hume's nationalist SDLP and finally obtaining the security cooperation that they had failed to achieve so far, despite the hopes they had entertained of Charles Haughey. The political developments that led up to the Good Friday Agreement of 1998 all flowed from this historic event.

Despite the fact that the very first words of Article One of the Agreement were a confirmation by both Governments that 'any change in the status of Northern Ireland would only come about with the consent of the majority of the people of Northern Ireland',[8] unionists, who at no stage had been consulted by the British Government, were stunned and outraged. Although they knew that something was in the wind, they knew nothing of its content or timing. John Taylor remembers returning home that evening to be confronted by an alarming piece of information from his children.

I didn't get home until the evening for dinner and my teenage children were watching television and they were all very stunned and quiet and I said, 'What's happened?' and they said, 'Oh, Mrs Thatcher is handing us over to Dublin.' I said, 'What?' I didn't know she was here in Northern Ireland. I said, 'But I'll tell you one thing, Mrs Thatcher is the Prime Minister today but she's not going to be the Prime Minister for ever. We've been in Northern Ireland for 300 years and we'll be here when she's gone, so don't worry too much.'

A week later a vast crowd, estimated to be over 100,000, packed the streets around Belfast City Hall to hear their political leaders, united as they had rarely been since 1974, attack the great betrayal. Loudest of all was Ian Paisley, seen by tens of thousands of loyalists as the prophet whose words had come true, who articulated the feelings and the anger of the vast multitude with three, simple words, delivered in a thunderous crescendo: 'Never! – Never! – Never!' He had said it before – and would say it again – but never with quite the same force and fervour as he did that day addressing the largest crowd that City Hall had seen since Carson signed the Covenant. Paisley had known the Agreement was coming although he was not aware of the detail. Paisley and the Ulster Unionists' leader, James Molyneaux, had gone to London and spoken to a worried member of Mrs Thatcher's Cabinet, Norman Tebbitt, who had been seriously injured in the Brighton bombing. Paisley and Molyneaux had tried to persuade Mrs Thatcher to embark on another course but she had refused. When Tebbitt had told his visitors that Ulster might soon regard some members of his Government as traitors, Paisley knew 'there must be something terrible in the pipeline'. There was. 'It was a complete surrender of Ulster's position,' Paisley told me. Action had to be taken.

At the beginning of December 1985, there was an ominous warning of what was to come when the RUC clashed with loyalist demonstrators as they marched to the gates of Maryfield, the headquarters of the new secretariat staffed by civil servants from Dublin. It was the day of the first meeting of the Anglo-Irish Conference at Stormont. Thirty-eight police-men were injured in the confrontations. But worse was to come. As the RUC held the line against the increasingly violent protests, the incongruity of which was epitomized on one occasion by the sight of a 'loyalist' attacking a member of the Royal Ulster Constabulary with a Union Jack, the loyalist paramilitaries started petrol-bombing the homes of policemen who lived in their areas. By May 1986, fifty policemen's homes had been attacked. Jackie McDonald made no apologies. 'We were taking the police and the army on almost hand-to-hand in the streets.' And weren't policemen being intimidated and burned out of their houses? 'Exactly,' he said. 'That was a sign of the times because this was a unique situation that no one had experienced before. We didn't want the Agreement but Maggie Thatcher was saying, "This is what you're getting."' Wasn't this a strange way to show loyalty? 'We always have been loyal', he replied. 'We've always been loyal to the Crown and we do want to remain British, but we just don't like people trying to take it from us, no matter what guise they would put it under.'

The Government stood up to the violence as did the RUC's Chief Constable, Sir John Hermon, and his officers, despite great dissatisfaction within the ranks. Mrs Thatcher was not the 'Iron Lady' for nothing. If the loyalists wished to re-run 1974, then the Government and the security forces were ready. Margaret Thatcher had not given in to the IRA hunger strikers and she was not going to give in to loyalists or their violence. They would not overturn the will of the British Government, this time they would not have their way. The Government's determination to stand by the Agreement, which it could never have done without Sir John Herman and the RUC's support, only inflamed loyalist tempers and convinced some of their leaders that drastic measures might have to be taken.

In the autumn of 1986, a meeting took place at a farmhouse near Omagh in County Tyrone. I understand that it was attended by five loyalist politicians and two members of the executive committee of the Ulster Clubs. Ian Paisley was not one of the gathering. They arrived in three separate cars and the meeting lasted between two and a half and three hours. The meeting was primarily a 'brainstorming' session to decide what action to take and assess how committed those who would lead it would be to seeing it through. The general view appears to have been that unless commitment was total, there was no point in going forward. Because the meeting was sensitive, it is difficult to assess precisely what was said and who said it. It concluded with a pledge that, whatever the cost to life or liberty, those present at the Omagh farmhouse intended to see it through. 'It', I was told, was what any reasonable judge would conclude to be a private or citizens' army prepared to fight to the bitter end. The organization they agreed to form, with Dr Paisley's support, became known as 'Ulster Resistance'. Once again, Paisley would be appearing to lead troops to the top of the hill. The question was now this time would he take them over the top?

Chapter Sixteen

Guns

As the first anniversary of the signing of the Anglo-Irish Agreement approached, there were rumbles of discontent in loyalist ranks about the failure of the campaign of street protests to have any effect on the Government. The paramilitaries in particular, who had played their part in burning out policemen's homes, were growing particularly restless at the lack of progress. The UVF wearily predicted the familiar scenario of yet another rally. 'The blood-curdling guldering of politicians threatening hell-fire, blood and damnation at 2.00 p.m. and the castigation of the mob at 2.30 . . . Where is it leading to? There's a short answer to that . . . nowhere. It's one great cul-de-sac . . . Now there has to be a different approach . . . The days of marching to God-knows-where are over.'[1] The UDA's Andy Tyrie expressed similar sentiments: 'We need some new tricks, not the same old ones we always use. We've become too predictable.'[2] The constitutional politicians of the Ulster Unionist Party (UUP), which had worked in unison with the DUP throughout the first year of the Agreement to preserve unionist unity, began to have second thoughts about the relationship. David Trimble, who was also connected with the Ulster Clubs, reflected the Protestants' dilemma and was aware of the dangers of the way the protests were going.

> If you have a situation where there is a serious attack on your constitutional position and liberties – and I regard the Anglo-Irish Agreement as being just that – and where the Government tells you constitutional action is ineffective, you are left in a very awkward situation . . . do you sit back and do nothing, or move outside constitutional forms of protest? I don't think you can deal with the situation without the risk of an extra-parliamentary campaign . . . I would personally draw the line at terrorism and serious violence. But if we are talking about a campaign that involves demonstrations and so on, then a certain element of violence may be inescapable.[3]

In the late autumn of 1986, invitations were sent out by the Ulster Clubs and the DUP for a special rally to be held at the Ulster Hall on 10 November, on the eve of the first anniversary of the Agreement. They indicated that 'Dress should be suitable for a religious service'. But the real purpose of the rally was to announce the formation of 'Ulster Resistance', yet another citizens' army to defend Ulster in her latest hour of crisis. It was the fruit of the meeting held in the farmhouse near Omagh a few months before. The media were excluded. The invitation was not completely misleading as 'defending Ulster' meant defending the Protestant faith, and the Reverend Ian Paisley was on the platform to give Ulster Resistance his blessing as flags and banners were paraded through the great hall. It was on a later occasion that Paisley, to the cheers of the crowd, was to don the red beret of Ulster Resistance. After the Ulster Hall rally, the organizers issued a statement of intent that was a potent mixture of politics, religion and defiance.

> We are not revolutionists or anarchists or murderers. We seek no fight with the forces of the Crown. Our cause is Ulster, the land of our birth . . . We make it clear to the British and Eire Governments that Ulster Protestants will not sit idly by while our future heritage and freedom are taken from us . . . No earthly power has the right to take from us our God-given heritage. Neither have we the right to surrender it. We call on the men of Ulster to rally to the cause and swell our ranks . . . Our cause is just. Let us with God's help match its justice with our courage and resolution.[4]

The Ulster Hall meeting had been chaired by the Lord Mayor of Belfast, the DUP's Sammy Wilson, with Paisley and his DUP deputy, Peter Robinson, alongside him. Paisley told me how he saw Ulster Resistance. 'It was designed to do simply what the Third Force should have done and give defence to people who were going to be subject to this campaign of murder that was going on at that present time. There was a large crowd of people there in the Ulster Hall. The mayor of the city presided that night and representatives of all the churches were there. We felt that we could depend on those that were leading this movement to do what was very necessary to be done to mobilize the people of Northern Ireland.' Paisley and his DUP colleagues shared the platform with Alan Wright, the Chairman of the Ulster Clubs, although there were a good many members of his organization who were opposed to the alliance with Paisley, believing that he would, yet again, prove to be the Grand Old Duke of York. Ulster Resistance was in effect the fusion of Paisley's Third Force and Wright's Ulster Clubs. Wright, too, drew on history and left few of his audience in any doubt about what he had in mind when he said, '. . . traditional unionism was shown in the 1912–1916 period when it was unconstitutional and illegal to form an army. But faced with treachery as we are today, I cannot see anything other than the Ulster people on the streets prepared to use legitimate force – only this will bring down the Agreement.[5] The DUP's Gregory Campbell was also present at the Ulster Hall.

I mean, there were no weapons there or anything like that. But it seemed to be the culmination of weeks and months of organization. I felt it was another rally in a similar vein to others but with an added dimension of people saying, 'Well, we are now organizing ourselves into a type of military unit.'

When you talk about organizing into a military unit, what did that actually mean? What was the organization planning to do?

Again, you have to understand the unionist psyche. By and large, the overwhelming bulk of the unionist community don't support or give any credence to paramilitary groups that are engaged in thuggery, vandalism and extortion and that sort of activity. But there is a degree of ambivalence towards people involved in paramilitary activity who do it for defensive purposes, who are seen as a bulwark against the IRA. Because, again, you've got to recall that the unionist community didn't give any degree of credibility to the British Government's assurances that they would defend them against the IRA. Given that, the bulk of the unionist community saw that there was a group of people who could defend them but that were looked upon with some contempt because of their involvement in all sorts of illegal activities – racketeering and so on. But if a defensive organization were to emerge that didn't have the unsavoury trappings of illegality and drugs and extortion, then that might actually be supported. I think people looked upon Ulster Resistance as that type – a sort of a clean-living paramilitary group that would be purely defensive and wouldn't single out innocent Catholics for murder. I think there was, amongst a large number of people, the hope – maybe not the expectation but the hope – that that's what could emerge.

But Ulster Resistance was seen to be a military organization, was it not? That was the plan behind it?

Oh yes. I think that, at that stage, the view was in most political circles that the logic of the British Government's intentions and their actions, over a period of years, would inevitably lead us into some form of quasi-united Ireland and that what had brought that about was the IRA's military actions. So the logic was that the way to stop it would be defensive military actions to try and ensure that the IRA didn't gain the upper hand either politically or tactically, but with this moral reservation that they would not resort to the killing of innocent Catholics or murder for the sake of murder. It would be a purely defensive mechanism.

But if that was the plan, the organization would need arms. It must have been recognized that at some stage Ulster Resistance would have to acquire them.

Yes.

There's no question of you marching up and down without arms if you were going to do what you were supposed to be doing.

Well, I suppose that at that stage there would have been the hope that a number of people who had personal weapons that were legally held may well wish to join so there would be some element of armament, even at an early stage.

There is no doubt that what most of the constitutionally minded politicians involved in Ulster Resistance at this stage envisaged was, as Gregory Campbell suggested, the creation of a citizens' army with weaponry in the form of legally held guns. That had been the point of Paisley's spectacle on the Antrim hillside almost seven years earlier when 500 men had waved their shotgun certificates in the air. But, by the time of the Ulster Hall rally, Paisley had already fired loyalists with the assurance that he was prepared to lead them into battle. At an Ulster Clubs rally in Larne on 24 June 1986, he was at his most unequivocal.

> If the British Government force us down the road to a united Ireland, we will fight to the death . . . This could come to hand-to-hand fighting in every street in Northern Ireland. We are on the verge of civil war . . . We are asking people to be ready for the worst and I will lead them . . . The people must prepare themselves as in the days of Carson, for a long struggle . . . The union is over.[6]

Despite the line about 'hand-to-hand fighting', few thought that Ian Paisley was talking about fisticuffs. There were elements within Ulster Resistance who took Paisley's powerful rhetoric literally, reasoning that if Ulster had to be defended and the IRA met on its own terms, then arms would have to be procured to do it. Paisley, by his association with such individuals in the organization to which he had given his blessing, was sailing into dangerous waters. His deputy, Peter Robinson, had already dipped his toe in them the previous August by leading 500 loyalists in the temporary 'takeover' of the tiny village of Clontibret, just across the border in County Monaghan. An Irish judge subsequently fined him 15,000 Irish pounds.[7]

It is not possible for legal reasons to reveal the precise details of how some members of Ulster Resistance set about procuring arms or the names of all those involved, but I have tried to piece the story together as best I can. South Africa, whose apartheid regime was at the time fighting a war on several fronts – Angola, Namibia and Mozambique – to maintain white minority rule, was pivotal. It was a pariah notion in the eyes of most of the world and anxious to make friends – besides Israel – and in particular to acquire missile technology to use against Soviet MIG-23 warplanes in the war in Angola. They were being flown by Cuban pilots in solidarity with the regime in Luanda against the South African-supported rebels. The latest ground-to-air missiles, like the new Starstreak developed and manufactured by Shorts of Belfast, would help neutralize the threat to South African forces on the ground. In particular, Pretoria wanted to get hold of Starstreak's advance guidance system. It appears that the loyalists' initial contact with South Africa was through Richard Wright, an Ulsterman who was the uncle of the Ulster Clubs' Chairman, Alan Wright, and who worked for the South African state weapons company, Armscor, which was in the business of replicating other nations' technologies in its own weapons industry crippled by sanctions. I understand that the initial contact was instigated by the UDA's John McMichael, who sat on the Ulster Clubs' executive and its 'security' committee along with the senior UVF commander from mid-Ulster. I am told that the UDA's intelligence officer, a former British soldier called Brian Nelson, was sent to South Africa to explore the possibility of an arms deal, perhaps sometime towards the end of 1985 between the formation of the Ulster Clubs and the signing of the Anglo-Irish Agreement. What the UDA did not know at the time was that Nelson was a British agent working for army intelligence. Nelson returned and reported back to McMichael and the UDA leadership, but as they had received reports from South Africa, presumably from Richard Wright, that Nelson's conduct left something to be desired, Nelson was cut out of the loop.

By 1986, as loyalist street protests raged against the Agreement, a number of individuals involved in the Ulster Clubs – on whose executive committee both the UDA and UVF sat – were made aware that arms might be available. I am led to believe these matters were discussed at various meetings, when those present were told what weapons could be obtained not from the back streets but from a variety of sources for a variety of prices. They were assured that those who would be involved in such an operation were serious people who knew what they were doing since it was thought that neither the UDA nor the UVF had the necessary expertise or finesse to carry out such a complex financial and logistical operation on their own. Paisley, I am told, was never present at any meetings when arms were discussed. There was not unanimity and while many thought the time was not ripe to start bringing in consignments of arms, there were those who did and who asked when would the time ever be right?

Talk of procuring arms continued into 1987 after the formation of Ulster Resistance with the UVF now particularly anxious to acquire new weapons as its oldest and most productive arms route had just been smashed when, on Christmas Day 1986, the Royal Canadian Mounted Police raided a house in Toronto, the city which was to the UVF what Boston was to the IRA. Over most of the previous decade, Canada had been the UVF's main source of arms, supplying loyalists with around a hundred submachine-guns, a hundred rifles, and thousands of rounds of ammunition. The mastermind of the Northern Ireland end of the operation had been a senior UVF Belfast commander, John Bingham. The organization's other main route from Scotland had been broken up in the spring of 1981.[8] Under the circumstances, the UVF found the prospect of a new arms supply route highly attractive.

By the spring of 1987, elements of Ulster Resistance, the UDA and the UVF had decided to go ahead and use the South African connection to procure arms on the basis of shared responsibility and a three-way split of the arsenal. Although Armscor was not directly involved in providing the weapons, it almost certainly knew about the deal and give it its blessing, no doubt in the expectation that, at some later stage, the loyalists might be useful given their potential access to Shorts' sophisticated missile technology. Most of the company's workforce were Protestants. If there was to be a deal at this stage, it was to be purely cash. I asked Jackie McDonald, who was McMichael's second-in-command at the time, what was involved.

There was contact made through various organizations. Channels were opened. Progress was made. Everything was in position through negotiations with different people and different countries, but obviously the embarrassing thing at the end of the day was when they said, 'It's going to cost so much up front.' Nothing was there so we had to resort to the tactics we did.

What sort of money were you led to believe was necessary to buy the arms that you needed?

How long's a piece of rope? You could be talking about one or two or three shipments of arms. But at that particular time, for one shipment of arms – you're talking a quarter of a million pounds.

The paramilitaries' part of the operation was to raise the quarter of a million and they did so in June 1987 by robbing a bank in Portadown of £325,313,00. The UVF in Portadown, who, I was told, probably knew more about the bank's alarm system than the bank manager himself, undertook the detailed surveillance of the premises and a UDA unit from Belfast carried out the actual robbery. The money was then divided three ways between the three organizations so it was not all kept in one place. Some paramilitaries, I understand, took their 'commissions'. Once the arms procurement itself was under way, only three people, one from each organization, knew the precise details, to minimize the risk of any breach of security, although both the Brigade Staff of the UVF and the Inner Council of the UDA were aware of the operation in general terms. I am assured that Brian Nelson, the army agent, knew nothing of the plans.

The deal was arranged through an American arms dealer based in Geneva called Douglas Bernhardt, with whom Richard Wright had worked when Bernhardt had a Mayfair-based company in London known as Field Arms, which had gone into receivership in 1986. The relationship between the two had endured and Bernhardt had become an agent for Armscor, scouring the world for up-to-date weaponry for his sanctions-strangled client. Bernhardt, it appears, looked after the financial side of the loyalist deal. I had often wondered how a quarter of a million pounds in cash was transferred from Northern Ireland to Swiss and other bank accounts in Europe. The answer, I was told, was simple. It was carried there 'by many people' in cash. Those who did the carrying were not loyalist paramilitaries, who might have been hard put to explain, if stopped, what they were doing with suitcases stuffed with tens of thousands of pounds in cash, but respectable Ulster Protestants involved in the world of banking, business and insurance, who knew their way round the financial world and what to say if questioned. Unlike the UDA and UVF, essentially working-class organizations, Ulster Resistance was deemed to be 'respect-able' and attracted loyalists from the middle classes. Although they might have had their suspicions, the couriers would not have asked what the money was for or where it had come from. Roughly a quarter of a million pounds was deposited via this route in mainly Swiss 'multi-signature' bank accounts to ensure that the money could be withdrawn only when both parties to the deal had signed their names since the international black market in arms is not known for its probity. Bernhardt arranged for the arms to be procured for a commission of £15,000 by a Lebanese arms dealer called Joseph Fawzi, working in Europe in the 'import-export' business, who operated as a 'fax jockey' locating and moving arms and other sought-after goods via a fax machine in accommodation addresses from London to the Benelux countries. Fawzi sourced the quantity of arms the loyalists wanted in the Lebanon, which, by the mid-eighties, was awash with weapons, some of which had been captured from the Palestine Liberation Organization (PLO) by the Israelis following their invasion of Lebanon in 1982 and handed on to their allies, the right-wing Christian Phalange. It is thought that some of the arms destined for Belfast may originally have come from this source since Fawzi is believed to have had links with the Phalange. The consignment was an eclectic mix of weapons, many of them from Eastern Europe, that appeared to have been put together from a variety of different sources. They were, nevertheless, a coherent and deadly package. Despite rumours that the Israeli secret intelligence service, Mossad, was involved – John McMichael had himself visited Israel – there is no evidence that that was the case, although it cannot be ruled out.

Once purchased, the weapons were to be shipped in from Lebanon via Liverpool in a consignment of ceramic tiles that had been ordered by a firm in mid-Ulster and paid for by the proceeds of the Portadown bank robbery. The tiles were real and cost the purchaser £5,000. So were the arms hidden beneath them and they cost considerably more. Although it is impossible to know for certain, it appears that the various intelligence services – notably the RUC's Special Branch and the Security Service, MI5 – may have known nothing about the containers of tiles or their contents. They finally arrived in Belfast docks some time between October and December 1987, cleared Customs and were collected by a haulier and taken to a location outside Portadown. The driver was unaware of the true nature of his load and thought in all innocence that it was tiles and nothing more. After he had gone, the tiles were unpacked and the weapons stashed away to await collection by the UDA, UVF and Ulster Resistance. The tiles themselves did not go to waste but were sold as a job lot to a dealer for roughly £5,000, the price that had originally been paid. The loyalists got their arms and their tile-money back into the bargain.

Arrangements were then made for representatives of the three participating organizations to collect their prizes: an estimated 200 AK 47 assault rifles, 90 Browning 9mm pistols, 500 anti-personnel grenades, RPG-7 rocket launchers and tens of thousands of rounds of ammunition.[9] I understand the weapons were distributed from a farmyard somewhere in mid-Ulster. Those involved were apparently surprised when, on 8 January 1988, Davey Payne, a leading UDA man from North Belfast, and two colleagues turned up in an Austin Maestro – that was to be the 'scout' car – and two maroon rented Ford Granada saloons and insisted on taking the UDA's share all in one go. Despite being told it was madness and that they could come back later for the rest, the collectors insisted on stuffing their share into the boots of the two Granadas and driving off. The distributors watched them leave the farmyard, I was told, with their noses in the air and their mud-flaps on the ground. Inexplicably, instead of taking a back route to Belfast, Payne drove past the Portadown security force base on the Mahon Road and was stopped at an RUC checkpoint. Again astonishingly, it appears that Payne, who was driving the lead 'scout' car, the Maestro, had no CB contact with the loaded Granadas behind him. The police opened their boots and found 61 AK 47s, 30 Browning pistols, 150 grenades and 11,500 rounds of ammunition – roughly a third of the total consignment. Payne was sentenced to nineteen years and the UDA lost most of its share of the arms it had robbed the bank to pay for. There is little doubt Payne was set up by a 'mole' within the UDA, but I was told that the information the source gave was not about the arms but about a bomb that Payne was thought to be carrying. Whether this was true or not, again it is impossible to say. The intelligence services may have been protecting their source within the UDA or they may indeed have had a blind spot. If so, it would not have been the first time.

Nine weeks earlier, on 1 November 1987, it was only a chance interception by the French authorities in the bay of Biscay that led to the seizure of the freighter *Eskund* with 150 tons of Libyan weapons on board destined for the IRA. In a staggering intelligence failure on the part of both the British and Irish, four other similar shipments from Libya had already got through in the previous two years and been landed along the coast of County Wicklow. If there was an excuse, it was probably that MI5 and MI6 were busy watching the Russians. A few weeks after the interception of Davey Payne and his two overweight Ford Granadas, the RUC uncovered another cache of the Lebanese arms in North Belfast, consisting of 38 AK 47s, 15 handguns, 100 grenades and 40,000 rounds of ammunition.[10] It appears that most of Ulster Resistance's share and a good part of the UVF's remained intact.

Ian Paisley and the DUP were acutely embarrassed when the activities of some elements in Ulster Resistance came to light. It was not the first time that Paisley had flirted with the loyalist paramilitaries – he had done so during the strikes of 1974 and 1977 – but it was the first time he had come perilously close to being damaged by them because they had become involved with the Ulster Resistance, the organization Paisley had helped form. I suggested he should not have been surprised at what happened given all that he had said.

When you were involved with Ulster Resistance, Ulster Resistance also became involved with the loyalist paramilitaries.
Immediately that happened we disassociated ourselves completely.
And they started procuring arms, robbing a bank.

Yes, well, we were disassociated from it at that time.

But if you're setting up a resistance movement, presumably you have to buy arms to arm the resistance, don't you? You shouldn't have been surprised they went out to buy arms.

No, no, no. You read the pledge of Ulster Resistance and you'll find that the pledge was no different from what Lord [Sir Edward] Carson said.

Lord Carson armed his troops. Ulster Resistance was in the business of arming its troops. You can't resist without arms, so you go and get arms.

No, no. We did not say that we were going to arm them. They knew perfectly well that there would be no support for that.

But how do you defend yourself without arms? It doesn't make sense.

Well, first of all many of the people of Northern Ireland have legally held weapons. That was the reason you asked about the [shotgun] certificates and that was the reason we produced the certificates. And let me tell you this, that as far as Ulster Resistance was concerned we had cut ourselves off. We had made it completely clear that because of the way it had gone, we couldn't do anything about it.

But again you and your colleagues started it. You unleashed forces that you couldn't control.

No, we didn't start it.

You were there at the foundation.

Oh yes, we were there at the beginning and that is right and we made it clear that if it kept on the line that we wanted it to keep on, they would have our support. We withdrew our support immediately it went off that line and now you're criticizing us and saying we're responsible for them going off the line. We're not responsible. Let me say something. All of them didn't do that. It was a very small number of them who had been already infiltrated by the paramilitaries because the paramilitaries were scared of it and they said we'd better infiltrate it and break it up.

But Davey Payne's arrest was not the end of the story. On his wrist the police found a telephone number that led them to a member of Ulster Resistance called Noel Little. Little, a former member of the UDR, had also been Chairman of the Armagh branch of the Ulster Clubs and subsequently a member of its executive committee. He was arrested, detained under the Prevention of Terrorism Act and released without charge. Little's family had suffered at the hands of the IRA when his mother's cousin, Ivan Hillen (46), was shot dead on 12 May 1984 on his farm in County Tyrone, when he went out to feed his pigs. His wife cradled his head on her lap as he died. Hillen was a member of the UDR and a personal friend of Little's. His killing hit at the heart of the family, and was no doubt one of the reasons why Little came to feel and act the way he did. But now, after the interception of some of the arms from the Lebanon, the police and intelligence services were watching.

Astonishingly in the light of the seizure of the Lebanese arms, Noel Little and others in Ulster Resistance were prepared to go further with an even more ambitious scheme. It seems they felt they could get away with it. The South African connection and Douglas Bernhardt had served Ulster Resistance well; they had paid the money and got the arms. The South Africans now wanted to use the relationship to serve their own ends. Armscor suggested a follow-up deal in which they were prepared to pay a million pounds if the loyalists could supply them with details of Shorts' missile technology, in particular in connection with its top-secret Starstreak project, the follow-up to the company's Blowpipe missile that had proved so effective against Argentinian aircraft in the Falklands war. As far as Armscor was concerned, what the loyalists did with their million pounds was up to them. Again, Douglas Bernhardt was involved in the transaction and stood to make a double commission, once on the missile-for-money deal and again on the arms that Ulster Resistance would use the money to buy.

The plan got under way on 31 October 1988 when loyalists entered Shorts' Castlereagh factory and made off with a training unit from the guidance system of a Javelin missile that was on display. When the theft was discovered, Shorts described it as 'an item of non-operational training material'. Soon afterwards during a search in the Markethill area of County Armagh, police uncovered components of a display missile, a weapons dump, red berets of Ulster Resistance (with the owners' names conveniently stitched inside) and documents that appeared to be linked to the South African connection.[11] Yet, despite these glaringly obvious signs that the police were on to their plans, Little and his associates blithely carried on in the hope of hitting the jackpot. On the night of 11 April 1989, a training model of a Blowpipe missile was stolen from a Territorial Army base in Newtownards. Almost a fortnight later, on 21 April, Noel Little and two other members of Ulster Resistance, Samuel Quinn, a UDR sergeant, and James King, a Free Presbyterian from Killylea, were arrested at the Hilton International hotel in Paris along with Douglas Bernhardt and Daniel Storm, a diplomat from the South African embassy in Paris. Officers from the French Intelligence agency, Direction de la Surveillance du Territoire (DST), presumably acting in concert with MI5 and MI6, had kept Little and his colleagues under surveillance during their visits to Paris, and had finally swooped when Storm had received two six-inch by four-inch cylindrical models of components from the stolen Blowpipe missile. Three days later, Storm, who claimed diplomatic immunity, and two other South African diplomats were expelled from France, and a week later the British followed suit by expelling three diplomats from the South African embassy in London. The same day, the South African Defence Minister, General Magnus Malan, explained his country's position. 'No South African weaponry is sold or delivered to terrorist organizations,' he said. 'Mr Storm was asked to act as a go-between on behalf of Armscor . . . our investigation has revealed that state officials were caught up in activities which did not have the approval of the Government and were not authorized'.[12] Little, King and Quinn were subsequently tried and convicted of arms trafficking and associating with criminals involved in terrorist activities. On 28 October 1991, they were given suspended sentences, having spent more than two years on remand. Little was fined £5,000, Quinn £3,000 and King £2,000. Bernhardt was also given a suspended sentence and the biggest fine of all of £10,000.[13]

Ulster Resistance had served its purpose, if not that envisaged by Dr Paisley. The UDA and the UVF now had the weapons necessary to intensify their campaign against the IRA and Sinn Fein by taking the 'war' to the enemy to convince them that they could not win.

Chapter Seventeen

Killing Time

While the Protestant community was in turmoil in the months following the signing of the Anglo-Irish Agreement, the loyalist paramilitaries were not only burning policemen's homes but killing Catholics in response to the IRA's campaign, whose strategy was no doubt to exacerbate loyalist feelings and provoke even greater instability in the province. The Provisionals were also determined to show the British Government that, despite the Agreement that was designed to undermine them, they were still a formidable enemy. In the six months that followed its signing in November 1985, the IRA killed twenty-four people: nine policemen, six serving members of the UDR and one former member, two soldiers and six civilians, including two suspected informers. The UVF was particularly active in the loyalist Ballysillan estate in North Belfast, sandwiched between republican Legoneil to the north and republican Ardoyne to the south. On 14 January 1986, Leo Scullion (55), a Catholic nightwatchman, was found shot dead at Legoneil Working Men's Club; on 15 March, the body of a Catholic, John O'Neill (25), was found beaten to death off Ballysillan Road; on 7 May, a Catholic woman, Margaret Caulfield (29), was shot dead at her home close by the spot where John O'Neill's body had been found (her husband had apparently been the target); and on 16 July a Catholic, Colm McCallan (25), died two days after being shot near his home in Legoneil. The IRA blamed the Ballysillan UVF and its commander, John Bingham, the loyalist who had coordinated the UVF's Canadian gun-running operation and who had been named by the loyalist 'supergrass' Joe Bennett in his evidence.

Later that summer, the IRA, probably the Third Battalion from Ardoyne, decided to put Bingham's wide-ranging activities to an end and take revenge on the man they believed was the architect of the killings in North Belfast. In so doing, the IRA was again able to present itself as the defender of the nationalist community. On 14 September 1986, an IRA unit smashed down the door of Bingham's home in Ballysillan Crescent with a sledgehammer, chased him up the stairs, and as he ran to a security door at the top shot him dead before he could open it.[1] The UVF was in no hurry to retaliate, preferring instead to wait and select an IRA target of Bingham's rank. Once he was chosen, the target's movements, associates and house had to be carefully watched to ensure that the attackers would find their potential victim at home, kill him and then make their getaway. The target selected was Laurence 'Larry' Marley, a close friend of Gerry Adams and a leading IRA man in Ardoyne. On 2 April, a UVF unit in a Cortina drove to his home at Havana Court in Ardoyne, dropped off the gunmen, one with an automatic shotgun and the other with a Browning pistol, who then walked up the path and knocked on the door. As Marley came to open it, they blasted their rounds through the door and sprayed the hallway with bullets. Marley died in hospital ninety minutes later. Eight spent cases were found in a neighbouring garden and there were eleven bullet holes through the door.[2] In a subsequent statement the UVF said, 'Laurence Marley had served a long prison sentence for IRA activities including blackmail and possession of arms and explosives. Upon his release, he became re-involved with the organization and this re-involvement cost him his life.'[3] Gerry Spence was one of the UVF men eventually charged with his murder. Just over a fortnight later, another UVF unit seriously wounded Alex Maskey, a leading Sinn Fein figure, at his home in Andersonstown.

Before April was out, the IRA took their revenge for Marley's death as the tit-for-tat killings spiralled. Their target was another high-ranking UVF commander, William 'Frenchie' Marchant, who, like John Bingham, had been named by the UVF 'supergrass' William 'Budgie' Allen. On 28 April 1987, Marchant was standing outside the offices of the Progressive Unionist Party (PUP), the political wing of the UVF, on the Shankill Road, when he was shot dead from a passing car by an IRA gunman. Again, it was to be several months before the UVF took revenge. This time the target was Anthony 'Bootser' Hughes, another suspected senior IRA man from Ardoyne. The person the UVF ordered to carry out the killing was Gerry Spence. I asked Spence what evidence he had for believing that Hughes was a senior IRA man. 'I'd seen his profile, his photograph, the things he'd done,' he said. 'I also knew from the nationalist community. They also gave us information that he was a high-ranking member of the IRA.' I asked why – if indeed it was true – nationalists should set up their own side. 'Because even they hated the IRA – or some of them did. They'd had enough of them.' 'Spence told me how he planned to kill 'Bootser' Hughes. The three-man UVF unit were going to walk up to Hughes' door, sledgehammer it in 'unless you touch lucky and he'd left the door open' and then 'execute' him. Spence was armed with a machine-gun but he never got as far as Hughes' door. On the way the unit was intercepted by the police, and Spence ended up in Castlereagh for six days and was eventually charged with the murder of Laurence Marley and the attempted murder of Anthony Hughes. He says he was also 'quizzed' about four other murders and two attempted murders. Spence told me he believed he had 'a legal right to defend my people and my country'. I suggested it was up to the security forces to do this by tracking down IRA suspects, arresting them and bringing them before the courts. 'They've tried for years and never got them,' he said. He also claimed that while he was in Castlereagh, the police tried to 'turn' him and recruit him as an informer. Spence alleged they wanted him to help them recover weapons recently stolen from a UDR base. 'They made the case that if I could help them, I could possibly walk free from the court.' Was that not better than getting a long gaol sentence? 'No. It would never happen,' he said. 'I can't betray my own people.' When the case came to court the following year, in April 1988, Spence was acquitted of the murder of Laurence Marley but sentenced to fifteen years for the attempted murder of Anthony Hughes. Passing sentence, the judge, Mr Justice Hutton, said that even if the intended victim was a high-ranking IRA man, there was no excuse for 'murderous acts of personal revenge'.[4]

While Gerry Spence was on remand in gaol for carrying out the UVF's personal vendetta against the Ardoyne IRA, the UDA was in deep trouble. On 22 December 1987, John McMichael had been blown up by an IRA booby-trap bomb and, less than three weeks later, Davey Payne had been stopped with most of the UDA's share of the Lebanese arms. Both these setbacks severely weakened Andy Tyrie's position as Supreme Commander of the organization, not least because there were suspicions that in both cases an informer had provided inside information. Tyrie was also unpopular with some sections of the UDA because, with McMichael, he tried to steer it down a more political path. A year earlier, the UDA had published a document called 'Common Sense – An Agreed Process', which was the brainchild of McMichael and Tyrie and a development of the UDA's discussion paper of 1979, 'Beyond the Religious Divide'. By advocating a form of power sharing within Northern Ireland in which nationalists recognized the state, it foreshadowed the political structures of the Good Friday Agreement more than a decade later. It recommended a written constitution and a Bill of Rights to protect *all* the province's citizens regardless of their religion and political affiliation. Again presciently, 'Common Sense' also suggested that such a package, once agreed by the politicians, should be put to the people in a referendum. This new political arrangement within Northern Ireland, McMichael and Tyrie argued, would help overcome the Protestants' siege mentality and the Catholics' fear of being dominated by the majority community. Its ideas and wording took many by surprise as it came from the deliberations of those most generally viewed as murderous sectarian killers and thugs. 'Majority rule in deeply divided societies is likely to be profoundly undemocratic,' the document said, 'and the only democratic system is one that allows participation in government by coalition of all groups, majority and minority, on a more or less permanent basis.'[5]

Andy Tyrie felt John McMichael's loss acutely. 'John was killed because he was the best person we had and the Republican Movement didn't like him. I didn't have anybody as astute in politics as he was,' he told me. 'They also didn't like him because he was being listened to and they knew the loss that we would incur with John being killed.' I asked Tyrie if he believed that Jim Craig had set him up. 'We had inquiries into that and we tried to found out,' he said, 'but we couldn't find any evidence that Jimmy Craig was responsible for the death of John McMichael. They were two good friends.'

But the political ideas emanating from the top of the UDA did not go down well with all the brigadiers on the Inner Council and their men on the ground. The UFF in particular saw its role as killing the enemy, be they IRA men or simply Catholics, and was not at this stage overly enthusiastic about advanced political theories while the IRA carried on slaughtering Protestants whether policemen, members of the UDR or innocent civilians. Tyrie had also made senior appointments in the UDA that were not universally popular. Tommy 'Tucker' Lyttle, the West Belfast brigadier, had enemies, as had his opposite number in North Belfast, Davey Payne, before his arrest. Suspicions that there was a highly placed informer – or informers – on the Inner Council served only to fuel the brigadiers' paranoia. The chief suspects were Jim Craig and Tommy 'Tucker' Lyttle, both of whom later died, Craig violently and Lyttle naturally. There was also concern about racketeering, which Tyrie seemed unable to control and perhaps, at least in his opponents' eyes, appeared to condone when they saw him appoint Jackie McDonald as brigadier in South Belfast following the death of John McMichael. However popular McDonald was and however effective a commander, there were those who, rightly, saw him as one of Jim Craig's henchmen in Craig's lucrative racketeering business. McDonald's subsequent conviction for blackmail, intimidation and making death threats, bore out their reservations. I touched a raw nerve when I asked Tyrie about what was clearly a sensitive subject. 'The UDA as an organization was not truly involved in racketeering,' he said. 'Some people in it were. You can't label the whole organization, that's totally unfair. I fought against it for years and years.' Although Tyrie was the UDA's Supreme Commander he did not exercise total control over his brigadiers, who tended to run their own areas as their personal fiefdoms.

When Andy Tyrie woke up on 6 March 1988, he was about to face a day he would never forget. The SAS shot dead three members of an IRA unit in Gibraltar who were planning to blow up an army band, and he found a bomb under his car. John McMichael's car had been booby-trapped by the IRA; Andy Tyrie's had been wired by one of his own men. He may smile about it now but was unlikely to have done so at the time.

> The bomb was put under my car because one man particularly felt that he would have made a better Chairman of the organization than me but he couldn't get the support. It didn't bother me. It didn't frighten me. Those who do the job I do, things like that do happen to them occasionally. You just have to be very aware and very careful of what's going on around you. When you've been in an organization as long as I had, people always feel they can do the job better.

The bomb sent Tyrie a clear message: to stay any longer as Supreme Commander of the UDA would not be good for his health. The writing was on the wall and, after fifteen years, he knew it was time to go. Five days later, on the night of 11 March 1988, he faced the brigadiers at his last ever meeting of the Inner Council. It was an emotional moment for him, having headed the organization for a decade and a half and having tried to educate its members to think politically, knowing that at some stage in the future the killing would have to stop.

> I felt changes were needed. I thought that by standing down, it would allow the membership to examine themselves and restructure the organization in exactly the way they wanted it. Within a very short period of time the people who had thought they could do a better job closed down all the important things like communication and public relations – everything that made an organization survive. What they did was expose themselves for what they were and the membership then turned on them.
>
> **Do you remember walking out of that meeting for the last time?**
>
> Yes, yes, it was very scary. A lot of people were in the room, a lot of them were still my friends. That's what kept me alive, the fact that they were my friends. When I walked out of the room and I came home to the house, I told my wife what had happened and she was quite well pleased. She was glad to see that I had resigned as the Chairman of the Ulster Defence Association.

There was to be no new Supreme Commander and from the moment Tyrie walked out, the UDA was to be run by a collective leadership. It was soon to face even greater upheavals.

Five days after Tyrie left, a horrified nation watched live killing on television as a loyalist paramilitary called Michael Stone single-handedly launched a grenade and gun attack on the funeral at Milltown cemetery of the three IRA Volunteers, Mairead Farrell, Sean Savage and Danny McCann, who had been shot dead in Gibraltar by the SAS. Stone had been waiting for the chance to strike at the heart of the IRA and try to kill Gerry Adams and Martin McGuinness and as many of the Provisional leadership as possible. He knew that the Gibraltar funerals would provide a unique opportunity to do so. It would also not only be revenge for the IRA's Remembrance Day massacre at Enniskillen the previous November, in which ten Protestant civilians and a policeman were killed, but also vengeance for the IRA booby-trap bomb that had killed John McMichael the previous December. After Enniskillen, there was a grim symmetry to massacring republicans as they commemorated *their* dead around the republican plot in Milltown that was the IRA's own Cenotaph. The UFF, with whom Stone was associated, told him they thought the attack was suicidal,[6] but he was determined to go ahead as such a collection of high-ranking republican targets was unlikely to present itself again in quite the same accessible way. Putting on a cloth cap, presumably to look ordinary, he collected a Browning pistol and a number of fragmentation grenades, allegedly provided by the UVF from their share of the consignment of Lebanese arms,[7] and prepared to launch his attack. The mourners, several thousand strong, were stunned as Stone, who had mingled among them, suddenly started to hurl grenades into the middle of the crowd before opening fire with the Browning. It was a cold, calculated and astonishingly brazen attack. People could not believe what they saw – nor could millions of television viewers. Most mourners dived for cover behind gravestones as the fragmentation grenades smashed the marble headstones causing injuries additional to those inflicted by the shrapnel. Others rushed to treat the wounded and dying, while Gerry Adams and Martin McGuinness, the leaders of the Republican Movement, shouted for calm above the chaos and confusion. An IRA man, Kevin Brady (30), and a father of two, John Murray (26), were both shot dead when Stone opened fire. Stone turned and ran towards the M1 motorway that skirts the bottom of Milltown cemetery, now chased by a hundred or so members of the crowd who were as fearless in their pursuit of Stone as he had been in his attack. Stone, still visibly cool, shot one of them, Thomas McErlean (20), dead. His pursuers caught up with him on the motorway and beat him almost senseless with frenzied cries of 'Orange bastard!' and assorted obscenities. The mob, now several hundred strong, would have finished him off had he not been rescued by an RUC patrol which intervened in time to save his life.

When Stone was being questioned in Musgrave Park hospital, where he had been taken to recover from his injuries, he told the police that he had acted alone as 'a dedicated loyalist freelance paramilitary' and that he had attacked the crowd at the funeral in retaliation for the IRA's atrocities at the La Mon restaurant, Brighton and Enniskillen.[8] Michael Stone was sentenced to life and entered the UDA wings at the Maze prison as a loyalist folk hero whom millions around the world had seen taking the 'war' to the enemy in a way that could hardly have been more dramatic. Stone was one of the last prisoners to be released under the 1998 Good Friday Agreement.

There was a horrific footnote to Stone's attack. When one of his victims, Kevin Brady, was being given an IRA funeral three days later, two army corporals, Derek Wood (24) and David Howes (23), who had been watching the cortège move along the Andersonstown Road from their silver Volkswagen Passat, decided it was time to make a hurried exit but in error found themselves driving into the crowd.[9] As they were surrounded, one of them pulled out his Browning pistol, a model like Michael Stone's, and fired a warning shot in the air. Not surprisingly, the crowd thought they were facing yet another murderous loyalist attack. The soldiers were dragged from their car, stripped naked and shot dead by the IRA. Again, the world's television cameras captured the scene, confirming the impression that Northern Ireland was peopled by savages. Few took the trouble to consider the mindset of Kevin Brady's mourners after Stone's attack at Milltown. The men convicted of the murders of corporals Wood and Howes were later released under the Good Friday Agreement – many months before Michael Stone saw freedom.

It is unlikely that Andy Tyrie would have been surprised at the attack because, although Stone claimed that he was a 'freelance' operator, the UDA knew what he was about to do. If the UDA had claimed responsibility their brigadiers – in particular those in North and West Belfast – would have exposed themselves to personal reprisals from the IRA, which was one of their abiding fears. I was led to believe that there was an implied understanding between the leadership of the loyalist and republican paramilitaries that each side's 'top table' enjoyed immunity. If there was, Michael Stone clearly swept it away. Because of this reluctance on the part of these powerful UDA and UFF brigadiers to sanction operations that might jeopardize their own health, frustration grew in the ranks of the younger members of the organization who, unlike the 'freelance' Michael Stone whose intended targets were Adams and McGuinness, felt they were being held back. A group of them had been groomed by Tyrie and McMichael as the élite and their own potential successors. Tyrie had set up a group within the UDA that he called the Ulster Defence Force (UDF), designed to make the organization more professional and capable of responding to any 'Doomsday' situation that might follow the imposition of the Anglo-Irish Agreement. Its motto was 'Sans Peur'. (The UDA's is 'Quis Separabit?' – Who will set us apart?) The training was done by former British soldiers who were sympathetic to the cause. I was told by one of its graduates, now a prominent loyalist on the Shankill Road, who passed out as 'best recruit' and was presented with 'a big cup by Mr Tyrie', that select members were picked out for training with arms and explosives. It was not something that Mr Tyrie mentioned.

If there was going to be a very serious war, a stand-up fight or military-type fight, we were not capable of dealing with it. We thought we knew war but we didn't have any proper structures. We didn't have any educational or communication classes and people dealing with public relations explaining how you would defend your area and how discipline could be managed without people being frightened. We needed training programmes so we could become more efficient in how we identified the enemy, get to know your enemy, all those things. I always felt that all the loyalist paramilitary organizations born out of the Troubles were very amateurish in their approach. Most people didn't even know [loyalist] strength in the province itself so if there had been an out-and-out conflict we might have been walking over the top of each other. The long-term aim of it was to create officer-type people who would replace the existing UDA commanders. Now I was accused of creating this force to remove the UDA's Inner Council and I would have been quite happy with that happening and even removing me because I felt that people like me had been there too long and a different approach was needed. I think it was time for change. Some people were a bit offended by that. But I felt the training was necessary. I didn't think that most of us were properly equipped to deal with the situation we found ourselves in.

Is it significant that some of the people who later took over the organization were graduates of the Ulster Defence Force?

Well, maybe it showed that the system was working and it was what I was trying to achieve.

It was a sort of advanced terrorist nursery.

I don't know about a terrorist nursery, but what it was meant to do was to stabilize the organization and take it in the direction it should go.

In time, 'graduates' of the Ulster Defence Force, most of whom had won their 'golden wings', were to become the 'Young Turks' who took over the leadership of the UDA and UVF in the nineties, as Tyrie had always intended.

Before being ousted from the UDA, Andy Tyrie, who had little control over the members of the Inner Council who tended to be laws unto themselves, was acutely aware of the frustrations of these young foot soldiers and the attitude of their brigadiers who had a different set of priorities.

> A few of them [the brigadiers], or most of them, had discussed with their own members that they felt they couldn't take up a higher profile within the organization because they felt they were making themselves targets. They felt it was all right for the ordinary members of the UDA to become targets but their attitude was that the ordinary members could become targets as long as they [the brigadiers] kept a low profile so they wouldn't become targets themselves.

The frustration felt by the younger members of the organization was even greater when they saw the Anglo-Irish Agreement bringing the UDA and UFF hundreds more eager recruits who were being constantly held back by the caution and self-preservative instincts of the old leadership that ousted Andy Tyrie. William 'Mo' Courtney, who was in charge of a West Belfast Active Service Unit (ASU) in the eighties and who became part of the new Shankill Road leadership in the nineties with John Adair and others, remembers the mood of the time.

> The recruiting drive the Anglo-Irish Agreement gave us was un-believable. The men just came flowing and flowing and flowing. We got all the men but there was a lot of frustration about. The hierarchy people upstairs seemed to be holding us back. They were holding the reins. They didn't want the bombings and the shootings. It just seemed to be, 'Just let things go. Let things settle down.' Whereas the young ones wanted to go and start killing republicans.
>
> **Why didn't the 'people upstairs' want it?**
>
> Sitting back and looking at it now, probably they were all sitting on a wee cushy number and just didn't want the hassle. They were getting their money, they were happy enough. They were sitting upstairs on their backsides all day, people giving them money left, right and centre. They had nothing to do.
>
> **Did that concern you, that the 'people upstairs' were in-volved in extortion and racketeering?**
>
> Me personally, yes, it was very, very frustrating. I mean, I was on the straight. I was on the go seven days a week. I couldn't even afford

a pint. These men were sitting upstairs having a cushy number. I was out carrying the war all day, couldn't do anything, and I would say there was a lot of young ones who felt the same as myself.

Did you and your colleagues confront the leadership at the time about your frustrations?

Yes, we did, we confronted them on numerous occasions but we just hit a brick wall. They didn't want to know. They were our leaders. They told us how to behave.

But you must have had some freedom because you say you were running around seven days a week.

No, no, no, no. We were actually out planning this or planning that as a potential [target] to attack.

And you weren't getting the OKs?

That's correct. We weren't getting the OKs at all. No.

So what did you and your colleagues decide to do?

We wanted the people coming through to take over the organization and get rid of the people upstairs and let the young ones take over and have a free hand.

You were planning a coup?

Yes, and I don't think it would have been bloodless.

But events did the job for them.

The sequence began on 25 August 1989 when a UFF unit attacked the home of a Roman Catholic called Loughlin Maginn (28) near Rathfriland, County Down, Maginn worked with his father in a poultry business and spent much of his time driving around the country collecting chickens. He was frequently stopped and questioned by the security forces, which he, like hundreds of other young Catholics, regarded as harassment. He once complained to his solicitor, Rory McShane, about being stopped by a UDR patrol, one of whose members said, 'I will stiff you when I get the chance.' Such allegations were commonplace and no doubt a good many were rooted in fact. 'The RUC are crucifying me,' he also told McShane. 'Every time I go out, I'm stopped.' His solicitor said it was a case of 'Give a dog a bad name and eventually the dog gets shot.'[10] Maginn had never been charged or convicted of any terrorist offences and his uncle was an SDLP councillor. That, however, was not how the UFF saw Loughlin Maginn. They smashed a window as he was sitting at home with his wife, opened fire and wounded him and then pursued him upstairs and finally shot him dead. The UFF had already killed four Catholics in the first six months of that year, 1989, including the republican solicitor Pat Finucane, and now faced another barrage of criticism that they had murdered yet another innocent Catholic. But the UFF rebutted the accusation and claimed that Maginn was an IRA intelligence officer and what was more, they insisted they could prove it. Jackie McDonald, the South Belfast brigadier, who was in prison on remand at that time, had no doubt. 'Due to information received, the UFF decided that Loughlin Maginn was an active member of the Republican Movement and he was eliminated as such.' I asked him how the UFF knew. 'Through information received from the security forces – the UDR,' he told me. He said the information the UFF had received was 'verbal, written and pictorial' and 'there was absolutely no doubt that he was a genuine target'. Four days after the killing, a BBC reporter, Chris Moore, was taken to a secret location by the UFF and shown confidential security documents and video tapes containing information on suspected terrorists. Among them were details about Loughlin Maginn. The classified information was thought to have come from a UDR base in County Down. In the wake of the revelations, other similar intelligence documents showered down on the press like confetti. To republicans and nationalists it was clear evidence of collusion between members of the security forces and the loyalist paramilitaries. It was what they had always said, that the 'loyalist death squads' were the puppets of British Intelligence.

On 3 March 1992, two UDR soldiers, Andrew Browne (27) and Andrew Smith (31), were given life for the murder of Maginn. They were also former members of mainland British army regiments. It was said in court that Smith had handed documents about Maginn to Browne, who in turn had passed them on to the UFF. The judge, Lord Justice Kelly, said, 'Those who set up victims for assassination by targeting their homes, their cars or movements, and pass this information on, are equally guilty of murder in law as the gunman who fires the fatal shot.'[12] The judge also gave life sentences for the murder of Maginn to two members of the UFF from Lisburn – a town covered by the UDA's South Belfast Brigade – Geoffrey McCullough (29) and Edward Jones (27). On 1 July 1992, the UDR ceased to exist and was amalgamated into the Royal Irish Regiment, to the relief not only of most nationalists but also of some very senior officers in the British army.

The huge outcry that followed the revelation that members of the security forces, or branches of them, were colluding with the loyalist paramilitaries, prompted the RUC's Chief Constable, Sir Hugh Annesley, to appoint the Deputy Chief Constable of Cambridgeshire, John Stevens, to investigate the theft and leaking of intelligence documents. In the course of his inquiry, Stevens finally uncovered the astonishing fact that the UDA's Director of Intelligence, Brian Nelson, was a British army agent. Nelson was the person the UDA had first sent to South Africa around 1985 to check out the possibility of acquiring arms. Stevens found out only after

Nelson's fingerprints were identified on some of the leaked security force documents that had been seized during police raids on UDA premises.[13] Nelson grew up on the Shankill Road and at the age of seventeen joined the British army's Black Watch regiment. In 1969 he was discharged and went on to enlist in the UDA as the organization emerged in the early days of the Troubles. In 1974 he was convicted of kidnapping and sentenced to seven years. On his release, he rejoined the UDA and volunteered his services to military intelligence, saying he was sick of the killing. The military, who probably could not believe their luck, enrolled him as an agent in the army's Force Research Unit (FRU), whose secret role, according to the officer known as 'Colonel J' who commanded it from December 1986 until March 1989, was 'to obtain intelligence from secretly penetrating terrorist organizations in Northern Ireland by recruiting and running agents and informants'.[14]

Nelson was a tremendous coup for the FRU: he had been selected to undergo training in Andy Tyrie's élite Ulster Defence Force and was clearly regarded by the UDA as one of its rising starts. In 'Colonel J's' words, Nelson was recruited 'to persuade the UDA to centralize their targeting through Nelson and to concentrate [it] on known Provisional IRA activists'.[15] Nelson's FRU agent code number was 6137. He had regular meetings with his army handlers after which they would draw up so-called 'contact forms' that leave no doubt as to what Nelson's purpose was. A 'contact form' dated 3 May 1988 states, '6137 wants the UDA only to attack legitimate targets and not innocent Catholics. Since 6137 took up his position as intelligence officer, the targeting has developed and is now more professional.' That clearly indicated the UFF was now targeting republicans as opposed to innocent Catholics. Nelson's handlers provided him with information that enabled him to draw up lists of prospective targets that he compiled as 'P' ('Personality') cards, which he then passed on to the UFF units who used them as the basis for their killings. Alex Maskey was one subject of Nelson's 'P' cards who survived; the solicitor Pat Finucane was one who did not. Finucane was targeted because many of his clients were republicans and he was believed to be close to Gerry Adams. While he was having supper with his family on Sunday evening, 12 February 1989, UFF gunmen smashed his door down with sledgehammers and shot him fourteen times, leaving him bleeding to death on the kitchen floor with his children running round in hysterics.[16] The UDA and UFF had no idea that Nelson was a British agent. As far as they were concerned, he was delivering the goods. Billy 'Twister' McQuiston claimed to know Nelson well, having first met him when he was released from prison in the mid-eighties after serving a sentence on the evidence of a 'supergrass'. Brian Nelson was the driver who came to collect him along with one of

McQuistan's friends. Whether 'Twister's' recollection of Nelson has the
benefit of hindsight is something that only he knows.

> I was always suspicious of him. It's hard to explain but he's one of
> those people that just didn't instil you with confidence. There was
> always something just not right about him. There were several people
> who also thought that there was something not right about him but
> when you were voicing your opinion you were told, 'Ah well, look,
> he's bringing in good stuff so who cares?'
> **The 'good stuff' being what?**
> Information regarding Provos etc. Good intelligence.
> **Where was he getting it from?**
> Well, people were asking that question but you were being more
> or less told, 'Who cares as long as it's coming in?' so nobody really
> answered it.
> **And how did you react when Brian Nelson was unmasked as
> an agent?**
> I think I was a wee bit worried because I thought to myself, 'He
> knows a hell of a lot about the organization. There's a hell of a lot of
> the boys going to be put away here.' To be honest with you it didn't
> come as a shock to me, but I was a bit worried because of what was
> going to happen next.
> **Was he going to name you?**
> Well, who was he *not* going to name, because physically he knew
> just about everybody. He knew something about everybody.

By this time 'Twister' McQuiston was back in gaol, having been caught
with hoods, masks and weapons in the Portadown area and sentenced to
eight years. When he was released in 1991, the IRA sledgehammered his
door down and almost succeeded in killing him with an AK 47, but he
managed to escape through the loft. 'Twister' took the attack in his stride.
'It's a war. I'm a soldier in the UDA so I'm entitled to be shot at now and
again. I think I was extremely lucky.'

Many of 'Twister's' colleagues from the UDA on the Shankill Road also
went to gaol after they had been arrested by John Stevens and his team.
One of them was the Ulster Defence Force's former 'best recruit', who was
charged and convicted of having documents 'likely to be useful to
terrorists'. The team's trawl picked up most of the senior UDA and
UFF members on the Shankill Road, as well as Jackie McDonald's
successor as brigadier in South Belfast. It was almost a point of honour
to be arrested. Some were convicted while others got off. But all were
remanded in custody, which, as with the 'supergrasses' earlier in the

decade, meant they were taken off the streets. The UDF's 'cup winner', whose 'dabs' were all over seventeen different documents, was sentenced and went to join his friend 'Twister' McQuiston in the Maze prison. The police had also tried to associate a child's novelty mask and a toy holster with him. Detectives said they were in his possession and were believed to have been used in killings. He denied it and was sentenced to four years for the lesser charges.

To the enormous embarrassment of military intelligence, Brian Nelson was also arrested by the Stevens team, and his collection of 'P' cards and the documents and photographs attached to them were taken away for analysis. According to my colleague John Ware, whose work on the Nelson case is unique, a combination of Nelson's own diaries and the army's records indicates that he was involved in at least fifteen murders, fifteen attempted murders and sixty-two conspiracies to murder during the two years when he was handled by the FRU.[17] At a short hearing in Belfast in January 1992, Nelson pleaded guilty to five counts of conspiracy to murder and was spared a potentially explosive cross-examination. Giving evidence, 'Colonel J' said that by his courage Nelson had saved a number of lives, including that of Gerry Adams, since the army had been able to foil many of the UFF's assassination bids. In the case of Adams that was true; in the case of many others, like Pat Finucane, it was not. The judge accepted 'Colonel J's' contention and said that Nelson had 'passed on what was possibly life-saving information in respect of 217 individuals'. Nelson was sentenced to ten years and, having been released, is now thought to be living somewhere in England under a new identity.

One of the key figures arrested in the Stevens swoop, along with his son, was Tommy 'Tucker' Lyttle, the UDA's West Belfast brigadier. Lyttle pleaded guilty and was given six years. 'He showed his true colours,' one of those sentenced with him told me, 'and the colour was yellow.' The younger men were not sorry to see him go as he epitomized the old leadership the 'Young Turks' felt had been holding them back. By 1989–90 information about operations was being kept from him 'because he was thought to be not reliable'. With the old leadership now out of the way – Davey Payne, the North Belfast brigadier, was already in gaol after the fiasco of the Granadas weighed down with Lebanese AK 47s – there was no need for the coup that had been planned. The way was clear for the new leadership to take over. 'Twister' McQuiston and his comrades felt that John Stevens and, ironically, Brian Nelson had done them all a favour.

The Stevens inquiry got rid of all the old guard within the UDA and fresher men took over, not people who had been in the organization from the start. The people who had lived through the eighties, a very frustrating time, were now in charge and were now bringing the war to the Provisional IRA. Whereas in the eighties the people in our area were calling us gangsters etc., in the nineties you were proud to be a part of the UDA, you were proud to be a member.

What effect did the renewed campaign have?

Well, we thought that we were now bringing the war to the Provisional IRA. We felt we were defeating the IRA. We were just filled with pride and were now at last starting to hit back and hit back seriously.

By 1992 and 1993, the loyalist paramilitaries were killing more people a year than the IRA and now, unlike so often in the past, many of their victims *were* republicans. Killing time was only just beginning.

Chapter Eighteen

Backstage

By the early nineties, the loyalist paramilitaries had embarked upon a strategy of killing and talking as a means of trying to bring the conflict to an end. I remember being surprised during a visit to the H–Blocks of the Maze prison during the summer of 1990 when a UVF prisoner from the Shankill, Denis McClean, sentenced to 410 years for an assortment of terrorist offences, told me that at some stage loyalists would have to talk to the Republican Movement. 'There'll have to be compromise,' he said. 'Everybody will have to give a little, which is something I would not have said a few years ago.' These talks, he added, would have to involve everybody, including the IRA, 'otherwise there's no solution. I wouldn't like to see this country still going through this in twenty years' time, which it will if the rising generation takes the path I took.'[1] But even as Denis McClean spoke, the next generation was already contemplating taking up arms and joining the UVF.

Seventeen-year-old Stephen Hull from the Shankill, who had never known anything but the Troubles, had, like Gusty Spence in the fifties, been reared on the stories of Carson's UVF and the Somme, which his grandmother used to relate to him on Sunday mornings when he visited her house. Stephen's father had served as a corporal in the UDR for seven years and no member of his family had ever been involved in any loyalist paramilitary group. Stephen did not know a great deal about the IRA, except what they were doing 'to the loyalist people as well as the British people both here and in England'. What he did know was that he hated them enough to want to join the UVF and 'get involved in the conflict and do whatever I can to help fight against the IRA as a Volunteer'. I asked Stephen why, if that was what he had wanted to do, he had not followed his father's footsteps and joined the UDR. I expected him to give the stock answer that their hands were tied, but he did not. At that time Stephen's problem was that he weighed twenty-three stone and the army would not take him, but the UVF would. 'It was a war,' Stephen said, 'and I was doing my bit.' I asked him if he was ready to go out and bomb and shoot and kill. 'Whatever was asked of me, I would have done it,' he said. The closest he had ever previously been to the UVF was helping paint a mural at the bottom of the street.

Stephen's parents, like so many others, had no idea their son had joined the UVF until one day the police came knocking on the door at half-past six in the morning when Stephen was asleep in bed. They said they had a search warrant for ammunition and explosives. He was almost as surprised as his parents. 'I was expecting to get up and go to work. I never thought once about my house being raided or else I wouldn't have had the stuff in the house. As far as I was concerned the house was safe. I was never involved in anything where the police would have me on record or anything like that.' While Stephen was detained downstairs and allowed to make his shattered parents a cup of tea, the police went up to his bedroom and turned it inside out. Behind a bookshelf with a television on top, they found a bag containing 700 rounds of ammunition, boosters for RPG-7 rocket launchers (almost certainly part of the UVF's share of the Lebanese arms consignment), some detonators and explosive substances and an A4 sheet of paper with the names and addresses of republican suspects. The police laid the haul out on his bed and summoned his puzzled father upstairs to take a look. He could not believe what he saw and started to bang his head against the bedroom wall in bewilderment and anger. Stephen was then brought into the bedroom and admitted responsibility, adding that his father had nothing to do with it. 'My father was just banging his head against the wall. He just couldn't believe what was happening. It was out of disappointment more than anything and frustration. He didn't know what to do or what to say. He would have liked to have been able to just let the police take the gear with them and have his son stay with him but that wasn't to be either.' I asked him what his father said to him. 'He didn't have to say anything,' he replied. 'He just looked me straight in the face and obviously I couldn't look back at him at the time because I felt a bit ashamed. In my eyes I was letting my parents down because of the respect they had for me. He just couldn't believe it. He just said my name and that was it.'

Stephen was interrogated at Castlereagh for five days and signed statements admitting possession of the contents of the bag, membership of the UVF and involvement in a punishment shooting. He had brought a mask and a gun for the kneecapping of a man who was going out with a prisoner's wife. Stephen told me he had no regrets for his part in what is now euphemistically known as 'street justice', the punishments that are administered widely, brutally and frequently by both loyalist and republican paramilitaries. 'Normally the fella himself would have taken care of it, only he was in prison and the prisoners and their families are looked after by the men outside. He had been warned and he deserved it because it was showing disrespect for the prisoner.' There is an acknowledged code on both sides that men do not mess around with prisoners' wives. If they do, they know the penalty. Stephen told me the man was shot in the leg only and not through the kneecap.

While Stephen was in Castlereagh, he says the police tried to recruit him. This was common practice as the Special Branch had everything to gain and nothing to lose because no one, except the suspect, would know that the attempt had been successfully made. Loyalists were usually easier to work on since both interrogators and their subjects shared a common enemy, the IRA. 'The detective sergeant that was questioning me offered me £25,000 at one time and a better life abroad. When he said "abroad" I pictured Spain or something like that, but in his eyes it was England. Maybe somewhere in the south or something like that. But I had no interest in it at all. I told them I was born in Woodvale [on the Shankill] and that's were I was going to die. I had no with to be anywhere else.'

Stephen was nineteen years old when he went to Crumlin Road gaol in 1992 on remand. When he was admitted and first weighed, he topped the scales and nearly broke them. They went up to only twenty-two stone so the prison officer wrote down, 'twenty-two plus'. During his time in the Maze, Stephen lost ten stone and became 'Loyalist Slimmer of the Year'. His parents and family stood by him throughout.

While Stephen Hull was in the Maze, loyalist gunmen outside carried on killing, following the pattern established in the late eighties when the British agent Brian Nelson set the agenda and the targets. In the critical four years between 1989 and 1993, the UVF and UFF killed twenty-six members of the IRA and Sinn Fein and relatives of republican families. The following were some of the targeted victims. In 1989: John Davy (Sinn Fein councillor), Gerard Casey (IRA), Liam Ryan (IRA) and Loughlin Maginn (disputed republican). In 1990: Samuel Marshall and Thomas Casey (both members of Sinn Fein). In 1991: John Quinn (IRA), Dwayne O'Donnell (IRA), Malcolm Nugent (IRA), Eddie Fullerton (Sinn Fein councillor), Padraig O'Seanachain (Sinn Fein), Thomas Donaghy (Sinn Fein), Martin O'Prey (IPLO – Irish People's Liberation Army, a tiny INLA splinter group), Bernard O'Hagan (Sinn Fein councillor), Sean Anderson (former IRA prisoner). In 1992: Kevin and John McKearney (members of an old republican family), Danny Cassidy (Sinn Fein election worker), Charles and Teresa Fox (republican family members), Leonard Fox (former IRA prisoner), Sheena Campbell (Sinn Fein), Malachy Carey (Sinn Fein). In 1993: Peter Gallagher and Alan Lundy (both Sinn Fein members) and James Kelly (IRA).

The killings, the majority of which still involved innocent Catholics as opposed to republicans, active or otherwise, reached a terrible climax in 1992 and 1993 when the loyalist paramilitaries actually surpassed the IRA in their number of victims. The pattern of killing in these years is instructive in that it provides the background to the secret political moves that were under way backstage. In 1991, loyalists killed thirty-nine people, most of them innocent Catholics, compared with the IRA's forty-one. In 1992, for the first time, loyalists out-killed republicans with the UDA and UFF killing thirty-seven people to the IRA's thirty-three; and in 1993, the worst year of all, loyalists again exceeded the IRA by killing forty-six people compared with the IRA's thirty-six.

The UVF had perfected its targeting of known republicans without Brian Nelson's help. On 3 March 1991, a UVF unit from mid-Ulster penetrated deep into the IRA heartland of East Tyrone and into the tiny village of Cappagh, whose IRA credentials and history are legend. The operation must have involved meticulous planning and was unlikely to have been carried out without some degree of assistance from the security forces. They, most likely in the form of the UDR, would have been the only agency in a position to pinpoint the movement of IRA Volunteers and pass on the information to the loyalist hit team. Also getting into and out of the village of Cappagh is not easy, as I know well, having got lost more times than I care to remember along its maze of narrow country lanes where signposts are a rarity – and deliberately so. Cappagh was the home of one of the ten dead hunger strikers, Martin Hurson, and a monument to what the village sees as his sacrifice stands at the top of its main street. The memorial is also dedicated to other young men from the area who gave their lives for the cause, most notably the four who were ambushed at Loughgall when the SAS eliminated eight members of an IRA unit, including some of its most experienced operators, in the biggest loss the IRA had suffered since the Anglo-Irish war of 1920–21.[2] Just below the memorial is Cappagh's local pub, Boyle's Bar, a white-painted breeze-block building, somewhat lacking in charm, which is not what its customers go there for. At 10.30 on a winter's Sunday night, 3 March 1991, a UVF unit shot dead three IRA men, John Quinn (23), Dwayne O'Donnell (17) and Malcolm Nugent (20), as they were sitting in their vehicle in the pub car park. Their car was riddled with bullets. A fifty-year-old civilian, Thomas Armstrong, was also shot dead. How the UVF hit team got into Cappagh – a village whose antennae are acutely attuned to strangers – and moreover got away again without detection, nobody knows. The word among republicans was that the hit was the work of Billy Wright, nicknamed 'King Rat' by his enemies, the notorious commander of the UVF's Mid-Ulster Brigade. I was informed, however, by senior UVF sources that Wright was not responsible.

By this time, the loyalist paramilitaries had become aware of the need to coordinate not only their military actions but their political responses as there was a feeling that the ground was shifting beneath them. While not letting up on its military campaign, there were signs that the Republican Movement was softening its traditional hard-line position on the way in which the conflict might be resolved. There were, for the first time, signs that the IRA might be prepared to compromise in response to signals being sent out by the British Government. In a landmark speech of 9 November 1990, the Northern Ireland Secretary, Peter Brooke, who played a critical part in pushing what became known as the 'peace process' forward, declared, 'The British Government has no selfish or strategic or economic interest in Northern Ireland: our role is to help, enable and encourage. Britain's purpose . . . is not to occupy, oppress or exploit but to ensure democratic debate and free democratic choice.'[3] Loyalists knew what Peter Brooke had said and studied it carefully but they were not aware that following the IRA's Christmas ceasefire of 1990 – the first of its kind in fifteen years – the MI6 officer Michael Oatley had secretly met Martin McGuinness in Derry and prompted the glacial movement in IRA thinking to thaw a little faster.[4] Nineteen ninety-one was not only the beginning of a new decade but the beginning of the process that might finally end the conflict for good. Loyalists were prepared to respond and meet the Provisionals on both fronts – military and political.

By this time, both the UVF and the UDA had developed their own political parties with their own political leaders. The UVF's political wing, which had been in existence for some years, was the Progressive Unionist Party (PUP), led by a group of former UVF and Red Hand Commando prisoners with a formidable array of gifted spokesmen like David Ervine and Billy Hutchinson, all of them graduates of Gusty Spence's Long Kesh political academy. The UDA's political wing was the Ulster Democratic Party (UDP), led by John McMichael's son, Gary, and a young UDA man from Lisburn called Davey Adams. Both were equally personable and articulate. Neither McMichael nor Adams had ever been to gaol and their relationship with the UDA was not umbilical like that of Sinn Fein to the IRA or the PUP's to the UVF, as Adams explained. 'The relationship is very much a voluntary one in terms of when the UDA leadership want political analysis from us. When they ask for our view on any given situation, then we will provide it, but we don't have a direct input as such in determining UDA and UFF policy. What we do is if we are invited, we go and make arguments from our position. But at the end of the day it's for the leadership of that organization to decide whether they accept our position or whether they don't.' In contrast, the UVF and PUP, like the IRA and Sinn Fein, are as one. Together these two political parties that sprung from the loyalist paramilitaries represented the new breed of loyalist politicians who wanted to reach a compromise that would end the 'war' but safeguard the province's place within the United Kingdom. They were in the business of saying 'Yes' – on certain conditions – instead of what had always appeared to be the loyalists' traditional 'No'. At the beginning of 1991, the UVF and the UDA, often enemies that had killed one another, buried their internecine past and formed a joint paramilitary organization under the umbrella of the Combined Loyalist Military Command (CLMC), with their respective political parties forming a similar alliance. From now on they were to make war or peace together.

On the night of 17 April 1991, twelve days ahead of the talks that Peter Brooke had finally persuaded the mainstream political parties to enter, the CLMC announced a ceasefire. Its statement said:

> In the light of the impending political dialogue and in common with a sincere and genuine desire to see a peaceful and acceptable solution to our political differences, the combined command of all the loyalist military organizations shall order a universal suspension of aggressive operational activities commencing midnight of the night preceding the political summit.[5]

It warned, however, that should the IRA attempt to disrupt this 'important and constructive political dialogue', the CLMC would order, where appropriate, retaliatory action that would be 'extremely discriminating and to grave effect'. The ceasefire began at midnight on 29 April and ended at midnight on 4 July. As the CLMC had anticipated, the IRA made no reciprocal gesture, and in the two-month period of the loyalist ceasefire killed thirteen people: three policemen and one former RUC officer; four members of the UDR; two soldiers; two civilians, one of them, Cecil McNight (32), a member of the UDP; and one suspected informer. For their part, the UFF killed a Sinn Fein councillor, Eddie Fullerton (56), who lived across the border in Donegal. The UFF said cross-border operations were not covered by its ceasefire and they would continue as long as the Irish Republic claimed territorial jurisdiction over Northern Ireland. When the ceasefire ended, the CLMC announced, 'We have proven that we have a desire for peace, which can be seen as genuine, and have no vested interest in the continuation of violence. We have also demonstrated since the start of the talks that we are disciplined organizations.'[6] The ceasefire ended the day the Brooke talks were wound up – without agreement. They had been conducted on the basis of three strands: relations within Northern Ireland, relations between North and South of the island and relations between London and Dublin. This, it was thought, was the most likely framework within which a settlement might be reached. All the main political parties had been involved, including Ian Paisley's DUP, and despite the failure to find agreement some progress had been made. The British and Irish Governments, building on the huge improvement in relations fostered by the Anglo-Irish Agreement, were determined to keep up the momentum and, after a decent interval, try again. The loyalist paramilitaries and their respective political parties, although not involved in the talks, believed that they had gained indirectly from them.

In 1989, the UVF had set up what it called a 'kitchen cabinet' – a paramilitary think tank to work out how it was going to end the 'war'. Its conclusion had been unanimous: the only way to end it was to escalate it. But the experience of the ceasefire made some of the kitchen cabinet, like David Ervine, think again.

> Tragically after the talks collapsed, the loyalist ceasefire collapsed and the kill rate was awful. That was sad. But from our point of view in practical political terms we had the theories of ceasefire in the bag. For the first time ever, this could be done. We had people thinking politically, people thinking strategically. It's always been perceived that nationalists are the only people who can think strategically: that they know what a loyalist or a unionist is going to do at every turn. So it was vitally important that Unionism had to try and take agendas and whilst the theories around our 'kitchen cabinet' about escalating the war was to take the military agenda from the Provos, well, it's equally valid to take the political agenda from the Provos.
>
> **And the 'kill rate'?**
>
> Well, let me identify again where there was a terrible loss of faith within the loyalists for the unionist politicians. Unionist politicians virtually ignored the loyalist ceasefire. One would have thought they would have taken the opportunity to use it as a cudgel to beat the IRA over the head with. The IRA didn't like that ceasefire because they started to plant bombs in loyalist housing estates and killed leading Orangemen [like Cecil McKnight] in order to try and provoke the loyalists off the ceasefire. They didn't like it, but yet the unionist politicians didn't make the capital out of it that they should have. The world wasn't watching, the world wasn't listening. Some might feel that the world wasn't even told. That then created another circumstance in that not only did we have to think for ourselves, we were going to have to talk for ourselves.

The loyalist ceasefire of 1991 was a watershed for the loyalist paramilitaries. In the political vacuum that followed the ending of the Brooke talks, violence flared once more as the two Governments had always feared it would, with loyalists, now freed from the inhibitions of their ceasefire, once again embarked upon a terrifying offensive. In the following six months they killed twenty-six people, including three members of Sinn Fein and one former IRA prisoner. The rest appear to have been innocent civilians. The IRA matched them shooting for shooting – or vice versa. The cycle of killing climaxed on 17 January 1992 at Teebane crossroads near Cookstown in County Tyrone when the IRA detonated a land mine under a bus carrying workmen home from a British army base. The IRA had previously announced that anyone who worked for the army helping to fortify or repair the bases its mortars had destroyed was a 'legitimate' target. It was all part of the IRA's strategy of denying ground to the enemy and trying to establish 'liberated' zones, Vietnamese-style, free from any military or police presence. Eight Protestants were killed in the savage attack. Most Catholics throughout the province lived in fear in the days and weeks that followed, knowing there would be retaliation. It was not a question of if but where and when. The answer came less than three weeks later when UFF gunmen walked into Sean Graham's betting shop on Belfast's Ormeau Road at the beginning of a race and sprayed its Catholic customers with bullets from a handgun and an AK 47 from the loyalists' Lebanese consignment. Five Catholics died, three of them teenagers, one of whom, James Kennedy, was only fifteen.

One of the wounded survivors described the awful scene. 'There was a right crowd in and I cracked a joke with a couple of them – they were like that, always laughing and carrying on. I had only been in for about twenty or twenty-five minutes when the shooting started – I was standing next to the door with a docket in my hand studying the form. At first I thought it was a hold-up but then the shooting started and somebody yelled, "Hit the deck." I just lay there and prayed that the shooting would stop. It seemed to go on for a lifetime. There wasn't a sound for a few seconds – everybody was so stunned, but then the screaming started. People were yelling out in agony. You could hardly see anything. The room was full of gun smoke and the smell would have choked you.'[7] When the UFF issued a statement claiming responsibility, it ended with the words, 'Remember Teebane'. The local residents later erected a plaque in memory of the five Catholics who had died. It bore the inscription, 'murdered for their faith'.[8] I asked Jackie McDonald, some of whose comrades in the UDA's South Belfast Brigade were believed to have carried out the attack, how it could possibly have been justified. 'You know I was in prison at the time and when it happened I wasn't horrified. I was trying to understand it. I knew that in John McMichael's time, John would have tended to go for a known republican or a few known republicans. But by this stage, at the time of the attack on Sean Graham's and after the attack on loyalists at Teebane, known Republicans knew to stay away so they weren't easily accessible. It was a message to the IRA and the republicans or the nationalist community, "If they're going to do that to us, we're going to do this to you, so you tell them to stop." And I believe it was the sheer violence and the escalation and the killings that brought about the ceasefires at the end of the day.'

At the beginning of 1992, it appeared that the province – or the paramilitary elements of it – had gone mad, with the tit-for-tat atrocities of Teebane and Sean Graham's only deepening the sectarian hatreds that were the product of almost a quarter of a century of killing. But amidst the carnage there were glimmers of political hope as the IRA, the loyalist paramilitaries and the political representatives of both realized that at some stage the slaughter would have to stop and some kind of political accommodation be reached. Ironically, the month after the massacre of the eight Protestant workmen at Teebane, Sinn Fein published a document called 'Towards a Lasting Peace in Ireland' in which the Republican Movement seemed to be offering an olive branch to their Protestant fellow Irishmen and women, however bloodstained its leaves may have been. It said:

> We recognize that peace in Ireland requires a settlement of the long-standing conflict between Irish nationalism and Irish unionism. We would like to see that conflict, often bloody, replaced by a process of national reconciliation, a constructive dialogue and debate . . . Unionists have democratic rights which not only can be upheld but must be upheld in an independent Ireland . . . Those democratic rights, however, must not extend to a veto over the national rights of the Irish people as a whole.[9]

Members of the UVF's kitchen cabinet, despite their suspicions, studied Sinn Fein's document along with Gerry Adams' writings and words with great care. David Ervine believed there had been a change. 'There were things happening within the Republican Movement,' he told me. 'It was slow, it was laborious, but we got our tentacles out and tried to understand what was going on. What was the debate? Where was it taking us? What did it mean? It meant that the Provos were inching ever, ever, ever so slowly to the recognition of the futility of the war and therefore the ending of it.'

Around this time was when it began to appear that, with the right encouragement in the right places, the political logjam that defied movement for so many years, might at last be broken. But it would need great sensitivity, care and courage to do so. The midwives of the loyalist paramilitary peace were an unlikely pair: a Presbyterian minister, the Reverend Roy Magee, and a Dublin Catholic, Chris Hudson, who came from a family with deep historical republican roots. Magee dealt with the UDA's Inner Council – and in the process became known as the 'eighth brigadier' – and Hudson dealt with the UVF's Brigade Staff on the Shankill Road.

Chris Hudson's father had been a member of the old IRA in the 1920s and a founder member of Eamon de Valera's party, Fianna Fail. There was also a macabre connection with the UVF in that he had been a close friend of Fran O'Toole of the Miami Showband, who had been murdered by the UVF in 1985. He came to be involved in the peace process quite by accident after meeting a member of the UVF who had been speaking at a conference in Dublin. In conversation afterwards, Hudson told the speaker how he felt about the massacre at Sean Graham's (for which the UFF not the UVF was responsible), and the person asked him how he would like to express his feelings face to face with the UVF leadership in Belfast. He was neither joking nor threatening. Hudson courageously said he would. A few days later, he was telephoned by his contact and told to come to Belfast where he would be met and taken up the Shankill Road. 'I was nervous, of course,' he told me, 'being very conscious of being from the South and speaking the way I do. However, I still felt that it was something that had to be done.' At his destination he was taken to an upstairs room and kept waiting for what must have been a tense twenty minutes before the UVF leaders finally came in.

They were not terribly friendly. When they came into the room we shook hands but I felt one of their handshakes was very limp. However, I found them incredibly candid during our discussion and in some ways I was fearful at the things they said. One of them mentioned that they could have carried out, or could continue to carry out, an indiscriminate, no-warning bombing campaign in Dublin. They pointed out that this had paid dividends for the IRA in London.

Did you think they were serious about what they said about wanting peace?

Yes, I did. I made a judgement call on one of the personalities that was there. I believed him in particular when he said to me, 'No matter what happens outside, trust us that what we're saying to you is the truth as we know it. We will always be honest with you. No matter what atrocities happen, we will be always honest with you, and we are equally trying to work our way towards peace.'

Did you believe what he said?
Yes, I did.

The person on whom Chris Hudson made the judgement call was David Ervine.

Hudson's role was to act as intermediary between the UVF and the Taoisach, Albert Reynolds, to convey to the Dublin Government that the UVF wanted to engage in dialogue with its enemies, but also to make it clear what they would and would not accept in any settlement. Much of Hudson's work was done over the telephone to Belfast, for which he devised a series of code-names: the CLMC became 'the full cricket team' and the UVF, 'half the cricket team'; the Irish Foreign Minister, Dick Spring, was 'the grocer' and his aide, Fergus Finlay, 'the grocer's assistant'; the second-in-command of the UVF, who, with Ervine, had been instrumental in pushing the process forward, became 'the craftsman'; and David Ervine himself was 'the milkman' – because he had once worked a milk round. Although 'the milkman' could deliver the analysis, Hudson knew that it was 'the craftsman' who could deliver the ceasefire. 'Hudson was absolutely vital,' David Ervine told me. 'He saved life, let us put it that way. In my honest opinion he saved life.'

The Reverend Roy Magee, being on the spot in Belfast, did not have to resort to code-words or convince the UDA and UFF of his loyalist credentials as he had once been the Chairman of William Craig's Vanguard. He had first encountered the UDA when they were vigilantes on the streets in the early seventies and had established relationships that had lasted down the years. He had met Andy Tyrie when he started to attend the Reverend Magee's church in Dundonald. Tyrie used to invite the minister down to his headquarters to talk to his men. When Tyrie and the old leadership went, Magee was sufficiently well established to be tolerated by the new 'Young Turks' at their Inner Council meetings. Magee was nothing if not outspoken.

> I challenged them that no one has the right to take the life of another human being. I even went further and said that what they were doing was not only against the law of man, it was against the law of God and that one day we would all give an account for our actions before God. We talked at times about the future – about their children and grandchildren, if they were spared to have them. Did they want them to grow up? That was a very telling meeting when we started talking about the future and children and grandchildren. The answer was that they certainly did not want their children and grandchildren to grow up in the atmosphere that they had grown up in, and we moved on from that.

Presumably they knew what your agenda was.

Yes, I think I made no excuse that I wanted to see them putting away their arms. That was where I was going. I was prepared to assist them in any way I could within the law to get them any assurances which they might have wanted in relation to their British ethos and identity. That was the thing that was worrying them so much. The whole issue of the 'consent' principle was coming into the picture, and I assured them that I was willing to do anything to try to get them satisfaction on those issues.

The 'consent' principle was, for loyalists and unionists alike, critical, as it meant that there would be no constitutional change in the position of Northern Ireland without the consent of the majority of its people. This was the principle that had to underpin any settlement if it were to be acceptable to Protestants and work. But Magee knew that he could only go so far and there was a limit to the political clout he could carry. If the loyalist paramilitaries wanted assurances, they would have to be given with a higher authority than his. With the approval – or it may even have been at the suggestion – of the CLMC, the Reverend Magee approached Archbishop Robin Eames, the Anglican Archbishop of Armagh and Primate of All Ireland, to see if he would be prepared to offer his services as a high-level intermediary with the British and Irish Governments. Eames was familiar with the loyalist paramilitaries, having been rector of one of the parishes in which the UDA was born. 'When the request came, I had tremendous heart searching,' he told me. 'Having condemned violence for years and years, having spoken against it, having done what I could to comfort relatives of those who had been butchered, literally, by para-militaries, had I the right to give even anything that could be interpreted as encouragement? The very fact that you meet people sends its own message.' Eames finally decided that he had to do all he could to try to end the killing and bring peace, however distasteful it would be to talk face to face with those responsible for murder. 'I had reason to believe that things were afoot that could have led us straight down the path into really bloody civil war. At that stage I saw danger signals in what I was being told because in the position that I was privileged to hold, people talked to me. People shared thoughts with me, people shared ideas with me. And if half of what was being told me was true [about what Dublin had in mind] then if it ever found its way into some sort of peace deal, I knew the Protestant/loyalist people of Northern Ireland couldn't live with it. And so for all those reasons I felt somebody has got to get to the bottom of this, and if it happens that they've approached me, I cannot at the end of the day shirk it.' But the Archbishop insisted that if he was going to talk to anyone, it had to be the military leadership of the loyalist paramilitaries. 'I wasn't interested in intermediaries,' he said. Meetings were held at his residence in Armagh towards the end of 1993 and the Archbishop remembers them well.

> When I knew they were coming, I wasn't sure what I would see. I saw a group of men well groomed, well dressed, nervous, I think possibly not knowing what they were going to meet when they met me. But I saw men with a sense of urgency, which encouraged me. I saw a group of men who had obviously agreed an agenda before they came to see me and were in agreement with it, which encouraged me. But most of all I saw a group of men who said, 'Look, the time has come to talk. The time has come to seek an alternative.' They said this wasn't a reaction [to the IRA's peace noises] because they were perfectly capable – as I think we all knew at the time – to go on wreaking mayhem if they wished to. So therefore I took their intentions very, very seriously.

Each side was blunt with the other as they explored their position. The Archbishop listened to the CLMC's concerns, most of which he himself shared, and knew that he had to ensure they registered where it mattered. In Dublin.

In the early summer of 1993, Eames travelled south to meet Albert Reynolds, who was working on the draft of a paper based on the thinking of John Hume and Gerry Adams, who had been working together with their respective parties on a solution since 1988. The document they drew up, generally known as 'Hume-Adams', outlined the nationalist and republican solution to the problem. Reynolds showed his version of it to the Archbishop, who was horrified that it was 'greener than green' and told the Taoisach it was 'a recipe for disaster'. 'I don't see one single piece of evidence in this draft you've shown me that leads me to believe that the importance of consent is there,' he told Reynolds. He said its contents would never be acceptable to the Protestant majority. 'If you really feel that you can make a long-term contribution to peace in Northern Ireland,' he went on, 'please think again and more deeply.' Reynolds said he would.

But in six bloody days in October 1993, all was almost lost and Northern Ireland came as close to the frequently prophesied civil war as it had ever been. The Chief Constable said the province was staring into the abyss – and Sir Hugh Annesley was not one to exaggerate. On Saturday 23 October, with the Shankill Road crowded with shoppers, the IRA planned to blow up what it thought was the leadership of the UFF, and its notorious West Belfast Commander, Johnny 'Mad Dog' Adair, whom it believed would be meeting in a room above a fish shop. The room was the office of the Loyalist Prisoners' Association (LPA) and Saturday morning was the time it was usually busy as money was paid out to prisoners' families. Two IRA men from Ardoyne carried a bomb into the fish shop with customers at the counter and it exploded prematurely, killing one of the bombers, Thomas Begley (23), and nine Protestant civilians, including the owner and his daughter. But the IRA's intelligence was hopelessly wrong and Adair and the UFF's high command were not there. The Shankill had never seen anything like it since the IRA's bomb attack on the Balmoral Furnishing Company in 1971. Billy 'Twister' McQuiston, who had recently been released from the Maze, was on the Shankill Road at the time doing some LPA business – but not in the LPA office – and had just gone into the pub on the next corner. 'Twister' had witnessed the Balmoral explosion all those years before and had helped rescue the wounded and dying. This time it was even worse.

We were only in the door and the explosion went off. The windows of the bar came in and automatically everyone there knew that the LPA offices had been blown up. So everyone ran out into the street. You couldn't see in front of you. There was dust everywhere. As the dust started to clear, everyone started to pull at the rubble. There were people in there. There was total confusion. People were on top of each other trying to dig people out. There were women screaming and crying and people walking about dazed. There was total mayhem and so I started shouting, 'Look, form a line and get back from there!' because part of the building was still just hanging there and I thought it was about to come down. Then my father came out of the building and came over to me. He was crying. He had just helped to drag someone out and he was covered in blood. He was numb and he just looked at me and the tears were rolling down his cheeks and he walked away.

I asked 'Twister' how people felt. 'Anybody on the Shankill Road that day from a Boy Scout to a granny, if you'd given them a gun they would have gone out and retaliated,' he said. Loyalists were even further outraged when they saw Gerry Adams carrying the coffin at the funeral of Thomas Begley, the dead IRA bomber.

The horror was not over. Two days later the UVF shot dead a seventy-two-year-old Catholic, Sean Fox, at his home in Glengormley, and the following day the UFF killed two Catholics, James Cameron (54) and Mark Rodgers (28), at the council depot where they worked in Andersonstown. But the worst was still to come. On Halloween night, 30

October 1993, masked UFF gunmen in boiler suits burst into the Rising Sun bar in the village of Greysteel just outside Derry, shouted 'Trick or treat' and opened up on the customers with an AK 47 and a Browning pistol. Yet again, as at Sean Graham's betting shop, the weapons had almost certainly come from the Lebanese consignment. Six Catholics, one of them aged eighty-one, and one Protestant were mown down. Billy McQuiston shed no tears. 'On that particular day, if the UFF had walked into a picture house or something on the Falls Road and killed 300 people I would have been quite happy to be honest with you at that particular point in time.' Among loyalists, that feeling was not unique. Roy Magee was devastated. These were the men he had trusted and with whom he felt he was finally making political progress. 'Greysteel blasted it out of the water completely,' he said. He could not understand, despite the Shankill bomb, how the UFF could have done what they did. He told them he was finished but they pleaded with him to come back. Eventually he did. Archbishop Eames also courageously stayed on board, recognizing that the alternative to not talking was unthinkable.

But the spirits of the two clergymen were lifted six weeks later when, on 15 December 1993, the British and Irish Prime Ministers, John Major and Albert Reynolds, stood together outside Number Ten and announced they had agreed a set of principles for a settlement. The document became known as the Downing Street Declaration. To Eames' and Magee's delight, they saw the principle of 'consent' enshrined five times within it. It was a meticulously balanced document with its every word weighed and measured by mandarins in London and Dublin. For nationalists the principle of 'self-determination' was established but, with separate referendums to be held North and South, only on the basis of consent. This meant that a majority of people in the North had to agree to any final settlement. But when Archbishop Eames next spoke to the CLMC leaders he was greeted not with relief but grave concern. Shortly before the Downing Street Declaration had been announced, word had leaked out via the incomparable Eamonn Mallie of the Belfast press corps that the British Government had been conducting a top-secret dialogue with the IRA. It was the culmination of the process that Michael Oatley had begun when he first met Martin McGuinness in January 1991. Immediately loyalists felt that the British Government had done a secret deal behind their backs. To reassure them – and presumably himself – the Archbishop went to Downing Street to see the Prime Minister. 'I looked John Major straight in the eye and said, "Can I go back to these people and can I tell them that you have not done a secret deal with the IRA? Can you give me your word of honour? I am an Archbishop and you're Prime Minister of the United Kingdom." I simply said, "Please, John, don't lie to me." He looked me straight in the eye and said, "You have my word." I said, "That's all I want. History will judge us both." I went back and I met them [the CLMC] again and said, "I am convinced the Prime Minister of Great Britain has not done a secret deal with the IRA," and they said, "That's all we want to know." End of question.'

The crisis that had almost brought the province to the brink of civil war was over and now, with the Downing Street Declaration in place, the stage seemed set for the final stretch of the road to peace. But the prize was still a long way off.

Chapter Nineteen

Ceasefire

In the wake of the Shankill bomb, an unidentified figure gave an interview to Ulster Television. The man was shown in silhouette and introduced as a spokesman for the UVF. The interview was brief but the message was clear: the slaughter was madness and both the IRA and the loyalists had to stop. 'Please lay down your weapons,' he said. 'The Loyalist paramilitaries have said they will lay down theirs. Call their bluff. Let our people move on together.' The shadowy figure was David Ervine making his television debut. I asked him how he felt at the time.

> Angry. Filled with anger and a sense of frustration because it was evident to me that we could do this to each other all day and twice on a Sunday – the Shankill bomb, Greysteel. You could effectively do that to each other any time you liked. That's how easy it would be. But where does that take us? Where does it ever end? Somebody had to put it up to the Provos and say, 'Where do you think you're taking us? Where is this going to go? Where does it end?' And I only hope that that interview was in some small way a contribution to maybe making people think, 'What are we doing here?' because that's what it was sent out to day. 'We're going over the edge here. Do we have to?'

But although David Ervine was the voice of the UVF talking about peace in that interview and basically saying to the IRA, 'If you stop, we will', the UVF was preparing for an intensification of the 'war' in case Ervine's plea came to nothing. It had sent one of its men to Europe to try to procure more arms with sights set on the Eastern European countries that had been Soviet satellites until the Berlin Wall came down. They were awash with arms desperately short of hard currency and some people there were ready to do business with anyone, even with loyalist 'terrorists' from Northern Ireland if they had the network and the money. Poland was the UVF's main hunting ground. It not only had arms but ports on its northern coast from which they could be shipped. On 24 November 1993, almost a week to the day after the Shankill bomb, a Polish freighter, the MV *Inowroclaw*, docked at Teesport in Cleveland on the north-east coast of England. It had left Gdynia on 19 November, called at London two days later and then made its way up the coast to its destination. The ship was bound to attract the attention of customs officers as their intelligence records showed that it had a history of smuggling vodka and caviar. When they searched the vessel and opened container number 2030255, they found 'ceramic tiles' bound for a builder in East Belfast. To customs *cognoscenti*, the words 'ceramic tiles' might have rung a bell. Inside the container they found not vodka and caviar but over 300 AK 47s, 20 tons of Semtex explosive and 60,000 rounds of ammunition. It was the biggest arms seizure ever made in Britain.

The weapons had been bound for the UVF in Belfast, who were eagerly awaiting delivery of the goods that had cost them over £200,000. They never got the arms or their money back. The operation was a 'sting' set up by MI5. Apparently, the UVF 'buyer' had been 'clocked' in a European capital, possibly Paris, and set up by the intelligence services, who had persuaded their Polish counterparts not only to go along with the sting but to help them set it up. The Polish Government was not overly enthusiastic at the prospect of being faced with the outcry that would result from Polish arms being found in the hands of loyalist terrorists, but eager to please its future NATO ally, it agreed to go along with the plan. Whether or not the Lebanese consignment had been anticipated by MI5 and MI6 in 1987, a sufficient number of AK 47s and Browning 9mm pistols had got through to cause mayhem at Milltown cemetery, Sean Graham's and Greysteel. British Intelligence could not take the same risk again and apparently assured the Polish authorities that the weapons would never get to Northern Ireland. They were true to their word. MI5's Polish equivalent, UOP (Urzad Ochrony Panstwa), helped set up a front company called 'Eloks' based in Warsaw in a small flat rented by an elderly pensioner who was unlikely to know much about Northern Ireland let alone black-market arms.[1] The weapons were duly ordered by the UVF emissary, supplied apparently from Polish Government stores and shipped to Gdynia by a reputable Warsaw company called 'Fast Baltic'. It was a perfect sting.

But what was the point when no arrests of loyalists were made, although the intelligence services would have known the UVF personnel involved? The likely explanation is that to have let the consignment run through to Belfast would have been too risky given what had happened to the Lebanese shipment, and it was out of the question anyway because of the undertaking that MI5 or MI6 appeared to have given the Polish Government. An even greater danger would have been the risk of exposing the MI5 source who had no doubt put them on to the case in the first place. The protection of that person's identity and life would have been the top priority. Nevertheless, as one of its senior commanders admitted to me, the UVF *was* damaged, not only by losing a large amount of money – and never getting the arms – but by the internal suspicions aroused by the sting that there was a British agent, a Brian Nelson-type figure, within their ranks. Paranoia in the ranks of the enemy is a powerful intelligence weapon. Disappointed but defiant, the UVF issued a statement saying that it wished 'to make it clear to the people of Ulster that whilst it was a logistical setback, it in no way diminishes our ability nor our determination, to carry on the war against the IRA. For as long as we are in receipt of the support of the loyalist people, in whatever form, so we will continue to put at risk our Volunteers to scour the world for arms to be used in their defence and for that of our country.'[2]

Some six months later, such protestations sounded empty as the UVF matched the UFF in blatant sectarian savagery. On 16 June 1994, one of the UVF's senior battalion commanders, 'Lt Colonel' Trevor King, was standing on a corner of the Shankill Road close by the empty space where the fish shop had once been. King was talking to two other men, one of them, Colin Craig, also a member of the UVF, who was posthumously disgraced in the eyes of the organization as an informer. As a result his name was removed from the Old Boyne Island Heroes' bannerette. A car drove by and INLA gunmen shot the three men dead. The Reverend Roy Magee was in the UVF's headquarters about a hundred yards away at the time discussing business for an imminent meeting of the CLMC.

> With some others, I ran down to where the men were. One was already dead and the others were in a very, very bad physical state. The road was in pandemonium at that stage. You could see that the leadership of the UVF was quite naturally very, very broken and disturbed about the shooting of their colleague. He was a senior commander. Trevor King was on a life-support machine and lived for three weeks or so. He himself took the decision that the life-support machine should be turned off, which was traumatic. I had visited him two days or so before and I was at the hospital that night when it happened. One doesn't easily forget those moments.

Retaliation was expected and came two days later at 10.20 on a Saturday night when most of the province was glued to its television sets watching Ireland play Italy in America in the football World Cup. UVF gunmen burst into the Heights Bar in the tiny County Down village of Loughinisland and opened fire on the customers who were having a drink and watching the match. Six Catholics were gunned down, one of whom, Barney Green, was eighty-seven years old. People who thought Greysteel had represented the

ultimate evil now saw it repeated. And they believed the Downing Street
Declaration was supposed to bring peace. To the vast majority, the attack
was incomprehensible, but to the UVF it was simply what they – and the
UFF – had been doing for years, retaliating for an attack on them or what
they saw as their community by killing innocent Catholics.

David Ervine, who had put so much effort into trying to bring the
slaughter to an end, now saw his own organization doing what he was
trying to stop. 'It was the worst day of my life,' he told me. 'I don't know
how I could remotely describe how I felt or how many around me felt. We
really felt we were getting somewhere. It was beginning to happen,
beginning to fall into place – then bang! I thought we'd lost it. I didn't
think that there was any point in being someone who was saying we need a
ceasefire. I just thought it had gone. But that day it became evident that it
hadn't gone – it hadn't. There were people who were saying, "This is *not*
the end – don't see this as you think you see it." I have to be circumspect
about my comments, but I'd have to say that very quickly it became not
something that was to damage us but something that was effectively to be
an impetus for a ceasefire.' In coded language Ervine appeared to be saying
that it was all part of the loyalist strategy to escalate the 'war' to bring it to
an end. It is by no means certain that the killings were authorized by the
UVF leadership because to give such an order would seem to have made
little sense, despite what David Ervine was implying, in the light of the
peace moves that were still ongoing backstage. In the event of an 'enemy'
attack, local UVF units had general autonomy to retaliate against what they
deemed to be an appropriate target and this is what may have happened at
Loughinisland. One UVF figure told me that the intelligence they had
been given was faulty and they had expected to find IRA men in the
Heights Bar. He said the intelligence had always been good before. It
might well have been an excuse or there might have been something in
what he said. It was no consolation to the dead.

Chris Hudson, who, with David Ervine, had done so much to push the
peace process forward, was equally horrified. 'David contacted me and I
really told him that I felt like walking away from it because I felt that they
[the UVF] had used honeyed words. I was beginning not to believe what
they were saying and felt that maybe I was just being sucked into
something that was false. I had to question what I was doing from the
point of view of meeting with these people [again] because this was just too
horrendous to comprehend. However, David reassured me that what he
had initially said to me was true, that what they were trying to achieve was
peace and for me not to walk away from it. So I agreed to meet them again
to continue the process even though I was going to attend a mass in
Loughinisland for the six men who were murdered. I found it extremely

difficult.' Archbishop Eames also thought of walking away, feeling that he too was wasting his time. 'I said to myself, "How can this be when they are talking peace?" And so within hours of that dreadful atrocity happening I was in touch with them to say, "Explain this to me because if you don't explain it to my satisfaction, you can forget about it." I understood later that in fact before I tried to contact them they were already trying to contact me to say, "Look, if you can possibly understand . . ." I think the words were "We did not commission this" or "We did not authorize this", some words like that. "You must believe us" and "This does not thwart our intentions in talking to you." At any rate, whatever words were used to me, my contacts were sufficiently sure in their own minds that it was worth going on with it.' Archbishop Eames decided to carry on. 'I had to because of my Christian belief,' he told me. 'Here was an opportunity to stop the killing, to save a few lives, to stop the mayhem. I couldn't change my mind then. I had to go on.' It is easy to forget the great courage shown and the risks that all took – and to the same degree on the republican and nationalist side too – to bring about the real possibility of peace.

After the horror of Loughinisland, the CLMC was on the brink of seizing the initiative and declaring its own ceasefire ahead of the IRA, partly to demonstrate that it had its own agenda and was not simply responding to the Republican Movement's. But the killing by the IRA of three prominent UDA/UFF members – Ray Smallwoods, Joe Bratty and Raymond Elder – in the weeks after Loughinisland put an end to the idea. To have declared a ceasefire after this would have been seen as a sign of weakness. Bratty and Elder were shot together on the Ormeau Road on 31 July 1994. Bratty had been charged in connection with the UFF attack on Sean Graham's betting shop but the charges were subsequently withdrawn.[3] Smallwoods, who was shot dead in Lisburn on 11 July 1994, was a spokesman for the Ulster Democratic Party and a close friend and political colleague of David Adams. Smallwoods had been gaoled for the attempted murder of Bernadette McAliskey by the UFF in 1981, but on his release from the Maze prison, he had continued the political work that Andy Tyrie, Glen Barr and John McMichael had begun with 'Beyond the Religious Divide' (1979) and 'Common Sense' (1987). When I asked David Adams about the death of his friend, he almost broke down. 'On a personal level, I was really devastated as were my family, who knew him very well. I think republicans felt that Ray was an articulate voice for loyalism. He posed a real danger in terms of having a real articulate political voice against them in the situation that they saw developing. They felt also that by murdering Ray, it would almost ensure that the UDA and UFF couldn't move to a ceasefire situation.' In political terms David Adams, like all his fellow political/paramilitary colleagues, believed that the strategy of escalating the 'war' to end it was working. 'The intensification of the UFF's campaign helped drive republicans to a position where they decided that the war had to be brought to an end. They had created a situation whereby those who they had been attacking for years had begun to attack them back in the same terms. To say the least, I think it was unsettling for them and I think their own communities were starting to put heavy pressure on Sinn Fein and the IRA to start thinking in terms of bringing their campaign to an end.'

On 30 August 1994, the IRA finally announced a 'cessation of military operations' from midnight that night. The loyalist paramilitaries' offensive, although republicans would deny it, undoubtedly played some part in the decision. Despite graffiti that sprung up in loyalist areas accepting 'The Unconditional Surrender of the IRA',[4] the IRA remained undefeated. The first building block of the final stage of the peace process was in place. It was now a case of fixing the second – the loyalist ceasefire.

By this time, late summer of 1994, the CLMC and their political associates in the UDP and PUP had asked Andy Tyrie and Glen Barr to come out of retirement and with the benefit of their long experience give advice at this critical stage in the process. Both men agreed. At the beginning of September 1994, shortly after the start of the IRA ceasefire, the loyalists called a three-day conference at Belfast's Park Avenue Hotel to discuss strategy in response to the IRA's cessation. But matters other than those of life and death were discussed, such as the question of funding. If the new loyalist political parties were to get their message across, they needed respectable money to do so. Barr and Tyrie were asked if they could help in any practical way, given the extensive contacts they had forged over the years, and they said they would see what they could do. They approached a Catholic businessman in Belfast whom they had known for a long time and met him in his office. 'He is a very devout Christian person who's always believed in supporting causes that are worthwhile and to bring about compromise and reconciliation,' Barr told me. 'He indicated yes, that money could be made available and was prepared to make £25,000 available to them and actually gave us £6,000 there and then in cash.'

On the spot?
On the spot, which we brought back and gave to the representative of the UDP.
With what words?
He was just delighted with anything that was gong to bring about peace and reconciliation and he certainly wanted to make his contribution to it and wished us all the best. He was prepared to do as much as he possibly could to help.

Glen Barr told me that the Catholic businessman was true to his word and the balance of £19,000 appears to have followed later as promised.

But the UVF and UDA/UFF could not contemplate calling a ceasefire without consulting their prisoners in the Maze. The first vote among the UDA and UFF prisoners showed that there was great hostility to the idea and ominously the opposition was led by the organization's Officer Commanding in the Maze, Adrian 'Adie' Bird. When the initial vote was taken, only three prisoners were in favour of calling a ceasefire and the rest were against. The general feeling was, 'Why should we let the IRA off the hook when we've got them on the run?' It reflected slogans that began to appear on some of the walls inside the prison and out: 'Stuff your Doves'. However, after much politicking and manoeuvring, engineered largely by the UDA/UFF on the Shankill Road, the vote was turned round. In the words of one of the loyalist prisoners I spoke to, who was not from Belfast, there was a coup within the gaol, Bird was ousted and Johnny Adair took over as effective OC. At the time Adair was in the Maze on remand awaiting trial on the new charge of 'directing terrorism' and, because he was on a separate remand wing, was apparently communicating with men on the sentenced wings via mobile phone. When, with Adair now in charge, a subsequent vote was held on the ceasefire the tables were turned and only around a dozen prisoners opposed it. I understand there was no or little debate. Adair was found guilty on 6 September 1995 and sentenced to sixteen years. Like Michael Stone, John Adair was one of the last prisoners to be released under the Good Friday Agreement.

Finally, in the historic setting of Fernhill House in Protestant West Belfast, where Sir Edward Carson had reviewed the West Belfast contingent of the UVF, the Combined Loyalist Military Command declared its ceasefire. Gusty Spence made the announcement. At his side were Gary McMichael, David Adams and John White of the UDP and David Ervine, William 'Plum' Smith and Jim McDonald of the PUP. The military commanders who had engaged in the critical dialogue with Archbishop Eames, and had made the ceasefire possible, chose not to stand in the spotlight. It was an emotional moment and as historic as the location in which it was held. Gusty Spence read the prepared announcement.

In all sincerity, we offer to the loved ones of all innocent victims over the past twenty-five years abject and true remorse. No words of ours will compensate for the intolerable suffering they have undergone during the conflict.

Let us firmly resolve to respect our differing views of freedom, culture and aspiration and never again permit our political circumstances to degenerate into bloody warfare.

We are on the threshold of a new and exciting beginning with our battles in the future being political battles, fought on the side of honesty, decency and democracy against the negativity of mistrust, misunderstanding and malevolence, so that, together, we can bring forth a wholesome society in which our children, and their children, will know the meaning of true peace.[5]

The significance of the fact that is was Gusty Spence who made the announcement was not lost on David Ervine. 'Here was the alpha and omega, perceived by many to be the first of the violent men of this recent era, reading out a statement that pulled the curtain down, or we hoped would pull the curtain down, on a brutal and awful past.' Did Gusty Spence speak for David Ervine? 'Absolutely. Without doubt,' he said. The Deputy Leader of the Ulster Unionist Party, John Taylor, who had lived through the Troubles with Gusty Spence, was also aware of the significance of the loyalists' ceasefire and the impact of their long and bloody campaign.

The loyalist paramilitaries achieved something which perhaps the security forces would never have achieved, and that was they were a significant contribution to the IRA finally accepting that they couldn't win.
Why do you say that?
The loyalist paramilitaries, of course, were illegal organizations operating outside the law and we disapproved of that. However, it has to be said – and sometimes people don't like to face this reality and some people say you shouldn't say it, but I always think it's important to say what is correct – that the loyalist paramilitaries, in their illegal activity, actually began to overtake the IRA as being the major paramilitary organization and terrorist organization in Northern Ireland. Indeed in the year before the ceasefire by the IRA the loyalist paramilitaries had killed more people that year than the IRA. So I think this got a message over to the IRA that no longer were they just going to be the one and only terrorist organization. There was a comparable one now on the loyalist side which was actually being more effective, and I think that would help people realize that there is going to be no victory in terrorism. Paramilitary killings are not going to win the day in Northern Ireland.

Remarkably, at the time of writing, the loyalist ceasefire has lasted – with some notable murderous infringements – for well over four years despite intense provocation such as the 'Real' IRA's bomb in August 1998 that slaughtered twenty-nine innocent people in Omagh. The IRA's ceasefire did not.

Chapter Twenty

Good Friday

In the early autumn of 1994, with the IRA and loyalist ceasefires in place, I was talking to a senior British official who had been one of the backstage architects of the peace process. To my surprise he told me it would be 'about five years' before the process on which he and his colleagues had worked so tirelessly would come to fruition. He warned that there would be many difficulties ahead and doubted that the violence was over for good. He clearly had a good crystal ball.

The first hurdle for the Prime Minister, John Major, who had welcomed both ceasefires, was to keep the process moving by getting the mainstream unionist parties, James Molyneaux's Ulster Unionists and Ian Paisley's DUP, to go along with the process and become involved. Ian Paisley flatly refused to have anything to do with it, believing the Government was dancing to the IRA's tune. At one stage he found himself being escorted from the Prime Minister's room after refusing to accept John Major's word that no deal had been struck with the IRA. The meeting had been cut short. Paisley returned to his tent where he waited for the opportunity to ambush his political opponents should they, like the Government, be enticed into what Paisley was convinced was the IRA's trap.

As a result of the secret dialogue conducted through an MI5 officer in the lead up to the Downing Street Declaration in December 1993, the IRA had been encouraged to call a ceasefire with the prospect of Sinn Fein being admitted to all-party talks that would be set up in an attempt to resolve the conflict. Gerry Adams and Martin McGuinness, who, with the close circle of republicans around them, had been the main advocates of the Republican Movement's strategy, were anxious to gain their admission ticket as soon as possible to demonstrate to the doubters in the IRA – and there were a good many – that the Government was delivering on its assurances. For months there was no political movement and the Provisionals became increasingly restless as they believed one hurdle after another was being placed in their way. The first hurdle, planted in their path by both Government and Unionists who wanted to cause the

Republican Movement as much discomfort as possible, was the insistence that the IRA should declare that their ceasefire was 'permanent'. This the IRA refused to do, the reality being that only the supreme authority of a General Army Convention – consisting of delegates from all IRA units throughout Ireland – could do that, and even then it could not speak for future generations. In the end the Government accepted the 'permanency' of the IRA's ceasefire as 'a working assumption'. No such pressure was ever put on the loyalist paramilitaries and their political parties.

But the biggest hurdle of all was what became known as 'decommissioning', the handing over of 'terrorist' weapons. It was the issue that was to haunt the peace process for months and years to come. Again, although it was meant to apply to both sides since loyalists too had amassed a formidable and deadly arsenal of weapons and explosives over the years, all the pressure was placed on republicans. When I spoke to senior Provisionals around that time, they made it clear that the IRA would surrender 'not one bullet'. 'Surrender' was the apposite word. That was the republican fear: that handing over weapons would be seen as surrender and, as the IRA pointed out, it had not been defeated. Republicans also reminded people that in 'conflict resolution situations' all over the world, decommissioning had never been part of the process. The ANC in South Africa had never decommissioned its arsenal, nor had SWAPO in Namibia nor ZANU in Rhodesia nor the PLO in Gaza and the West Bank. The IRA, which had never in its history handed over weapons at the end of its several campaigns, was not going to act any differently now. The arguments became fierce. The logic of the Government and the unionists was that if the Republican Movement was sincere about wanting peace and if, even as a working assumption, its ceasefire was 'permanent', then it had no need of guns. To refuse to hand them over, its critics charged, was proof of the Provisionals' insincerity. Ian Paisley had a field day. Once more, the UVF and the UDA/UFF got off lightly, although they too had said they would not hand over a single weapon. In reality, decommissioning was more a political issue than a security one. Even if the IRA and the loyalists handed in every weapon and ounce of Semtex or Powergel (the loyalists' equivalent) in their lockers, they could still go out and buy more. Furthermore, most of the IRA's 'big boomers', the huge bombs that had devastated the City of London in 1992 and 1993, were made with home-made explosives (HME), a potent mixture of fertilizers and chemicals, both of which were readily available and produced a very large bang. Even the Chief Constable, Sir Hugh Annesley, told me he was surprised it had been allowed to become such a dominant issue. 'It was perfectly clear from the intelligence assessments that the Provisionals were not going to hand in their arms,' he said. 'In pragmatic terms, the issue of decommissioning was less important for the security forces than it was on the political front'.[1] For both sides, the issue became a powerful symbol, and the more it was discussed the more intractable it seemed to become. The best solution, some wise observers said, was a four-letter word – rust. On 8 March 1995, the Northern Ireland Secretary, Sir Patrick Mayhew, seemed to make a resolution even more unlikely when he said that the IRA would have to decommission some of its weapons at the *beginning* of the all-party talks as 'a tangible, confidence-building measure'.[2] Again, the emphasis was on republicans not loyalists – not that they minded watching their enemies being given a hard time.

In December 1995, with President Clinton about to arrive in Belfast, well over a year into the ceasefires and with no sign of political progress, John Major opted for a 'twin-track' approach in the hope of putting decommissioning on the back burner while talks about talks continued. An International Body was established to try to solve the problem that refused to go away and draw up a list of principles of non-violence to which all those participating in the proposed all-party talks would have to agree. The chairman was the former United States Senator, George Mitchell, who was to work alongside General John de Chastelain, the Canadian Chief of the Defence Staff, and Harry Holkeri, a former Finnish Prime Minister. These three wise men were posed a difficult task and when they accepted the challenge had no idea their contracts would be so long. Senator Mitchell did have some experience of Northern Ireland as President Clinton had appointed him his Special Adviser on economic initiatives in the province. 'It was supposed to be for six months, a day or two a month and maybe one trip to Northern Ireland and that would be it', he told me. 'Little did I know what was in store for me.' When he arrived in Northern Ireland, he knew that with the ceasefires in place he faced a unique situation. 'The loyalist ceasefire was very important, as was the IRA ceasefire. In the past, there had been many efforts to bring about a resolution of the conflict but never before had there been, at the same time, negotiations *and* a ceasefire. There had been negotiations without a ceasefire. There had been a ceasefire without negotiations, but it was not until most recently that both were able to exist at the same time.' Decommissioning was the knot he and his colleagues had to untie to end the stalemate and move forward the situation that the twin ceasefires had made possible. Mitchell knew it would not be easy.

The Unionists quite rightly wanted some reassurance. They did not want to have talks occur in a setting in which the threat of violence or the use of violence influenced the negotiations. That's the reason for the request for prior decommissioning. It became obvious to us, very soon into our consultation, that prior decommissioning, however desirable, was simply not a practical approach. It wasn't going to happen. The British Government wanted prior decommissioning and they wanted inclusive negotiations and it became clear that they could not have both. And so we sought a way to provide to the Unionists the reassurance that they were appropriately seeking to come into the talks – that there would not be negotiations under the gun, so to speak, or subject to the threat or use of violence. And it was from that process that the [Mitchell] 'principles' emerged. We thought that we could get as a requirement to participate in the negotiations a commitment to principles of democracy and non-violence and thereby provide the assurance and eliminate the threat of violence as an influence on the negotiation process. We made that suggestion in our report and those principles of course were eventually embraced by the British and Irish Governments, as the joint sponsors of the negotiations, and became a requirement for participation in the talks.

The issue was fudged but it refused to go away. By February 1996, eighteen months into the IRA ceasefire without any sign of political progress, the Provisionals decided they had had enough. They were tired, according to their analysis, of being strung along by a Government and Prime Minister whose wafer-thin parliamentary majority at Westminster meant their survival depended on Unionist support. However neat the theory, the reality was far more complex than that. John Major realized that getting Sinn Fein to the negotiating table was one thing, getting the Ulster Unionists to join them was another. The Prime Minister pursued a hard line, not just because he believed in what he said – that if the IRA was genuinely serious, decommissioning should not pose a problem – but to ensure that in the end Unionists would join in too. He had to create the circumstances in which they would do so. Without it, the peace process simply would not work. But to the IRA, the issue was black and white. At 7.10 p.m. on 9 February 1996, the IRA exploded a huge bomb that had been placed in a vehicle in the car park of a building near Canary Wharf in London's Docklands. It killed two men, injured more than a hundred and caused £85 million worth of damage.[3] Showing great restraint, the loyalists did not respond. Perhaps the fact that the bomb was in England – as were the IRA's other attacks, such as the one that devastated the centre of Manchester on 17 June 1996 – made it easier for the UVF and UDA/UFF to resist the temptation to take out their guns.

By the early summer of 1996, the frozen political process had at last started to move. On 30 May elections were held to a Peace Forum from which it was intended to draw those who would finally participate in all-party talks. Although Sinn Fein won seventeen seats, the party was automatically ruled out of any such talks because the IRA had returned to its campaign and the inclusion of its political wing would have been a breach of the Mitchell Principles. The complex voting system was deliberately engineered to guarantee the inclusion of the UDP and PUP and other fringe parties like the increasingly visible Women's Coalition. The PUP and the UDP won two seats each. Compared with the Ulster Unionists' thirty, the DUP's twenty-four, the SDLP's twenty-one and the Alliance Party's seven, the political representatives of the UVF and the UDA/UFF were a small minority – but, critically, they were there. To the loyalists' military commanders, their strategy had not been in vain.

But one event threatened to disrupt the progress that now appeared to be gradually getting under way. The name became synonymous with loyalist defiance – Drumcree. The issue of the Orangemen's return march from their church service at Drumcree had first surfaced in 1985 when their traditional route was changed from the nationalist flashpoint of Obins Street to the nearby Garvaghy Road. But only the route, not the problem, had been moved, as most of the Garvaghy Road was nationalist too, running through estates largely controlled by Sinn Fein. It was a confrontation waiting to happen. As Orangemen saw the IRA call a ceasefire and the British Government seemingly follow a 'green' agenda, Drumcree became the issue around which all loyalist frustrations exploded. Frustrations on the Garvaghy Road exploded too as its residents saw Sinn Fein excluded from the political process because, in their eyes, the IRA had been forced back to the 'war' by British and unionist intransigence. The previous year, in July 1995, there had been violence as Orangemen were prohibited from returning down the Garvaghy Road until they finally agreed to do so in silence, without the thunder of fifes and drums. When they reached the bottom of the road and the haven of Protestant territory, there were triumphant scenes of wild rejoicing led by Ian Paisley and the local Unionist MP for Upper Bann, David Trimble. To nationalists, it meant that the 'croppies' (ancient Irish peasants) had been forced to lie down. As July 1996 approached, Drumcree looked like being even more explosive. Joel Patton, a member of Vanguard in the seventies, of the Ulster Clubs in the eighties and in the nineties the founder of a radical movement known as the 'Spirit of Drumcree', explained what Drumcree meant to Protestants.

In many ways it's not about 800 Orangemen marching down a road. It's about the survival of a culture, of an identity, of a way of life. It's about our ability to still hold on to parts of the country. The Ulster people have their backs to the wall. They're in retreat. They have been chased from quite a large area of the country and they feel that [Portadown], the citadel of Orangism, where Orangism was born 200 years ago, that is the place where they want to take their stand. Drumcree represents that.

But the vast majority of people cannot understand why marching a few hundred yards down a road is such an issue.

But it isn't about marching a few hundred yards down a road. It's about the freedom of people to come from a church into a town, a Protestant town where they feel that they can express their culture in an open and free manner. They believe intensely that if it's taken away from them there, then there isn't anywhere in Ulster that will be safe. If they're beaten in Portadown then they believe that they can be beaten anywhere and that's why I don't think they're about to give in.

Again, in July 1996, the Orangemen were prohibited from marching down the Garvaghy Road and this time the mid-Ulster UVF, under its charismatic leader, Billy Wright, were present in force on the ground. Again, as in 1995, Orangemen from all over the province flocked to the fields around Drumcree church to put pressure on the authorities to let them through. There was intelligence that Billy Wright and his UVF heavies were about to light the fuse by attacking the police and army who were blocking the Orangemen's way, which would have been risking another 'Bloody Sunday' in which Protestants not Catholics would have been the victims. I was in the church hall at Drumcree at the time, drinking tea supplied by the army of Orangemen's wives who were providing sandwiches and scones for their menfolk, dug in for the long wait outside. Suddenly the crowd inside the hall parted as a short, muscular man with close-cropped hair, gold earring, crisp white tee-shirt and neatly pressed jeans walked in with two much larger men who were clearly his bodyguards. It was Billy Wright. Young boys and girls looked on in awe as he passed by without a word and went upstairs to a room at the back of the hall. His minders sat at the top of the stairs outside. Shortly afterwards, David Trimble entered the hall, attracting comparatively little attention, and went upstairs to meet Wright. I was astonished to see it happen as Trimble had always said he would never talk to 'terrorists'. The meeting went on a long time. Despite what some might have thought, I suspected Trimble was asking Wright and his men to 'cool it' and not ignite the powder keg that was waiting to explode outside. If that was the case, he succeeded. At Drumcree no guns were in sight. But blood was spilled elsewhere.

On 8 July 1996, the body of a Roman Catholic taxi driver, Michael McGoldrick, was found a few miles away near Lurgan. Although no organization claimed responsibility, few had little doubt he had been shot dead by Billy Wright's UVF. Shortly afterwards, Wright was stood down by the UVF's Brigade Staff in Belfast, perhaps more for internal political reasons than because his men might have broken the ceasefire. When the Portadown unit was ordered to stand down, Wright took most of its members with him and set up a rival organization, the Loyalist Volunteer Force (LVF). Wright was now establishing an alternative centre of power to the UVF in mid-Ulster which, in the eyes of the leadership in Belfast, came close to treason. On 1 September 1996, he was served with an ultimatum: leave the country or be killed. Typically, he treated the threat with the contempt he thought it deserved and stayed in Portadown, enhancing his reputation still further.

In 1996, the Orangemen were finally allowed down the Garvaghy Road with a heavy police escort to protect them from the fury of the nationalist crowd who lined the road behind the police barricades and pelted the marchers with missiles. For the second year running, loyalists were triumphant. The crisis continued for the summers of 1997 and 1998 with each confrontation threatening to derail the peace process. A resolution to the yearly stand-off seemed as remote as agreement on decommissioning. But in 1996, despite the ugliness of the clashes, the killing of Michael McGoldrick, and the continuing IRA violence, John Major pushed ahead, knowing that not to do so would play into the hands of those who wished to destroy the peace process. Shortly afterwards, he invited the PUP and UDP to Downing Street for talks. On the fine, sunny morning of 22 July a smiling delegation consisting of John White, Gary McMichael, David Ervine and Hugh Smyth walked into Number Ten for an hour's meeting with the Prime Minister. He was anxious to keep the loyalist ceasefire intact and perhaps show the Republican Movement that the Government was prepared to engage in dialogue with 'terrorists' once they had put down their guns. Encouragingly for John Major, the sky did not fall in at the sight of John White, who had savagely murdered Senator Paddy Wilson and Irene Andrews in 1973, and his colleagues walking cheerily into Downing Street, smartly dressed in suits, collars and ties. For John White and the process itself it was a historic moment that showed that given the absence of violence, nothing was ruled out. In previous decades many other 'terrorist' leaders from Britain's former colonies and elsewhere had walked through the doors of Number Ten; now those from Northern Ireland were doing the same. It took courage on John Major's part given his slender parliamentary majority and the fierce opposition he was facing from the Eurosceptic wing of his own party, who felt the same about terrorism as they did about Europe: it should not be dealt with. John White shook hands with John Major.

I certainly felt very proud that I was going there to represent the Loyalist community, and also because of my background. It sort of justified the nature of loyalist violence, that it was political and not criminal. Here was a long-term member of the UFF going to meet the British Prime Minister and despite all the criminalization policy, I think this sent a message clearly to people like myself that the conflict they were caught up in was political and wasn't criminal.

Did the Prime Minister know he was shaking hands with a double murderer?

I think he did because obviously the press homed in on that issue and saw it as a way to divert attention from what that visit was about but I'm certain that he knew. He was well briefed on my background. But I think he also knew of the positive role I was playing in bringing about the loyalist ceasefire in the first place and also sustaining it and bringing the prisoners and the loyalist paramilitaries along the line of political, democratic dialogue rather than violence.

Do you think that there could have been a Good Friday Agreement without the groundwork that John Major had done?

No. I think John Major was under extreme pressure to collapse the talks at a very early stage and I think he held out. Without his determination, there wouldn't have been a conclusion and I think this is something that really hasn't been recognized. He was the man who started the process and endeavoured to persevere through very, very difficult times.

Nevertheless, there was an outcry in the press, although muted in comparison with what it might have been. Most of what had once been Fleet Street, like Major's potential political opponents at Westminster, were broadly supportive of his controversial initiative. The son of Paddy Wilson, John White's victim, was outraged at the sight of his father's murderer being welcomed by John Major. 'How could the British Prime Minister shake hands with a man who knifed my father to death thirty times?' he asked. 'All I can think about when I see that man is how my father must have fought in vain for his life. When I look at his face, I think about the screams of pain he must have listened to when he was mutilating my father. The screams must haunt him . . . mustn't they?'[4]

John Major's efforts to bring the peace process to fruition continued. Talks had got under way at Stormont the previous month, June 1996, under the chairmanship of Senator Mitchell but they were not 'inclusive' since Sinn Fein was excluded because of the resumption of the IRA's campaign, and progress was hampered by the continuing failure to reach agreement on decommissioning. For almost a year the talks dragged on, getting nowhere as the violence continued. The loyalist ceasefire, however, remained intact. On 1 May 1997, Tony Blair took over following Labour's sweeping election victory. With a crushing majority of 179, Tony Blair did not face the problems of parliamentary arithmetic that had so restricted John Major's room to manoeuvre – and not just on Ireland. From the very beginning, Northern Ireland was the priority for the new Prime Minister and his Secretary of State, Dr Maureen 'Mo' Mowlam, who stunned everyone with her energy and unconventional political approach. Whereas her predecessor, Sir Patrick Mayhew, had seemed aloof and patrician, Mo was warm and accessible. She would conduct meetings with her shoes off, rubbing cream on her face. Some thought it was a deliberate act but Mo Mowlam was for real. The province's politicians who had emerged from the streets related to her straight away but the Ulster Unionists, accustomed to the formalities of her predecessor, were not quite sure what to make of her. Tony Blair signalled his commitment to carrying on where John Major had left off by visiting Northern Ireland almost immediately and making it clear that the Government would talk to Sinn Fein once the IRA had reinstated its ceasefire. He also hinted that decommissioning would not become an obstacle.

On 19 July 1997, almost three months after Blair's election victory, the IRA declared its second ceasefire on the basis of the assurances that Sinn Fein had received from the new Government. A date – 15 September 1997 – was set for the resumption of the all-party talks. Now, with Sinn Fein admitted, they were for the first time fully inclusive as the former 'men of violence' from both sides were sitting round the table with the mainstream politicians. With great difficulty and no small degree of political courage, the new leader of the Ulster Unionists, David Trimble, sat down with Sinn Fein's Gerry Adams and Martin McGuinness, although he refused to address them directly. But his own grave reservations were nothing compared with those entertained by many members of his party. Following James Molyneaux's retirement in 1995, David Trimble had won the leadership of the Ulster Unionist Party (UUP) over John Taylor not least because of the highly visible stand he had taken over Drumcree that summer, when television cameras had shown him triumphantly joining hands with Ian Paisley after the Orangemen had finally marched down the Garvaghy Road. But one loyalist politician was not at the table. Two days after the IRA's new ceasefire, Ian Paisley and the DUP walked out in protest at the Government's clear intention to fudge the issue of decommissioning. Once again, Paisley was outside the tent, a dangerous focus for unionist opposition to the road down which Tony Blair and Mo Mowlam were taking the peace process. The 'Big Man' had been written

off many times over almost three decades, but although now in his
seventies he remained a force to be reckoned with. The joke was that
he had had more comebacks than Lazurus. What Paisley had predicted
finally happened when, on 11 December 1997, Adams and McGuinness
walked into Downing Street to meet Tony Blair. They were the first Irish
republican leaders to do so since the legendary IRA leader, Michael
Collins, met the Prime Minister, David Lloyd George, during the Treaty
negotiations of 1921. To Paisley, this encounter between Prime Minister
and 'terrorists' symbolized the British Government's final surrender to the
IRA. He had been sounding the warnings since 1966 and few could say
they had not heard him. But, although now outside, Paisley would remain
a major player in the drama that was about to unfold, triggered by a few
seconds in the Maze prison.

The law had finally caught up with Billy Wright, at whose door popular
myth had laid many atrocities but for which there was little evidence. The
police had charged him with menacing behaviour and he was sentenced to
the H–Blocks of the maze where he demanded – and got – a separate wing
for the other LVF prisoners and those dissident members of the UFF who
had cast their votes against the loyalist ceasefire in 1994. Wright and his
men were moved to H-Block 6 as that was the only available wing at the
time. The other one in the block was already occupied by INLA prisoners.
It was a potentially combustible mixture. Neither the INLA nor the LVF
were on ceasefire. At 9.15 a.m. on 27 December 1997, as Wright was
sitting in a van in the forecourt outside the block waiting to be taken for a
visit, INLA prisoners who had escaped from their wing via the roof
overlooking the exercise yard shot him several times in a few seconds at
point-blank range. Wright died fifty-four minutes later.[5] The gunmen
then returned to their wing and admitted what they had done. The killing
of Billy Wright provoked yet another awful cycle of tit-for-tat killings that
dragged in both the UFF and IRA and resulted in their respective political
parties, the UDP and Sinn Fein, being suspended, albeit temporarily, from
the talks. It was Senator Mitchell's most difficult moment.

I was deeply concerned. I knew immediately that there would be
retaliation. It was inevitable. I think that the setback of December of
1997 was the most difficult of all to take because hopes had been, for
the first time, high. We had got not all but more inclusive negotiations than before with the entry of Sinn Fein into the talks in
September of 1997. We hadn't been able to get agreement on a
preliminary agenda in December of '97. I tried very hard. I changed
the format. I restricted the meetings to just two political leaders. I
made them much less formal and we tried to get an agreement just on

the key questions to be asked and answered and we couldn't even get that. Well, if you can't get agreement on the questions, how can you ever hope to get agreement on the answers? I remember flying home for Christmas in 1997, feeling particularly discouraged because I'd been so hopeful before and then when I got the news – I was in the United States at the time for the Christmas break – of Billy Wright's death, I knew that there were troubled times ahead.

As 1997 drew to a close, the Secretary of State, Mo Mowlam, was faced with a political crisis as well as a security one in the wake of the sectarian killings that Billy Wright's death had provoked. On the evening of his death, the LVF in retaliation shot dead a Catholic, Seamus Dillon, an ex-prisoner working as a doorman at a hotel just outside Dungannon. Four days later, on New Year's Eve, another Catholic, Eddie Treanor, was killed in the Clifton Tavern in North Belfast. At first it was also thought to be the work of Wright's LVF, but forensic tests on the weapon showed that the UFF was responsible. Not only were the UFF's gunmen outside getting restless, but their comrades inside the Maze were on the point of mutiny. On 4 January 1998, the UDA and UFF loyalist prisoners voted by two to one to withdraw support from the peace process and sent out an instruction for the UDP to leave the talks which were about to move to Lancaster House in London.

The leaders of the UDP, Gary McMichael, David Adams and John White, whose influence over the UFF in general and their prisoners in particular was limited, knew the situation was critical. 'We got to a point where we had tried to negotiate with the prisoners who had said that they were withdrawing support from the peace process and quite frankly we'd failed which was an indictment upon us,' McMichael admitted. He travelled to London with his colleagues to see Mo Mowlam in her office and outline to her face to face just how serious the situation was. The Secretary of State instinctively knew her visitors were not bluffing. 'It was a very, very difficult time. Absolutely no doubt about it,' she told me. 'We had infighting then between the loyalist groups, minimal but it was there, and there was a real anger among loyalism that they were getting treated unfairly compared to the nationalists. I think the murder of Billy Wright was symptomatic of those difficulties. It was tough and in the end, it was particularly hard on the UDP and Gary McMichael. By this time, we'd been talking for six months and I was convinced they were serious about wanting to find another way other than the violent route. They said, "The prisoners don't believe us and if we don't take the prisoners with us, we're in very serious trouble." I've seen negotiating ploys of "This is serious" before but this was different. They were seriously in trouble and to say they were "deeply concerned" doesn't express what was almost fear. And they said, "We can't make the prisoners believe what we're saying. You say it to us, but they don't believe us. Will you go and say it to them?" '

The Secretary of State consulted her officials and made the highly controversial decision to go to the Maze and meet Johnny Adair, Michael Stone and the leadership of the UFF in the prison. It was an unprecedented scene: the hard men of the Shankill and East Belfast talking across a table in a bare room in the prison with the Secretary of State. A lot of straight talking was done and, in the end, Mo Mowlam convinced them that there was no 'sell-out' and the Union was safe. Adair and his colleagues were impressed, not only that she had come to meet them on their playing field – which, despite what critics said, was not the purpose of the exercise – but that she had been genuine in what she had said. They believed her and reinstated their support for the UDP and its role in the all-party talks. If Mo Mowlam had not taken the huge political risk of talking to the prisoners face to face – which would probably have been terminal had she not succeeded – the process might well have collapsed. But although the talks were now back on course with all the participants still at the table, violence continued to threaten to tear the peace process apart.

With loyalists once again killing Catholics, the IRA retaliated, concerned that the INLA, that was not on ceasefire and had started the tit-for-tat killings by shooting dead Billy Wright, was presenting itself as the defender of the nationalist community, the role that had first brought the Provisionals into being in 1969. Although the IRA took out its guns again, it never admitted doing so, on the basis of 'no claim, no blame'. The IRA wanted to have it both ways: to maintain the ceasefire which gave Sinn Fein its ticket to the talks and to take reprisals for the loyalist killings whether they be perpetrated by the LVF or the UFF. In one retaliatory shooting on 10 February 1998, the IRA shot dead Robert Dougan, a member of the UDA's South Belfast Brigade, as he sat in a car outside a factory in Dunmurry.[6] Jackie McDonald, who came from the same area as Bobby Dougan, knew him well. He also knew another victim from the South Belfast Brigade, Jim Guiney, who had been shot dead by the INLA three weeks earlier on 19 January outside his carpet shop. Eight hours after the killing, the UFF shot dead a Catholic taxi driver, Larry Brennan (52), as he sat in his cab on the Ormeau Road. McDonald had no problem in justifying the UFF's retaliation.

It's the nature of the beast. Some people would call it a knee-jerk reaction but it's just a product of the times. If somebody attacks us, we have to attack back.

But there was a ceasefire. Your political party, the UDP, is

involved in the talks. The ceasefire is broken and the UFF goes out and starts killing Catholics again.

Yes. Again, I have to repeat, it's the nature of the beast. We developed because of IRA violence. We came into being because of what the IRA was doing to this country. We agreed to hold a ceasefire, but once people attack us, although we are on ceasefire, we still have to respond against the people who attacked us.

As a result of the killings that were a clear breach of the Mitchell Principles, the UDP and Sinn Fein were both suspended from the talks – but for only a few weeks. The UDP walked before it was officially suspended in January 1998 for a month. The UFF admitted responsibility. The IRA never did. Sinn Fein was suspended in February for two weeks. The Government and Senator Mitchell wanted both parties back as soon as possible as there would only have been three legs on the stool. 'The Governments made it clear to me that they regarded an important part of my job description as keeping the process going, keeping hope alive, keeping some optimistic view of it,' he told me. 'Among those who were most insistent about keeping the process going, for precisely the reasons I have suggested, were the loyalist political leaders. Gary McMichael many times said to me, "Senator, you have to keep this process going because the alternative is conflict", as did David Ervine and many others.' Senator Mitchell told me that he regarded David Ervine as 'one of the most impressive political figures I've met, in Northern Ireland or anywhere else. I think he made a very powerful contribution to the process and I think he will be a political leader in Northern Ireland for a long time to come.'

After the suspensions, Senator Mitchell flew back to America, concerned that the talks were increasingly vulnerable to being destabilized by outside violence. He had just been through two meetings in London and Dublin, each of three days, and seen all the valuable time taken up with discussing expulsions rather than an agreement. 'I felt this process would disintegrate unless there is a specific deadline, unless there is a firm commitment to reach an agreement by a certain time. And I recall getting back to my home in the United States and the next day I took out a calendar and I sat and looked at it for a long time, thinking about how and where is the best place to bring this to a conclusion.' Mitchell's first thought was to make Easter Sunday 1998 the deadline on the basis that relating it to some external event, like Easter, helped concentrate minds even more. Then it occurred to him that Easter Sunday would give him no margin for error, so he thought of Easter Saturday, then midnight on Good Friday and finally, to provide the greatest flexibility possible, midnight on Thursday. When he returned to Belfast, he discussed his proposal with all the parties who, to his surprise, responded positively. Midnight on Thursday 9 April was the agreed deadline.

The talks continued with the UDP and Sinn Fein now back again and the violence outside caused by associates of the parties inside largely absent. Predictably, as the deadline approached, there was little progress, and the political temperature inside the talks was raised by a further series of killings by the LVF and INLA, groups who were not on ceasefire, designed to destabilize the process. On 3 March 1998, masked LVF gunmen burst into the Railway Bar in the tiny village of Poyntzpass, County Armagh and shouted, 'On the floor you bastards!' before shooting dead two innocent young men who were having a drink, Philip Allen (34) and Damien Trainor (25). Philip was a Protestant and Damien a Catholic. They had grown up together in a village that had never known sectarian hatred, and were close friends. Mrs Allen was at her son's side as life slowly left him. 'He was just lying on the floor of the pub,' she told me. 'I just kept talking to him. I asked him if he was all right and he just said, "I'm dying, I'm dying." '[7] Their parents – simple, dignified people – made moving pleas for peace. Many had done the same before and some were to do so after. Among those who came to pay their respects were the Leader of the Ulster Unionist Party, David Trimble, and the Deputy Leader of the SDLP, Seamus Mallon. Together, united in sorrow before the television cameras, the two men who were traditional political opponents echoed the families' plea for the violence to stop.

LVF suspects from the nearby town of Banbridge were arrested shortly afterwards. A fortnight after the killings, one of them, David Keys (26), was found hanging in his cell in the Maze prison. He was thought to have been tortured and murdered by his LVF colleagues for 'grassing' on the operation. Two days before the Thursday midnight deadline, the INLA also struck, shooting dead Trevor Deeney (34) in his car outside his home in Derry. His brother, Geoffrey (27), was serving life for the UFF massacre at Greysteel and his other brother, Robert (30), had been sentenced to nine years in 1992 for possession of ammunition. But the killings in Poyntzpass and Derry, perpetrated by gunmen of both sides, far from derailing the talks only brought home more starkly the urgency of reaching agreement.

As the clock ticked, the two Prime Ministers, Tony Blair and Bertie Aherne, who was now Taoisach, offered to come to the Government buildings at Stormont, where the last leg of the talks was being conducted, to see if they could assist in the final stages. George Mitchell was happy to see them do so but gave them a warning.

I told Prime Minister Blair and Prime Minister Aherne, when they arrived in Belfast, that the one thing I ask of you, the one thing I insist upon, is that when we go into session on Thursday April 9th, we will stay in session until we finish. There will be no breaks. We will either get an agreement or we will fail to get an agreement but I told them I will not even consider a request by anyone to say, 'Well, we're nearly there, we're tired now. Let's break and come back next week.' And they were very willing, eager.

Did you tell them to bring their toothbrush?

I didn't have to tell them that. They were both terrific. I had not personally seen a finer example of leadership in a democratic society than that exhibited by Tony Blair and Bertie Aherne in these talks. In modern diplomacy usually everything's scripted before national leaders get involved. They go in after the assistants have all drafted what is to be signed and they effectively finalize it. They put their signatures down and they have a large celebration. That was not the case here. When Bertie Aherne and Tony Blair came here, there was no agreement. They worked. They didn't supervise the negotiations, they *conducted* the negotiations, word by word, sentence by sentence, provision by provision. There would not have been an agreement without them. They both were superb.

But without George Mitchells' patience and personal, political and diplomatic skills, it is unlikely that the Good Friday Agreement would ever have been finalized.

The deadline came and went as the lights burned through the night in Stormont and the press shivered in the cold Portakabins outside. Even the hot drinks machine had broken down, which seemed to reflect the general mood as the various parties and Tony Blair's spokesman came and went through the long hours giving their particular 'spins' to the press. There was no mood of optimism. Dawn broke, morning came and the snow and the sleet lashed down. By lunchtime there were reports of a breakthrough, which were dashed a few hours later when we heard that final agreement had stumbled over the hurdle of decommissioning. Again, the issue was fudged when Tony Blair handed David Trimble a letter promising him that if the 'intention' of decommissioning implicit in the emerging agreement was not met, the Government would introduce legislation to make it more effective.[8] David Trimble bought it. His colleague and rival for his leadership job, Jeffrey Donaldson MP, did not and walked out, putting down a dramatic marker for the succession should Trimble ever fall. David Ervine said Donaldson's action 'took the cream off my bun.' John Taylor stayed by his leader's side. Senator Mitchell finally received the confirmatory call from David Trimble at 4.45 in the afternoon of Good Friday.

I picked up the phone and he told me that they were ready to go and I congratulated him. I said, 'Well, David, I don't think we ought to wait. My experience always told me, when you've got the votes, you vote, you don't wait because there might be a last-minute change of mind.' By then it was nearly ten to five. I said, 'I'd like to call a meeting for five o'clock. How's that suit you?' He said, 'That's fine with me.' And I said I'd like to have a short meeting. 'We can do all the talking we want afterwards but let's get the agreement approved.' He agreed and we went in at five o'clock and we had an agreement by 5.30 and I felt a great sense of relief, gratification and really genuine happiness. I have spent three and a half years in Northern Ireland. I've come to know the people very well. I like them. I admire them. They're tremendously energetic and productive. They're good people. They deserve better than the violence and the anxiety and the fear that they've had over the past several decades, and feeling that I had been able to be helpful to them in reaching this agreement was a great sense of relief and satisfaction and happiness.

When I asked Mo Mowlam, who had played an equally important part in cajoling, persuading, charming and no doubt bullying, how she felt, she laughed and said, 'Tired! It had been a long, hard slog and I was too tired for elation. What I mainly did was sleep at every opportunity afterwards.' Billy Hutchinson said, 'I was very emotionally drained and I just remember breaking down.' Gary McMichael said, 'It was very important to me and I think to everyone around that room that our efforts over those two years had borne fruit. But there was by no means a clear smooth road ahead.' His words were prophetic, not least for the fortunes of his own party. David Adams was more upbeat, 'I was exhausted and delighted. It was almost miraculous how it happened, and as in all things in Northern Ireland, it went right to the wire. It was only three-quarters of an hour before the agreement was actually signed that all of us knew that the Ulster Unionists were going to go along with it. We were all so exhausted that all we really wanted to do was get the agreement signed, get home and get to bed. And it was only a day or two later, when I had a brief couple of days away with my wife and family, that it actually dawned on me the magnitude of what had been achieved.' But Ian Paisley, who had disassociated himself and his party from the talks months earlier because he saw them as capitulation to the IRA, felt very differently. He told me the Agreement was 'the saddest day that Ulster has seen since the founding of the province. A lot of people thought I was mad.'

What became known as the Good Friday Agreement was, like the Downing Street Declaration on whose principles it was based, a meticulously worded document that remarkably gave both sides just enough of what they wanted to make a deal possible. Most important of all to loyalists and unionists, it guaranteed the security of the Union as long as the majority of the people of Northern Ireland wanted to remain part of the United Kingdom. For thirty years, this was what unionist politicians had been fighting for and loyalist paramilitaries had been killing for. Andy Tyrie, who had survived for so long as leader of the UDA, saw the efforts that he and John McMichael had made over the years finally show results. 'The Union is secure,' he told me. 'The Union is the people themselves and if we can get the two communities to work together, the Union doesn't become important any more, neither does the link with the rest of Ireland. It doesn't become important. People become important in what they do for the betterment of that community. These two things are no longer important and they won't be important in the future.' I asked him if he thought his community had won. 'Yes,' he said. Jackie McDonald also had no doubt the Union was secure, nor any doubt about who had helped make it so. 'I would take great pride in believing and thinking and saying that our organization [the UDA and UFF] has played a great part in this.' A critical part of the Agreement for Protestants was that the Irish Government for the first time recognized the right of Northern Ireland to exist and indicated its willingness to change the articles in its constitution that laid territorial claim to Northern Ireland. To John Taylor this now underpinned the Union. 'In my opinion, the Agreement is a defeat for republicanism because I believe that the Union is now more secure and the [1800] Act of Union remains intact. We were told it was going to be renegotiated. It hasn't been touched. Northern Ireland is part of the United Kingdom and now accepted by Dublin for the first time.' Nor had the astonishing fact been lost on unionists and loyalists that the IRA had effectively accepted partition, at least for the time being, by giving Sinn Fein dispensation to sit in the new Northern Ireland assembly. Such an idea would have been unimaginable only a few years earlier. It was a measure of how far the Republican Movement had come to reach an accommodation that it believed would lead them on to the united Ireland they had fought for.

Republicans and nationalists also got much of what they wanted in terms of the Irish Dimension which both saw as a stepping stone on the road to a united Ireland. There was to be a power-sharing assembly (although that emotive word was never used) with an executive drawn from politicians of all parties in proportion to their strength in the assembly. There was to be a North–South Ministerial Council and cross-border bodies set up to oversee matters such as agriculture, education, transport, social security, health, environment and urban and rural development.

However, the most controversial aspects of the Agreement had nothing to do with political structures but were gut issues that every person in Northern Ireland could identify with and had intense and passionate feelings about – the release of prisoners and decommissioning. As far as the British Government was concerned, although it never openly said so, it was a deal in which the paramilitaries on both sides would agree to give up their arms in return for the release of their prisoners. Although the word 'amnesty' was never used (for that, like 'power sharing', had emotional connotations), effectively that was what it was. Prisoners were to be released on licence, which could be revoked were they ever to transgress. Technically, therefore, it was not amnesty. These releases were specifically set out in the Agreement. Decommissioning was not and again the issue was fudged. All the Agreement itself says on the subject is that parties (that is the loyalist UDP and PUP and Sinn Fein) agree 'to use any influence they may have to achieve the decommissioning of all paramilitary arms within two years.'[9] There was no clause that said that the IRA (or the UDA/UFF or UVF) *had* to decommission, nor was there any specified linkage between Sinn Fein taking seats in the executive (should their election results merit their inclusion) and the handover of weapons. This critical issue was blurred even more with the words, 'Those who hold office should only use democratic, non-violent means, and those who do not should be excluded or removed from office under these provisions.'[10] In response to this Sinn Fein would simply say that it was not the IRA and that its party *was* committed to using only 'democratic, non-violent means'. Although the Agreement would never have been possible without the fudging of decommissioning, it did mean that potentially it carried the seeds of its own destruction if the IRA refused to decommission and David Trimble's Unionists refused to accept Sinn Fein in the executive without some gesture on the IRA's part. But such grim thoughts were not entertained in the euphoria and exhaustion of Good Friday.

The other key section of the Agreement stipulated referendums North and South to ratify what had been agreed. The exercise was to be seen as the expression of the will of the people of the whole of Ireland, in whose name the IRA claimed the legitimacy of its 'war'. If the vast majority on both sides of the border voted for peace, the two Governments calculated that the IRA would be stripped of whatever moral authority it claimed to be acting on behalf of the Irish people.

The date set for the dual referendums was 2 May 1998. The campaign was intensely fought, with Ian Paisley and Robert McCartney of the UK Unionist Party, once Paisley's foe but now his ally, representing the opposition to the Agreement. The years had hardly blunted Paisley's powers. To most people, in particular those outside the province, he was yesterday's man fighting yesterday's battles, but they wrote him off at their peril. I put to him the question that seemed to sum up most people's feelings about him, especially those in the rest of the United Kingdom.

Many would see you as the person who fanned the flames of the Troubles, the person who was the wrecker, the person who always said 'No'.

Well, they can say what they like about me. I will not be here when they're saying that so it'll not affect me nor my eternal whereabouts. I lived my life before God, before my country and, to tell you the truth, I couldn't care less about what people say about me, either when I'm living or dead. All I can say is, I'll not be changing. I will go to the grave with the convictions I have.

Anyone who thinks they can change Ian Paisley is simply wasting his or her time.

After a campaign in which Paisley and the 'no' camp made most of the running, the 'yes' parties, who were in the majority, finally got their act together in the last few days, encouraged by Tony Blair who came to the province to lend his support, sensing that what had been achieved on Good Friday might be slipping away. He knew the result was finely balanced, not least after the IRA's 'Balcombe Street Gang', who had terrorized London in 1975, appeared in the glare of television cameras on 10 May at Sinn Fein's special conference in Dublin. They had been transferred from prison in England to custody in the South as part of the lead up to the Agreement and as a gesture to the peace process had been given leave for a few days, which they used to make their tumultuous appearance before the packed hall of Sinn Fein delegates. They were given an ecstatic reception, with cheering and stamping of feet that it seemed would never end. It was the last thing the 'yes' campaign needed. Equal unease was caused a few days later when the loyalist Michael Stone, who had attacked the IRA funeral at Milltown cemetery in 1988, appeared at a UDP rally at Belfast's Ulster Hall. He too received a rapturous welcome but certainly not stage-managed by the UDP and UDA leaders who were on the platform. The last thing they wanted was a loyalist hero returning in triumph like the 'Balcombe Street Gang' had done in Dublin because they knew the electoral damage such scenes might cause. Their assessment was correct.

On referendum day, 22 May 1998, the pro-Agreement parties managed to pass the critical 70 per cent figure but only just – by 1 per cent. Anything less than 70 per cent would have been seen as a defeat. Voters in the Irish Republic endorsed the Agreement with a staggering 94 per cent.[11] Without having time to catch breath or recharge their emotional and political batteries, the parties then launched themselves into the campaign to elect the new Northern Ireland Assembly on 25 June that was to run the province after Westminster devolved powers. The campaign was anti-climactic, as if all passion and energy had been spent in the referendum showdown. To the relief of the two Governments and the parties endorsing the Agreement, the result indicated 75 per cent support for what had been achieved on Good Friday. No one could have been more relieved than David Trimble, whose party won the greatest number of seats – twenty-eight – thus making him the first Prime Minister of Northern Ireland (or First Minister, as he was called) for more than a quarter of a century. Ian Paisley and his supporters, however, followed close behind with a combined total of twenty-seven seats. Trimble's majority, given the problems that inevitably lay ahead, was dangerously thin. Sinn Fein made the greatest advance of any party, receiving its highest percentage of the vote at 17.6 per cent and winning eighteen seats, thus giving it the right to have at least one place in the new executive. David Trimble now faced the prospect of having Gerry Adams, and possibly Martin McGuinness as well, sitting alongside him in Cabinet. But the parties whose efforts had made the loyalist ceasefire possible – without which there would have been no Agreement – did not fare as well as expected, or as they had hoped given the efforts they had made. David Ervine and Billy Hutchinson won two seats in the assembly for the PUP but the UDP did not win any. David Adams was bitterly disappointed.

> I felt dejected and rejected. In personal terms I found it very hard to get over. I felt almost as though all the effort and risks that people like myself and John White and Gary McMichael have taken over these last few years counted for nothing. I was tempted for a while just to say, 'That's it, bye-bye.' But I put far too much into this process and I think there is still much work to be done for the UDP. What we'll do is just continue to work for the people on the ground and continue to try and push the process forward and in the direction we feel it should go.
>
> **Isn't there a danger also because you didn't win any seats that the UDA and the UFF feel left out in the way that you do and not part of the process?**
>
> Well, I think that it's up to us, the leadership of the UDP, to ensure that the views of the largest loyalist paramilitary organization in Northern Ireland aren't left outside the door in the process, that that organization isn't allowed to feel as though it's been isolated.
>
> **That's a danger, isn't it?**
>
> It's a danger. It is a danger that we're aware of and that's one that we will be trying our best to counter.

The first test of unionist and loyalist support for the Agreement came a week later over the now regular July showdown at Drumcree. The Government had set the election date so close to the referendum to ensure that the result was not affected by the emotions generated by the issue which, for many loyalists, had come to epitomize everything that Ian Paisley articulated – that the IRA had won and Ulster was finished. Drumcree was the loyalists' Alamo, their last stand. Drumcree 1998 was also a test of the loyalist ceasefire and the commitment by their para-militaries to peaceful means. They passed the test and anxieties that the UDA/UFF, having seen their politicians emerge from the election without a single seat, would abandon the peace process and take out their guns again, were ill-founded. Again the Orangemen mustered at Drumcree and this time they were stopped permanently from marching down the Garvaghy Road by a phalanx of police and army. Ian Paisley and Robert McCartney came to lend their support, and so too did Jeffrey Donaldson, who had made the dramatic eleventh hour exit on Good Friday. But David Trimble, the local MP, was nowhere to be seen. In 1995, he had been the hero marching with Ian Paisley down the Garvaghy Road and at the end clasping hands with him in triumph. In 1998, Trimble was the arch-traitor, the 'Lundy' who had sold out both his own Orangemen and Ulster. Had he put in an appearance, few could have vouched for his safety. Yet again, the stand-off seemed set to escalate.

Then, as violence spread around the province, three little boys, the Quinn brothers, were burned alive in their beds in a petrol-bomb attack on their home near Ballymena. Most people, including the Government, put two and two together and connected their deaths with Drumcree, although that was not necessarily the case. The mood immediately changed. In his sermon the Reverend William Bingham, the Orange Order chaplain of County Armagh in whose area Drumcree lies, bravely attacked the violence that he believed had arisen from the protest and declared with great emotion from the pulpit that 'no road is worth a life'. However strong his devotion to the Orange Order and belief in all it stood for – his grandfather and great-grandfather had both been Orangemen – in the summer of 1998 the Rev. Bingham put other things first.

> I believed in my heart and before God that the time had come where the protests had got out of our control and were actually damaging all that we stood for and undermining considerably our just cause because I certainly believe that the cause is just.
>
> **And you said no road is worth a life.**
>
> Yes. I've been a Presbyterian minister for about seven years now and I've buried members of my congregation, people who have been

blown up by the IRA. I have had to bury children, I've had to bury folk killed in accidents, and for me life is very, very precious. I believe Portadown district has the right and I hope they will have that right restored to go down the Garvaghy Road. We will work tirelessly until that happens, but life is more precious.

This time, unlike in previous years, the Orangemen were now allowed down the Garvaghy Road. The area was saturated with an even more formidable array of policemen and troops and it was clear that the Government was not going to let the Orange Order and the individuals it attracted – not all of whom were welcome to its leaders – destabilize the Good Friday Agreement. The protesters refused to be beaten and vowed they were going to say there and at some stage march down the road. When asked how long they were prepared to wait, they said, 'As long as it takes'. Like their Protestant ancestors at the Siege of Derry, the Orangemen were ready to hold out against what they regard as the same threat. Again, the loyalist paramilitaries passed the test of Drumcree, maintaining their ceasefire and refusing to become involved in the stand-off. Their leaders expressed a common thought, that politicians would use, and then abandon them as they had so many times before. They said they had learned their lesson and were not getting dragged in.

The following month, the UFF and the UVF passed an even bigger test when they did not retaliate in the wake of the 'Real' IRA's Omagh bomb on Saturday 15 August, when twenty-nine people died and more than 200 were injured. (The 'Real' IRA was a splinter group that had left the Provisional IRA along with its Quarter Master General after disagreeing with its support of the peace process).[12] The temptation to retaliate in kind, as they had done so often before in the wake of IRA atrocities, was resisted. Times and strategies had changed.

Through the autumn and early winter months of 1998, the Agreement not only seemed to be working despite the inevitable odd hiccup but also had a knock-on effect, with both the INLA and LVF declaring ceasefires. They did so not because they supported the Agreement but because they too wanted their prisoners out. As far as the 'Real' IRA was concerned, the universal condemnation heaped upon it after Omagh – and the draconian legislation the two Governments rushed through in its wake – effectively put an end to its activities, at least for the time being. But at the time of writing, with 1999 only a few days away, the Good Friday Agreement is about to face its biggest test. David Trimble has said that Sinn Fein cannot enter the Cabinet of Northern Ireland unless the IRA makes some gesture on decommissioning. On three occasions during 1998 – April, September and December – the IRA has made it clear it will not be handing in any weapons. The loyalist paramilitaries are adamant too and say they will not give up any arms as long as there is a threat to their community from the IRA. The issue has been fudged many times before but it will soon have to be confronted and resolved if the Agreement is to survive. Nineteen ninety-nine, the year that marks the thirtieth anniversary of the deployment of British troops and the re-involvement of the British Government in the Troubles, will decide the future of David Trimble, the Good Friday Agreement and perhaps even of Ulster itself.

But despite the grave problems that the loyalist paramilitaries always knew would lie ahead, most agree with Tony Blair that all parties, not least their own, have come too far to turn back. Gusty Spence, the 'alpha and omega' of their violent tradition, agrees. 'As far as loyalists are concerned, the war is over. There is no need to prosecute it any more. Of course the war is over.' Bobby Morton, the UVF gunman who was almost killed in a hail of RUC bullets, has no wish to return to being a 'soldier' again. 'I'll be glad to see the back of it. I think I am not the important issue here,' he said. 'The important issue is our children. A better future – jobs, security – a different way of life for them, especially those who have known nothing but bombs and bullets. If there's never another shot fired, it will not be too soon.' I asked him would he not miss the excitement, and the danger, and the adrenaline. 'No, I will not,' he said emphatically. 'If someone on all sides will declare the war over, I will rejoice. And I look forward to the day – whether it will ever come in my lifetime I don't know – when I can even have a pint on the Falls Road. Now that would be something to look forward to, wouldn't it?'

Notes

Introduction: Billy

1. See *Provos. The IRA and Sinn Fein*, Peter Taylor, Bloomsbury Publishing, 1997, Chapter Thirteen.
2. See Chapter Thirteen.
3. *Irish Independent*, 22 November 1982.
4. *Belfast Telegraph*, 22 November 1982.
5. Ibid., 28 May 1985; *Irish Times*, 15 June 1985.

Chapter One: Under Siege

1. *No Surrender. The Siege of Londonderry 1689*, Tony Gray, Macdonald and Jane's, 1965, p. 21.
2. *The Green Flag. A History of Irish Nationalism*, Robert Kee, Weidenfeld & Nicolson, 1972, pp. 16–17.
3. *A Circumstantial Journal of the Siege of Londonderry*, Captain Thomas Ash, reprinted from the edition of 1792; thought to have been reprinted in 1888 on the bicentenary of the siege, p. 98.
4. *No Surrender*, op. cit., p. 175.
5. *A Circumstantial Journal of the Siege of Londonderry*, op. cit., p. 99.
6. There had long been sectarian fighting around County Armagh between gangs of Protestants known as the 'Peep o' Day Boys' and the Catholics known as the 'Defenders'. Following an exchange known as the 'Battle of the Diamond' near the village of Loughgall, the victorious Protestants withdrew to an inn and formed the Orange Order.
7. *The Ulster Covenant. A Pictorial History of the 1912 Home Rule Crisis*, edited by Gordon Lucy; The Ulster Society, New Ulster (Publications) Ltd, 1989, p. 10.
8. *Irish Historical Documents 1172–1922*, T C Curtis and R B McDowell, Methuen and Co. Ltd, reprinted 1977, p. 304.
9. *The Ulster Covenant*, op. cit., p. 11.
10. *The Ulster Crisis. Resistance to Home Rule 1912–14*, A T Q Stewart, The Blackstaff Press; reissued paperback 1997, p. 77.
11. *The Ulster Covenant*, op. cit., p. 88.
12. Ibid., p. 89.
13. *The Ulster Crisis*, op. cit., p. 78.
14. Ibid., p. 72.

15. *The Oxford Companion to Irish History*, edited by S J Connolly, Oxford University Press, 1998, p. 131.
16. *The Ulster Crisis*, op. cit., pp. 233–5.
17. Ibid., p. 240.
18. Technically, the rebels who took over the Post Office were members of the Irish Volunteers, originally formed to counter Carson's Ulster Volunteers. It was only in 1919 that they were officially constituted as the Irish Republican Army with Michael Collins at its head.
19. *A History of Northern Ireland 1920–1996*, Thomas Hennessey, Macmillan Press Ltd, 1997, p. 6.
20. Ibid., p. 11.
21. *The Troubles. The background to the question of Northern Ireland*, edited by Taylor Downing, Thames/MacDonald Futura, 1980, p. 110.

Chapter Two: Gathering Storm

1. *Paisley*, Ed Moloney and Andy Pollak, Poolbeg Press Ltd, 1986, p. 125.
2. Ibid., p. 111.
3. *Paisley. Man of Wrath*, Patrick Marrinan, Anvil Books Ltd, 1973, p. 82.
4. *Persecuting Zeal. A Portrait of Ian Paisley*, Dennis Cooke, Brandon Book Publishers Ltd, 1996, p. 142.
5. *Paisley*, op. cit., p. 117.
6. *Persecuting Zeal*, op. cit., p. 144.
7. *Provos. The IRA and Sinn Fein*, op. cit., p. 25.
8. *Paisley. Man of Wrath*, op. cit., p. 94.

Chapter Three: Murder

1. *UVF*, Jim Cusack and Henry MacDonald, Poolbeg Press, 1997, pp. 5–7.
2. *The UVF 1966–73. An anatomy of loyalist rebellion*, David Boulton, Torc Books, 1973, p. 40.
3. *UVF*, op. cit., p. 9.
4. *The UVF 1966–73*, op. cit., p. 49.
5. Ibid., pp. 49–50.
6. Ibid., pp. 50–53.
7. Ibid., p. 57.

Chapter Four: Insurrection

1. *Provos. The IRA and Sinn Fein*, op. cit., p. 31.
2. Ibid., p. 31.
3. Ibid., p. 32.
4. *Disturbances in Northern Ireland. Report of the Commission appointed by the Governor of Northern Ireland*, September 1969, Belfast HMSO, Cmd. 52, p. 15, para 12. This is often known as the Cameron Report after its Chairman, Lord Cameron.
5. *Violence and Civil Disturbances in Northern Ireland in 1969. Report of the Tribunal of Inquiry*, Chairman the Hon. Mr Justice Scarman, Vol 2 (Appendices), Belfast HMSO, Cmd. 566, p. 53. This is also known as the Scarman Report.
6. *Disturbances in Northern Ireland*, op. cit., p. 38.

7. Ibid., p. 39.

8. *Paisley*, op. cit., p. 8.

9. *Disturbances in Northern Ireland*, op. cit., p. 40.

10. Ibid.

11. *A History of Northern Ireland. 1920–1996*, op. cit., p. 148.

12. *Disturbances in Northern Ireland*, op. cit., p. 44.

13. Ironically, Major Bunting's son, Ronald, did not adopt his father's loyalist politics but became a republican political activist and joined the Irish Republican Socialist Party (IRSP). He was shot dead by the Ulster Freedom Fighters (UFF) on 15 October 1980.

14. *Disturbances in Northern Ireland*, op. cit., p. 46.

15. Ibid., p. 47.

16. Ibid., pp. 89–90.

Chapter Five: Explosion

1. *Paisley*, op. cit., pp. 170–71.

2. The Lambeg is a huge drum beaten incessantly with twin canes to produce a mighty roar. It was traditionally regarded as the Protestants' 'war' drum.

3. William McGrath was subsequently at the centre of the scandal surrounding the Kincora boys' home in Belfast whose young residents were sexually abused by McGrath and others. See *The Kincora Scandal. Political Cover-Up and Intrigue in Northern Ireland*, Chris Moore, Merino Books, 1996.

4. John McKeague was shot dead by the INLA on 29 January 1982.

5. *Belfast Telegraph*, 18 February 1970. Account of the trial of Samuel Stevenson and co-accused.

6. *The UVF 1966–73. An anatomy of loyalist rebellion*, op. cit., p. 92.

7. Ibid., p. 98.

8. *Belfast Telegraph*, 23 October 1969.

9. Ibid., 25 October 1969.

10. Ibid., 24 October 1969.

11. *Provos. The IRA and Sinn Fein*, op. cit., p. 44.

12. Ibid., p. 48.

13. *Violence and Civil Disturbances in Northern Ireland in 1969. Report of the Tribunal of Inquiry*, op. cit., p. 84. Also known as the Scarman Report, it is the most accurate and comprehensive account of this contentious and critical week. I use it as the framework for my account.

14. Ibid., p. 84.

15. Ibid., p. 119.

16. *Provos. The IRA and Sinn Fein*, op. cit., p. 50.

17. *Violence and Civil Disturbances in Northern Ireland in 1969. Report of the Tribunal of Inquiry*, op. cit., p. 120.

18. Ibid., p. 123.

19. Ibid., p. 126.

20. Ibid., p. 135.

21. For a more detailed account of the state of the IRA in Belfast at the time see *Provos. The IRA and Sinn Fein*, op. cit., pp. 52–3.

22. *The Last Post. Details and Stories of the Irish Republican Dead 1916–1985*, National Graves Association, Dublin, p. 173.

Chapter Six: Defence

1. For a more detailed account of the emergence and rise of the Provisionals see *Provos. The IRA and Sinn Fein*, op. cit., Chapters Four, Five and Six.
2. Ibid., p. 53.
3. Ibid., p. 63.
4. Ibid., p. 66.
5. For more details about the ideological reasons for the split over the principle of 'abstentionism' see *Provos. The IRA and Sinn Fein*, op. cit., Chapter Five.
6. Fianna Fail is the Irish for 'Soldiers of Ireland' and is the party founded in 1926 by Eamon de Valera who was one of the leaders of the 1916 Easter Rising.
7. *States of Terror*, Peter Taylor, BBC Books, reprinted as Penguin paperback 1994, p. 214.
8. Ibid., p. 230. For a detailed account of these financial complexities that led to the prosecution of Dublin Goverment Ministers for gun-running see ibid., Chapter Seven.
9. *Provos. The IRA and Sinn Fein*., op. cit., p. 62.
10. *The UVF 1966–73*, op. cit., p. 114.
11. Ibid., p. 123.
12. For a detailed account of these riots at the beginning of 1970, see *Provos. The IRA and Sinn Fein*., op. cit., pp. 72–4.
13. Ibid., p. 91.

Chapter Seven: Tit for Tat

1. *Memoirs of a Statesman*, Brian Faulkner, Weidenfeld & Nicolson, 1978, p. 78.
2. *Provos. The IRA and Sinn Fein*, op. cit., p. 92.
3. Ibid., p. 93.
4. *An Index of Deaths from the Conflict in Ireland 1969–1993*, compiled by Malcolm Sutton, Beyond the Pale Publications, 1994. This is an invaluable work of reference.
5. *Belfast Telegraph*, 'Inquest told of Four Step blast horror', 16 December 1971.
6. Ibid., 2 October 1971.
7. *Irish Times*, 6 December 1971.
8. *Memoirs of a Revolutionary*, Seán MacStiofáin, Gordon Cremonesi, 1975, p. 222.
9. *Belfast Telegraph*, 6 September 1978.
10. *Memoirs of a Revolutionary*, op. cit., p. 243.

Chapter Eight: Escalation

1. For a detailed account of 'Bloody Sunday' see Chapter Nine of *Provos. The IRA and Sinn Fein*, op. cit.
2. Hansard, Vol. 833, c. 1860, 24 March 1972.
3. *Northern Ireland. A Chronology of the Troubles 1968–1993*, Paul Bew and Gordon Gillespie, Gill and Macmillan, 1993, pp. 47–8.
4. *Sunday Times*, 28 January 1973. Interview with Denis Herbstein.
5. *The Red Hand. Protestant Paramilitaries in Northern Ireland*, Steve Bruce, Oxford University Press, 1992, p. 59.
6. Ibid.
7. The Official IRA ceasefire was declared following widespread nationalist revulsion at the Officials' killing of Ranger William Best, a young serving British soldier from Derry's Creggan estate who was home on leave at the time. The Official IRA said they

had ordered an immediate cessation of hostilities in accordance with the wishes of the people they represented. Its statement said: 'The overwhelming desire of the great majority of all people in the North is for an end to military actions by all sides.' It was to be more than another twenty years before that happened. But although the Officials put their guns away, a breakaway group that called itself the Irish National Liberation Army (INLA) carried on a military campaign with support from its political wing, the Irish Republican Socialist Party (IRSP), of which Bernadette McAliskey (formerly Bernadette Devlin) became the most prominent member.

8. For a detailed account of the IRA ceasefire and the Whitelaw meeting see *Provos. The IRA and Sinn Fein*, op. cit., Chapter Ten.

Chapter Nine: Killing Fields

1. *Provos. The IRA and Sinn Fein*, op cit., p. 149.
2. *The UVF 1966–73*, op. cit., p. 168.
3. *Northern Ireland 1968–73. A Chronology of Events*, Vol. 2, 1972–3, Richard Deutsch and Vivien Magowan, Blackstaff Press, 1974, p. 236.
4. *The Red Hand*, op. cit., pp. 106–8.
5. *Belfast Telegraph*, 26 June 1973.

Chapter Ten: Returning the Serve

1. *The Oxford Companion to Irish History*, edited by S J Connolly, Oxford University Press, 1998, p. 526.
2. *Northern Ireland. A Chronology of the Troubles 1968–1993*, op. cit., p. 61.
3. *Northern Ireland 1968–73. A Chronology of Events*, Vol. 2, op. cit., p. 314.
4. Ibid.
5. Ibid., p. 270.
6. Ibid., pp. 356–7.
7. Ibid., p. 76.
8. *UVF*, op. cit., p. 129.
9. *This Week: The Price of Peace. The Protestants*, Thames Television, January 1974.
10. *Northern Ireland 1968–74. A Chronology of Events*, Vol. 3, 1974, op. cit., pp. 4–5.
11. Ibid., p. 54.
12. Ibid., p. 39.
13. Ibid., p. 44.

Chapter Eleven: Strike

1. *The Point of No Return. The Strike which broke the British in Ulster*, Robert Fisk, Times Books, André Deutsch, 1975, p. 19.
2. *14 May Days. The Inside Story of the Loyalist Strike of 1974*, Don Anderson, Gill and Macmillan, 1974, p. 20.
3. Ibid., p. 27.
4. *Five Long Years, This Week Special*, Thames Television, 8 August 1974. Also quoted in *The Point of No Return*, op. cit., p. 152.
5. *The Point of No Return*, op. cit., p. 109.
6. *Northern Ireland. A Chronology of the Troubles 1968–1993*, op. cit., p. 86.
7. *The Point of No Return*, op. cit., p. 201.

Chapter Twelve: Inside and Out

1. *UVF*, op. cit., p. 150.
2. *Belfast Telegraph*, 8 May 1975.
3. For a detailed account of the IRA ceasefire and the IRA's secret talks with MI6 and the British Government see *Provos. The IRA and Sinn Fein*, op. cit., Chapter Thirteen.
4. *Irish News*, 18 March 1975.
5. Ibid., 20 October 1976 and *Belfast Telegraph*, 19 October 1976.
6. *The SAS in Ireland*, Raymond Murray, Mercier Press, 1990, p. 138.
7. *Combat – The Journal of the Ulster Volunteer Force*, August 1975.

Chapter Thirteen: Heroes and Villains

1. 'The Sash My Father Wore' is the best known and most traditional of all the Orange songs and refers to the Orange sash that all Orangemen wear around their necks.
2. Brian Robinson was part of a two-man UVF team that had killed a Catholic from Ardoyne, Patrick McKenna (43), and made their getaway on a motorcycle. The UVF claimed that McKenna was a member of the Provisional IRA, a fact his family denied. It would appear that an undercover unit of the British army had been monitoring the operation and opened fire on the motorcycle as the gunmen were escaping.
3. Colin Craig was shot down by the INLA on the Shankill Road with the UVF's battalion commander for West Belfast, Trevor King, on 16 June 1994. Their killings provoked the UVF's retaliation at Loughinisland.
4. Lenny Murphy had been sentenced to three years on 20 June 1973 for the attempted escape. His accomplice, who had faced the same murder charge and had been persuaded to turn Queen's evidence, was Mervyn Connor. The murder for which Murphy was charged and acquitted was that of a Protestant, Edward Pavis, on 28 September 1972. The killing had been ordered by the UVF. The best and most detailed account of Lenny Murphy and his gang is in Martin Dillon's definitive book, *The Shankill Butchers. A Case Study of Mass Murder*, Hutchinson, 1989.
5. Ibid., p. 41.
6. Ibid., pp. 55–7.
7. Ibid., p. 226.
8. It was the shooting of Lenny Murphy that made Billy Giles bring forward his killing of Michael Fay. See Introduction p. 00.
9. *The Shankill Butchers*, op. cit., p. 53.

Chapter Fourteen: Bad Years

1. Special category status had been granted by William Whitelaw on 13 June 1973 following a hunger strike in Crumlin Road gaol by the veteran IRA leader, Billy McKee. It gave both republican and loyalist prisoners special privileges, among them more visits and letters, but the most important concession was the right to wear their own clothes. This was the issue that led to the IRA hunger strikes of 1980 and 1981. The prisoners saw the Government's granting of special category status as an admission that they were political prisoners. The Government never accepted the fact.
2. For a detailed account of this period and the abuses at Castlereagh see *Beating the Terrorists? Interrogation in Omagh, Gough and Castlereagh*, Peter Taylor, Penguin Special, 1980.

3. Ibid., pp. 76–7. The case in point was that of a young man from Derry called Michael McNaught. The case is covered in detail in Chapter Three of *Beating the Terrorists? Interrogation in Omagh, Gough and Castlereagh*, op. cit.

4. *Provos. The IRA and Sinn Fein.*, op. cit., p. 205.

5. Ibid., pp. 206–7.

6. *Northern Ireland. A Chronology of the Troubles 1968–1993*, op. cit., p. 122.

7. Ibid., p. 119.

8. 'Beyond the Religious Divide', New Ulster Political Research Group, Paper for Discussion, March 1979.

9. *The Provisional IRA*, Patrick Bishop and Eamonn Mallie, Corgi Books, 1993, p. 389.

10. *Provos. The IRA and Sinn Fein*, op. cit., p. 201.

11. *Northern Ireland. A Chronology of the Troubles. 1968–1993*, op. cit., p. 133.

12. *Provos. The IRA and Sinn Fein*, op. cit., p. 228.

13. *Belfast Telegraph*, 16 May 1980.

14. *The Red Hand. Protestant Paramilitaries in Northern Ireland*, op. cit., p. 142.

15. Joe Bennett was released and secretly resettled in England under another name, John Graham. On 22 July 1986, he was sentenced to ten years for armed robbery at Nottingham Crown Court.

16. These were the killings that John Stalker, the Deputy Chief Constable of Greater Manchester, investigated and that led to a highly controversial series of events. For the full details see *Stalker. The Search for the Truth*, Peter Taylor, Faber and Faber, 1987. Also John Stalker's own book, *Stalker*, Harrap, 1988.

17. *INLA. Deadly Divisions*, Jack Holland and Henry McDonald, Torc – A division of Poolbeg Enterprises Ltd, 1994, p. 154.

18. Ibid., pp. 158–9.

19. *The SAS in Ireland*, Raymond Murray, The Mercier Press, 1993, p. 264.

20. *Man of War, Man of Peace? The Unauthorised Biography of Gerry Adams*, David Sharrock and Mark Devenport, Macmillan, 1997, p. 220.

21. Ibid., p. 222.

22. *The Red Hand*, op. cit., p. 245.

Chapter Fifteen: Betrayal

1. *Paisley*, op. cit., p. 381.

2. *Northern Ireland. A Chronology of the Troubles 1968–1993*, op. cit., p. 158.

3. *Paisley*, op. cit., p. 387.

4. *Persecuting Zeal*, op. cit., pp. 191–2.

5. Fine Gael is, like Fianna Fail, a party that grew out of the Irish civil war and means 'Irish race'. Its founders had supported the Anglo-Irish Treaty of 1921.

6. *Northern Ireland. A Chronology of the Troubles. 1968–1993*, op. cit., p. 181.

7. Ibid., p. 184.

8. *Provos. The IRA and Sinn Fein*, op. cit., p. 285.

Chapter Sixteen: Guns

1. *Unionist Politics and the Politics of Unionism since the Anglo-Irish Agreement*, Feargal Cochrane, Cork University Press, 1997, p. 158. Reference to UVF statement in *Combat* magazine.

2. Ibid., p. 157.

3. Ibid., pp. 157–8.
4. Ibid., p. 159.
5. Ibid.
6. Ibid., p. 154.
7. *Northern Ireland. A Chronology of the Troubles 1968–1993*, op. cit., p. 200.
8. Three Ulstermen living in Canada – Billy Taylor, Howard Wright and Albert Watt – who had organized the shipments in Canada, were arrested. William Cubbon was picked up in Liverpool for the part he played in the UVF conspiracy. For further details of UVF gun-running in Scotland and Canada see *UVF*, op. cit., Chapter Seven, pp. 195 ff.
9. *Jane's Intelligence Review*, 1 November 1997.
10. *Daily Telegraph*, 22 April 1989.
11. Ibid., 24 April 1989.
12. *The British Broadcasting Corporation Summary of World Broadcasts*, 5 May 1989. Source: SAPA (South African Press Association).
13. *Independent*, 29 October 1991.

Chapter Seventeen: Killing Time

1. *UVF*, op. cit., p. 244.
2. *Belfast Telegraph*, 9 May 1988.
3. *UVF*, op. cit., p. 247.
4. BBC Northern Ireland news report, 2 June 1988.
5. *Unionist Politics*, op. cit., p. 218.
6. *Stone Cold. The True Story of Michael Stone and the Milltown Massacre*, Martin Dillon, Arrow, 1993, pp. 142–3.
7. Ibid., p. 146.
8. Ibid., p. 184.
9. *Provos. The IRA and Sinn Fein*, op. cit., pp. 298–301.
10. *Daily Telegraph*, 1 September 1989.
11. Ibid., 22 September 1989.
12. *Daily Mail*, 4 March 1992.
13. I am indebted to the remarkable work of my colleague John Ware who has made the Nelson story his own, along with his former *Panorama* producer, Geoffrey Seed. Most of my account is based on their work, notably their joint article for the *Sunday Telegraph* on 29 March 1998 and John Ware's article for the *New Statesman* on 24 April 1998.
14. *Sunday Telegraph*, 29 March 1998.
15. Ibid.
16. *New Statesman*, 24 April 1998.
17. *Sunday Telegraph*, 29 March 1998.

Chapter Eighteen: Backstage

1. *The Maze. Enemies Within, Inside Story Special*, BBC1, 20 November 1990.
2. For details of Cappagh and Loughgall see Chapter Nineteen of *Provos. The IRA and Sinn Fein*, op. cit., pp. 266 ff.
3. Ibid., p. 318.
4. Ibid., p. 320.
5. *Behind the Lines. The Story of the IRA and Loyalist Ceasefires*, Brian Rowan, The

Blackstaff Press, 1995, p. 20. This is an invaluable and authoritative first-hand source work of reference for the period.

6. Ibid., p. 23.
7. *Belfast Telegraph*, 9 March 1992.
8. *Irish News*, 6 February 1995.
9. 'Towards a Lasting Peace in Ireland', Sinn Fein, February 1992, p. 14.

Chapter Nineteen: Ceasefire

1. *Evening Standard*, 'How MI5 spiked the loyalist guns', Keith Dovkants, 22 December 1993.
2. *The Herald* (Glasgow), 25 November 1993.
3. *Behind the Lines*, op. cit., p. 111.
4. Ibid., p. 124.
5. Ibid., p. 127.

Chapter Twenty: Good Friday

1. *Provos. The IRA and Sinn Fein*, op. cit., p. 349.
2. Ibid., p. 350.
3. Ibid., p. 352.
4. *Belfast Telegraph*, 25 July 1996.
5. *Provos. The IRA and Sinn Fein*, updated paperback edition, Bloomsbury, 1998, pp. 366–7.
6. Newsletter, 17 February 1998.
7. *Provos. The IRA and Sinn Fein*, updated paperback, op. cit., p. 372.
8. Ibid., p. 374.
9. Ibid.
10. Ibid.
11. Ibid., p. 377.
12. For the background to the 'Real' IRA see *Provos. The IRA and Sinn Fein*, updated paperback, op. cit., Chapter Twenty-five.

Glossary

ADI	Assaults During Interview
ASU	Active Service Unit
CIA	Central Intelligence Agency
CLMC	Combined Loyalist Military Command
CRA	Civil Rights Association
CSM	Company Sergeant Major
DCI	Director and Controller of Intelligence
DST	Direction de la Surveillance du Territoire
DUP	Democratic Unionist Party
ECM	Electronic Counter Measures
FBI	Federal Bureau of Investigation
FRU	Force Research Unit
GHQ	IRA's General Headquarters
GOC	General Officer Commanding
GPMG	General Purpose Machine Gun
HME	Home Made Explosives
HMG	Her Majesty's Government
ICJP	Irish Commission of Justice and Peace
INLA	Irish National Liberation Army
IRA	Irish Republican Army
IRB	Irish Republican Brotherhood
IRSP	Irish Republican Socialist Party
LPA	Loyalist Prisoners Association
LVF	Loyalist Volunteer Force
MOD	Ministry of Defence
NICRA	Northern Ireland Civil Rights Association
NIO	Northern Ireland Office
NLF	National Liberation Front
Noraid	Irish Northern Aid (Committee)
OC	Officer Commanding
PAC	Provisional Army Council

PIRA	Provisional IRA
PO	Prison Officer
POA	Prison Officers' Association
POTA	Prevention of Terrorism Act
POW	Prisoner of War
PRO	Public Relations' Officer
PUP	Progressive Unionist Party
REME	Royal Electrical Mechanical Engineers
RHC	Red Hand Commando
RIC	Royal Irish Constabulary
RSF	Republican Sinn Fein
RTE	(Irish Television Network)
RUC	Royal Ulster Constabulary
SAM	Surface-to-air missile
SAS	Special Air Service
SBS	Special Boat Service
SDA	Shankill Defence Association
SDLP	Social and Democratic Labour Party
SLR	Self-loading rifle
SPG	Special Patrol Group
SYT	Shankill Young Tartan
TCG	Tasking and Co-ordinating Group
TUC	Trades Union Congress
UCDC	Ulster Constitution Defence Committee
UDA	Ulster Defence Association
UDF	Ulster Defence Force
UDP	Ulster Democratic Party
UDR	Ulster Defence Regiment
UFF	Ulster Freedom Fighters
UOP	Urzad Ochrony Panstwa – The Polish Security Service
UPV	Ulster Protestant Volunteers
USC	Ulster Special Constabulary
UUP	Ulster Unionist Party
UUUC	United Ulster Unionist Coalition
UVF	Ulster Volunteer Force
UWC	Ulster Workers' Council
UYN	Ulster Young Militants
VPP	Volunteer Political Party
WDA	Woodvale Defence Association
YCV	Young Citizens Volunteers

Index